proclamation 2

**Aids for Interpreting the
Lessons of the Church Year**

pentecost 3

**Victor Paul Furnish
and
Richard L. Thulin**

series a

editors: Elizabeth Achtemeier · Gerhard Krodel · Charles P. Price

FORTRESS PRESS   PHILADELPHIA

Library of Congress Cataloging in Publication Data (Revised)

Main entry under title:

Proclamation 2.

Consists of 24 volumes in 3 series designated A, B, and C which correspond to the cycles of the three year lectionary plus 4 volumes covering the lesser festivals. Each series contains 8 basic volumes with the following titles: Advent-Christmas, Epiphany, Lent, Holy Week, Easter, Pentecost 1, Pentecost 2, and Pentecost 3.
    CONTENTS: [etc.]—Series C: [1] Fuller, R. H. Advent-Christmas. [2] Pervo, R. I. and Carl III, W. J. Epiphany.—Thulin, R. L. et. al. The lesser festivals. 4 v.
    1. Bible—Homiletical use. 2. Bible—Liturgical lessons, English.
[BS534.5.P76]   251   79-7377
ISBN 0-8006-4079-9 (ser. C, v. 1)

8559K80   Printed in the United States of America   1-4098

Contents

Editor's Foreword

Christians borrowed the Feast of Pentecost from the Jews. One of the three major festivals prescribed in the Law, Pentecost was originally known as the Feast of Harvest or the Feast of Weeks, because it was connected with the summer wheat harvest which fell seven weeks or fifty days after the Feast of Unleavened Bread (cf. Lev. 23:16). It had no great theological significance before the Exile and was not rooted in redemptive history, but was probably borrowed from Canaanite cultic tradition.

After the Exile, however, the Priestly writers connected Pentecost "in the third month" with the events at Mount Sinai (Exod. 19:1), and the Chronicler pictured it as a solemn Feast of Covenant Renewal (2 Chron. 15:10–14). This connection of Pentecost with the renewal of the Sinai covenant is confirmed by the late traditions in the Book of Jubilees.

It is therefore appropriate that Acts 2 pictures the establishment of the church through the gift of the Spirit as having taken place on Pentecost. As Israel was constituted the people of God at Sinai and given the covenant commands, so also was the church constituted the new Israel in Christ on Pentecost, and it is now the lessons of the season of Pentecost which spell out our Lord's covenant commands to us. In this season we learn from the Scriptures what it means to be the people of the New Covenant.

Guiding our endeavor are Victor Paul Furnish, the exegete for this volume, and Richard L. Thulin, the homiletician.

Dr. Furnish has been Professor of New Testament at Perkins School of Theology, Southern Methodist University, since 1959. A graduate of Cornell College of Iowa, Garrett-Evangelical Theological Seminary, and Yale University, Dr. Furnish has also done research abroad in Germany and Athens. He is the author of three books, of which the latest is *The Moral Teaching of Paul: Selected Issues,* 1979, and he has written numerous scholarly articles.

Dr. Thulin is Professor of the Art of Preaching at Lutheran Theological Seminary in Gettysburg, Pennsylvania. During pastorates in Massachusetts and Connecticut he spoke frequently on radio and television and has had wide experience in Christian broadcasting. He has taught at Yale, Hamma School of Theology, and Winebrenner Theological Seminary. Dr. Thulin is a graduate of the University of California at Berkeley, of Augustana Theological Seminary, and of Boston University School of Theology.

Richmond, Va.   ELIZABETH ACHTEMEIER

The Twentieth Sunday after Pentecost

Lutheran	Roman Catholic	Episcopal	Pres/UCC/Chr	Meth/COCU
Isa. 5:1–7	Isa. 5:1–7	Isa. 5:1–7	Isa. 5:1–7	Isa. 5:1–7
Phil. 3:12–21	Phil 4:6–9	Phil. 3:14–21	Phil. 4:4–9	Phil. 3:12–21
Matt. 21:33–43	Matt. 21:33–43	Matt. 21:33–43	Matt. 21:33–43	Matt. 21:33–43

EXEGESIS

First Lesson: Isa. 5:1–7. This "Song of the Vineyard" is actually a skillfully developed parable about God and Israel. The parable is introduced in v. 1a, presented in vv. 1b–6, and interpreted in v. 7. The parable itself ends suddenly (v. 6), and so does the interpretation that follows. There is no "application" in the form of a call to repentance, as one might expect. As the Book of Isaiah now stands, however, these verses constitute an appropriate introduction to 5:8ff., a series of woes pronounced over those in Israel who ignore the law of God by practicing iniquity and exploiting their fellow human beings.

As v. 7 indicates, the parable portrays Israel as a vineyard and Yahweh as its owner and keeper. Another level of imagery is also involved here, however, because the vineyard was a familiar metaphor for a bride (see Song of Sol. 2:15; 8:12, etc.). Thus, Yahweh is portrayed as a bridegroom and Israel as his bride (cf. Hos. 2; Jer. 2:2). Furthermore, Isaiah himself assumes the role of "the friend of the bridegroom" who sings of the love his friend ("my beloved," v. 1a) has for the bride.

Yahweh's love for Israel is emphasized by the degree of detail which enters into the depiction of his cultivation of the vineyard. It is carefully dug up, cleared of stones, and planted with the best vines. The guard on the watchtower protects it from the ravages of thieves, beasts, or birds, and a wine vat stands ready for the harvest. But there is no harvest, only wild grapes, despite all the best efforts of the owner

7

(vv. 1b–2). In vv. 3–4 one seems to hear the bridegroom himself pleading with Israel that the fault is not his but hers: What more could he have done? Now the unproductive vineyard is destined to be ravaged and laid waste, and its keeper will no longer cause the clouds to bring it rain (vv. 5–6).

In the final verse one discovers that this has been, in effect, a parable about God's love and care and about the people's unfaithfulness. In place of the "justice" and "righteousness" which were to have been Israel's destiny, there has been "bloodshed" and "a cry" (RSV; there is a play on words here that cannot be reproduced in English). This parable is the more exquisite and compelling precisely because the prophet has declined to allegorize or moralize it. The hearers/readers are confronted only with the poignant reality of God's great love and Israel's unworthiness.

Second Lesson: Phil. 3:12–21. This passage stands within a section of exhortation that runs from 3:2 on into chap. 4. Some commentators believe that these materials are from a letter that was originally distinct from the one represented by chaps. 1—2. Whatever the case may be, the present verses are closely related to 3:2–11. There, in opposition to certain false teaching, Paul has reaffirmed his conviction that true righteousness comes from God and is received by faith (v. 9). Although the first person singular predominates in vv. 2–16, the appeal of v. 17 shows that Paul is presenting his own life as an example of what faith should mean for all believers. It should mean knowing Christ and being in him as one who shares his sufferings and death and hopes for resurrection from the dead (vv. 9–11).

It is first of all to the hope of ultimate resurrection that Paul refers in vv. 12–16 when he writes of the Christian life as a "pressing forward" in disciplined pursuit of that which is always in faith's future (cf. Rom. 6:5, 8). However, the apostle is more interested in describing the future's claim on the present than he is in describing the future in and of itself. He stresses, first, that faith requires forgetting the past (v. 13). As vv. 4–8 show, he is thinking of one's past accomplishments. Whatever religious or moral credentials one has are to be regarded as worthless insofar as righteousness is concerned. Thus, "straining forward to what lies ahead" does not mean the devoting of one's energies to the achievement of some religious or moral goal.

That pressing on is in response to what God has already given in Christ (v. 12). Being "perfect" means, fundamentally, being whole and wholly devoted to God's service. Even so, faith does not exult in how far it has advanced toward God, but only in how far God has come to claim and to call believers.

When Paul urges his readers to join in imitating him (v. 17), one must remember that he seeks to live his own life in imitation of Christ's (1 Cor. 11:1, cf. 1 Cor. 4:16). In this context imitating Paul means, specifically, living by faith in God's righteousness and in obedience to God's call in Christ Jesus (vv. 9, 14). Those who do not are called enemies of the cross of Christ (v. 18) because they decline the gift of unmerited love God proffers there (Rom. 5:6–11). Those who do receive that love know that their lives belong to God's kingdom, from whence Christ will return with a transforming power (vv. 20–21).

The athletic imagery of vv. 12–16 shows what awaiting Christ's return (v. 20) means for Paul: energetic obedience to God's call. Faith means abandoning the world's claims, but not abandoning the world. It means living within the world as a transformed and transforming person (see Rom. 12:1–2).

Gospel: Matt. 21:33–43. This parable of the wicked tenants also appears in Mark 12:1–10 and Luke 20:9–17, and, in its simplest form, in the Gnostic Gospel of Thomas, Log. 65. In both Matthew and Mark the narration of the parable has been influenced by the Song of the Vineyard (Isa. 5:1–7).

The Gospel of Matthew was written perhaps a decade or more after the Romans destroyed Jerusalem in A.D. 70. One of this evangelist's major concerns was to arrange, formulate, and interpret the teachings of Jesus in a way that would be of maximum utility for the church of his day. Thus, after recounting Jesus' birth, baptism, and temptation (1:1—4:16), the evangelist devotes the second part of his Gospel (4:17—16:20) to Jesus' teaching, opening it with the formula, "From that time Jesus began to preach . . ." (4:17 RSV). A similar formula opens the third and final section of the Gospel: "From that time Jesus began to show his disciples that he must . . . suffer many things . . . , and be killed, and . . . be raised" (16:21 RSV).

There is still much teaching material in these later chapters, but now it is all organized and presented in relation to Jesus' destiny as the crucified and risen Lord.

The parable of the wicked tenants stands in the last of these three sections and has become an allegory in which the whole history of salvation is recapitulated. The "vineyard" is the kingdom of God (see v. 43). The "tenants" are the Jews, and the owner's "servants" (vv. 34–36) are the prophets of Israel. The two separate groups of servants may represent the "former" and "latter" prophets, respectively. The "son" and "heir" who is sent last (vv. 37–38) is Jesus (cf. Heb. 1:1–2), and his murder (v. 39) is an allegory of the crucifixion: He is killed outside the vineyard (outside the walls of Jerusalem).

As it stands in Matthew, this allegorized parable emphasizes the importance of bearing the "fruits" appropriate to God's kingdom. It is because the present tenants have not cultivated "the fruits in their seasons" that the owner expels them (v. 41). The evangelist probably has in mind here "the fruit that befits repentance" (3:8 RSV) which for him is, above all, a life lived in accord with the higher righteousness of God's kingdom (see 5:17–20; cf. "fruits of righteousness," Prov. 11:30; Amos 6:12; Phil 1:11; James 3:18). The citation of Ps. 118:22–23 (v. 42) and the final warning (v. 43) underscore this message: The Kingdom of God no longer belongs to unproductive Israel, but to the Christian church—provided it produces "the fruits of it."

HOMILETICAL INTERPRETATION

Matthew's account of the parable of the wicked tenants is highly allegorized. Its use on this day suggests that the First Lesson is to be read in the light of the salvation history which the NT allegory rehearses. Thus the focus is finally in the church, to whom the Kingdom of God now belongs. Inasmuch as the season of Pentecost can be seen as the "time of the church," it seems appropriate to develop this theme homiletically. The Philippian passage makes its own contribution to such a development.

There ought to be a time when church members simply sit in awe at "that wonderful and sacred mystery" of which they are a part. It is an "immense journey" (to borrow a phrase from Loren Eiseley) to which they have been joined. The journey started with God's choosing of Israel, and it includes everything that has occurred in the centuries that have followed that initial act. We are linked to Israel and to the prophets as well as to the "son" and "heir" (Matthew's parable). We are the inheritors of the vineyard (Matt. 21:43), and thereby the inheritors of all that God's love and care have wrought for and through his people. The results of all the digging, clearing, planting, and watching-over are ours (Isaiah). God could not do more than he has done—and we are the full recipients of his activity.

Loren Eiseley looks at the human hand and marvels at the long journey through which it has come, a journey through "fin and scaly reptile foot and furry paw" *(The Immense Journey* [New York: Random House, 1957], p. 6). Perhaps we need to learn from the anthropologist's sense of wonder, derived as it is from a close look at the "long way we have come." As God's people we are in continuity with the whole of his past activity. At times we are far too episodic in our look at the "way we have come," jumping from the present, back to the sixteenth century, back again to the first century, and stopping there except for a sweeping glance at what came before. In doing that, however, we cut ourselves off from the fullness of our inheritance. We are part of all that came before us, all of the persistent and loving cultivation by God of his people. God's care is not simply manifested in what he does for us in the present moment; it is also manifested in what he has done throughout long centuries to bring us to this moment.

The church has been joined to a future as well as to a past. The vineyard, the kingdom, is ours through the "son" and "heir" whose own future was not cut off by death (Matt. 21:42; Phil. 3:9–11). The immense journey of which we are a part does not end until the resurrection, when we are met by the returning and transforming Christ. We enter the journey at a point where we receive both what has gone before (Israel's hope fulfilled) and what is promised for the future (a new hope).

The present time of the church is to be a time of productivity. Claims are made upon us by both our past and our future. We are to live in the light of what God's love has wrought for us in what has gone before, and we are to live in the light of what is yet to come. It is this present time of productivity which is of central concern to both Matthew and Paul.

It is important that any exhortations to produce be made in the right context. That which presses on us as Christians is in response to what God has already given. The vineyard's grapes are its natural produce and an expression of, and response to, the owner's care. Likewise, a Christian's activity grows out of his or her identity in Christ and is an expression of, and response to, the care of God which embraces all past, present, and future moments.

It is also helpful to remember that the production of wild grapes is not simply an act of disobedience. And it is certainly not a refusal to "knuckle under" to the arbitrary demands of a detached lawmaker. To bear wild grapes as one born and bred to do otherwise is a kind of self-mutilation. It is an abandonment of origin and of identity. It is a disfigurement in which the genuine nature can no longer be discerned. But the production of wild grapes is not only an offense against the self. It is most of all an offense of monstrous proportions against God. It is to betray God's love (the lover's lament in Isaiah). It is to trample on all of God's expressions of care and affection (Matthew). It is the fracturing of a relationship in which the one most loved chooses to become an enemy (Paul). Isaiah writes of such offense with pathos and St. Paul writes of it with tears.

The texts suggest at least three types of "good grapes." The first type is pointed to by Isaiah and is one of justice and righteousness (the "wild grape" counterpart is that of iniquity and exploitation). While Isa. 5:1–7 provides little context for these words, it should be noted that they have a central function in Isaiah's preaching. It is not difficult to locate descriptive meanings. These words are of God, for he is exalted in justice and shows himself holy in righteousness (Isa. 5:16). In terms of human relationships they mean positively "to do good . . . correct oppression; defend the fatherless, plead for the widow" (Isa. 1:17; cf. Isa. 10:2). Negatively, they refer to such acts as acquitting the guilty for a bribe and depriving the innocent one of rights (Isa. 5:23). The behavior patterns outlined here are not optional. To refuse to do them is an annihilation of the self and an offense to God.

A second type of "good grape" is clearly set forth by St. Paul. It is that of a life of faith in God's righteousness rather than in our own. It means forgoing all claims to worthiness apart from God. It means living "in Christ" and in what he is for us rather than in ourselves and in what we have done for ourselves—our past or present accomplishments, our proper goals, our intended achievements. To do other than this is to decline the unmerited gift of God's love. It is also to claim more than we ever could, that is, that we are the owners of the vineyard and that the kingdom is ours by right.

A third type of "good grape" is further suggested by St. Paul, and combines the content of the other two. Christians share in a kind of twin membership. To use the metaphors of the lections, they live in an earthly vineyard and yet have their commonwealth in heaven (Phil. 3:20). Depending on God's righteousness and justice rather than on their own, they are to live out lives of righteousness and justice (obedience) in a world peopled by "wicked tenants" and "harlots." They are to abandon the world's claims, but not the world. They are to live as transformed and transforming people, knowing that thereby they will share the fate of the prophets and of the Son. The Christian life is a life of "in-betweens"—in between the gift of the already and the gift of the not yet, in between the no of rejection and the yes of affirmation, in between the cross and the exaltation.

The journey of God's kingdom cannot be stopped. No amount of wild grapes or wicked tenants can destroy it. Nor can it be destroyed by any refusal of church members to produce the proper fruit. The question is whether or not we will continue on the journey to which we have been joined. The everlasting kingdom will always belong to someone. And this is more of a fact than a threat.

The Twenty-first Sunday after Pentecost

Lutheran	Roman Catholic	Episcopal	Pres/UCC/Chr	Meth/COCU
Isa. 25:6–9	Isa. 25:6–10a	Isa. 25:1–9	Isa. 25:6–9	Isa. 25:1–10a
Phil. 4:4–13	Phil. 4:12–14, 19–20	Phil. 4:4–13	Phil. 4:12–20	Phil. 4:4–20
Matt. 22:1–10 (11–14)	Matt. 22:1–14 or Matt. 22:1–10	Matt. 22:1–14	Matt. 22:1–14	Matt. 22:1–14

EXEGESIS

First Lesson: Isa. 25:6–9. Chaps. 24—27 of Isaiah did not originate with the eighth-century prophet Isaiah, but sometime in the

postexilic period (fifth to third centuries B.C.). In this series of eschatological poems, hymns, and prayers one overhears Israel affirming the coming righteous judgment of God over all iniquity (see 24:5,
6). In these same chapters, however, there are songs of praise to the
majesty of the Lord (for example, 25:1–5), and the affirmation that
God's salvation shall come to the righteous (for example, 26:1ff.).
Moreover, in conscious counterpoint to Isaiah's own poignant Song
of the Vineyard (5:1–7), one now finds a new, eschatological vineyard
song (27:2–6): "A pleasant vineyard" where "Israel shall blossom and
put forth shoots, and fill the whole world with fruit" (vv. 2, 6 RSV).

In Isa. 24:23 there had been a reference to the coming reign of God
on Mount Zion and in Jerusalem, and it is this coming enthronement
of the Lord of Hosts which is the subject in 25:6ff. V. 6 depicts the
enthronement feast, vv. 7–8 indicate what God's reign will mean for
all peoples, and v. 9 reports the festal song. V. 10a, which many
commentators would include as part of this passage, may be either a
part of the song of thanksgiving (v. 9) or a final word of explanation
for it.

The references to "this mountain" in vv. 6, 7, and 10a presuppose
the earlier reference to Mount Zion (24:23). Now the coming day of
Yahweh's enthronement there is portrayed as a time of pilgrimage for
"all peoples," when they will acknowledge and celebrate God's rule
and share in the banquet the King himself will provide. The veil
mentioned in v. 7 is the veil of mourning. Its final destruction is
correctly interpreted in v. 8 as the destruction of death itself. At the
same time, God's people will be rescued from all the reproaches they
have suffered in this world. Similar promises are extended in Zeph.
3:16–20 and elsewhere.

The vision of an eschatological banquet to celebrate the coming of
God's kingdom is familiar from the synoptic Gospels (for example,
Matt. 8:11; 22:1–14; Luke 14:15; 22:18) and Revelation (for example,
19:9). Both Paul (1 Cor. 15:54) and John of Patmos (Rev. 21:4) draw
on Isa. 25:8 when writing of God's final victory over the powers of
death. However, in earliest Christianity a sense of mission to all
peoples has replaced the vision of their eschatological pilgrimage to
the mountain of the Lord. In Matt. 28:16–20, for example, the mountain is the place from which Jesus' disciples are *sent out* to all nations
to baptize and to teach.

Second Lesson: Phil. 4:4–13. This lesson is composed of three distinct parts. If, as some commentators believe, our canonical Philippians is actually a composite of several originally separate letters, this lesson may be drawn from two, or even three, of those. The summary-exhortations to rejoice and pray in vv. 4–6 read like the final paragraph of a letter, and they are even followed by a benediction (v. 7). However, the same may be said of vv. 8–9, where there is another benediction (v. 9b). V. 10, on the other hand, opens a whole new topic, and that is concluded with yet another benediction (v. 19) and a doxology (v. 20).

Most interpreters, regardless of their theory about the composition of Philippians, agree that vv. 4–7 belong to the same letter represented in 1:1—3:1. This letter, even though written from prison (see 1:7, 12–14, etc.), is punctuated with repeated expressions of thanksgiving and admonitions to rejoice (for example, 1:3–5, 18, 19; 2:17, 18; 3:1). That theme is also present here, in vv. 4 and 6. Despite his own present circumstances, and despite the dangers with which the Philippians are themselves beset (see 1:28–30), Paul can rejoice that he and they are partners in the gospel (1:3–11), that the gospel is still being preached (1:12–18), and that God is at work completing salvation (1:6, 19–20; 2:13). The "forbearance" commended in v. 5a is supported by a reference to the Lord's imminent return (v. 5b), and the appeal to "have no anxiety about anything" (v. 6) may echo a traditional saying of Jesus' (see Matt. 6:25 and parallels).

The admonitions of vv. 8–9 are so general that it is impossible to associate them with any specific theme elsewhere in Philippians. The qualities listed in v. 8 are representative of the noblest virtues enjoined by the Hellenistic moralists of Paul's day, and one should not presume that the apostle is here reducing his ethical teaching to a few selected principles or norms. He is saying, rather, that every genuine "good" should be espoused and practiced. The appeal of v. 9a is more typically Pauline, and may be put alongside other passages in which his apostolic conduct, itself conformed to Christ's, is offered as a pattern for all believers (3:17; 1 Cor. 4:16; 11:1).

Although v. 10 introduces the subject of the aid Paul has received from the Philippians, that topic is only developed in vv. 14–20. What intervenes (vv. 11–13) is in a sense parenthetical, because the apostle is testifying that he knows how to survive whatever his worldly circumstances. Self-sufficiency was a great ideal in Paul's day, and he uses the technical term for that in v. 11 (RSV: "content"). Paul, however, is using the word in a radically different way: His sufficiency is not from himself (or the Philippians), but from God, who is his strength and stay in all things (v. 13; cf. 2:13).

Gospel: Matt. 22:1–14. In this passage the evangelist has combined two parables as if they were one, using one introductory formula (v. 1) and adding one generalizing conclusion (v. 14). There are parallels to the first parable (vv. 2–10) in Luke 14:16–24 and in the Gospel of Thomas, Log. 64. The second (vv. 11–13) does not appear elsewhere in Christian sources, although there is a similar rabbinic parable.

Of the three versions of the first parable, that in the Gospel of Thomas is the simplest, and probably provides the best idea of what may have been intended by the story in its original form. There Jesus speaks of a man who sent his servant out with dinner invitations for four friends. Each of them declined, however, pleading a prior commitment. When the master heard this, he commanded the servant to "go out to the roads" and bring back for dinner whomever he could find there. As told by Jesus, this parable could have been directed as a challenge to his hearers: They have no reserved seats at the banquet table in God's kingdom. They must respond now to the invitation to come, or it will be too late. In the context of Jesus' ministry and message, then, this is a parable that challenges to decision; one must respond without delay or excuse.

In its Matthean version this parable has been transformed into another allegory about the history of salvation. The two sets of servants sent out by the king (vv. 3 and 4) represent God's prophets and apostles, respectively, and some of the latter are martyred (v. 6). On the basis of v. 7 this Gospel must be dated after A.D. 70, because in this verse the evangelist interprets the Roman destruction of Jerusalem, which occurred in that year, as God's judgment upon the Jews for having rejected the gospel. The king's subsequent order to his servants to extend the invitation to others (vv. 8–10) represents the institution of the church's gentile mission: It should preach to all and should gather whomever it can find.

The appended parable, vv. 11–13, expresses a typically Matthean concern. Since there are both bad and good in the church (v. 10), the church itself stands under God's judgment, and at the last "harvest" the "weeds" will be separated from the "wheat" and destroyed (13: 36–43). The evangelist has attached this parable to that of the marriage feast in order to make the same point: only those who are prepared for the Last Judgment will be spared. The evangelist may well be thinking of the prophet's reference to the "robe of righteousness" (Isa. 61:10), because elsewhere he emphasizes that righteousness is the fundamental requirement of the Christian life (5:6, 10, 20; 6:33).

HOMILETICAL INTERPRETATION

The symbol of the eschatological banquet, or feast, dominates the First Lesson and Gospel for this day. While the Second Lesson does not make conscious use of the image, its content (the return of the Lord) nonetheless provides the orientation out of which Paul writes. All three lessons therefore enable the preacher to emphasize the salvation of God as that which is anticipated (as well as present) and to helpfully elaborate at least part of the complex of ideas connected to such a proclamation. Such themes are clearly at the liturgical center of the Pentecost season.

God's people live in the light of what is yet to come, and what is yet to come is the consummated rule of God. As described by the prophet, this rule will be both a vindication and the fulfillment of all hope for God's people. Judgment will be made on all iniquity, and all injustices will cease. "God's people will be rescued from all the reproaches they have suffered in the world" (see exegesis), and they will no longer be insignificant. All reasons for mourning will be removed and death itself will be overcome.

The consummated rule of God will come of itself, quite apart from anything we may do or say or believe. The prophet, who describes the end time in such splendid images, makes this quite clear. It is the Lord of Hosts who will do it, the one waited for. The Matthean version of the parable also makes it clear. The host in the story is a king who is not dependent upon the whims, the approbation, or the attendance of others. The feast is his. His will is determinative. His plan for a great supper will not be blocked by anyone for any reason. From beginning to end, the feast, the power, and the offensive belong to him.

If God alone is the host, then our participation in the feast occurs only by means of an invitation. We are not the hosts. We don't even help plan the menu or prepare the food. The first words we hear are the ones which announce that everything is ready. The invitation is intensely personal. It speaks our names, and it tells us to come now, without preparation, without probation, and without credentials. Entrance to the festal celebration is free.

The invitation to the banquet is an invitation to joy. The somber tone of the Matthean story should not stifle the call of both prophet and apostle to rejoice (Isa. 25:9; Phil. 4:4). However tempting it might be for the preacher to stress the indifference and negligence portrayed in the Gospel text, such an emphasis would finally be a disservice to the three-text lection and to the dominant symbol of the feast. Even in the parable, in spite of the refusal and the rejection, there is joy. The wedding hall *was* filled with guests and the wedding celebration *was* held.

Just as the texts state and describe what is yet to come, so also do they suggest something of what it means to live in the light of that coming event. It should be noted that the anticipated rule of God, spoken of here in terms of a banquet, is the *consummation* of that rule. Not only has it been promised, but it has already begun. This "already . . . not yet" quality is suggested most clearly perhaps in the lection from Philippians and its context. Paul invites his readers to rejoice, to share in the joy of that which is already present but is also yet to come. Paul himself rejoices because of the church at Philippi, because of what is occurring there even as he writes. In spite of Paul's imprisonment, the members of the Philippian congregation are still his partners. The gospel is still being preached. God is at work among them completing salvation (see exegesis). But Paul also rejoices because the Lord is at hand, because the Lord's return is not very far ahead. Paul lives in anticipation of that coming, the day of great celebration when God will be all in all. The apostle rejoices both because God waits with his kingdom, and because God's kingdom shines into this life.

The festal celebration is for all peoples. The prophet visualizes an eschatological pilgrimage of all nations to the mountain of the Lord. God's victory is not meant for Israel alone. It is a victory which extends through Israel to all people. But this extended victory receives a far more active interpretation from the evangelist. God's people are not to sit and wait for the nations to come. They are, rather, sent to the nations, sent to preach and to gather whomever they can find. To live, therefore, in the light of an all-inclusive banquet is to live with a keen sense of mission. What we have been given is not for us alone. It is to be shared. In the Matthean parable we find ourselves not only as guests but also as servants. We are commanded to go and to find other people in other places. We are to cross the nicely defined barriers (such as good and bad) which separate the streets from the banquet halls. We are to bear an invitation to a feast not of our own making, to people whose worthiness is never up to us to decide. We are even to share the disappointment and the pain of rejection.

To live in the light of the coming rule of God is also to wear the proper wedding garment, a "robe of righteousness." In the Matthean context, this suggests doing God's will by loving both God and the neighbor. What this means can be demonstrated more precisely from the Second Lesson. To love God means to depend on God, to know, to live out the fact that one's sufficiency is from him rather than from oneself. Paul's acknowledgment that God is his strength and stay in all things is an expression of such love. What love toward the neighbor involves is pointed to in Paul's appeal that every genuine "good" be espoused and practiced, and in his appeal that the Philippians do what they have learned, received, heard, and seen in him. More particularly, to love the neighbor means to show forbearance and to show it toward hostile opponents as well as toward fellow Christians (a readiness to forgive, and an unwillingness to insist upon personal right to the detriment of another). A further specific meaning is suggested by the OT lection. If the consummated rule of God which is to come signifies the end of all injustice, then to live in its light is to work for the elimination of all social oppression.

Because of the central image of the eschatological banquet, an appropriate focus for this day may well be that of the Lord's Supper (the Eucharist). Two elements in particular seem highlighted by the texts. When Paul, for example, writes that "the Lord is at hand"

(Phil. 4:5b), he is making reference to the eucharistic prayer. The church's liturgy anticipates the return of Christ. More specifically, the eucharistic prayers look forward to the coming of the Lord in glory ("Christ has died. Christ is risen. Christ will come again"). The remembrance *(anamnesis)* is not only of past events become present. It is also an anticipation of the fulfillment of Christ's work. The meal is one of eschatological expectancy, a meal which begins to realize what is to happen in its fullness at the eschaton.

Again, the improperly dressed banquet guest in Matthew's parable suggests the necessity of preparation for the meal. Consciences should be examined. Guests should be open toward all other guests. External preparation such as prayer and fasting may be of help. But the one who is truly well prepared is the one who, as Luther said, believes these words: "for you" and "for the forgiveness of sins."

The Twenty-second Sunday after Pentecost

Lutheran	Roman Catholic	Episcopal	Pres/UCC/Chr	Meth/COCU
Isa. 45:1–7	Isa. 45:1, 4–6	Isa. 45:1–7	Isa. 45:1–6	Isa. 45:1–7
1 Thess. 1:1–5a	1 Thess. 1:1–5b	1 Thess. 1:1–10	1 Thess. 1:1–5	1 Thess. 1:1–5a
Matt. 22:15–21	Matt. 22:15–21	Matt. 22:15–21	Matt. 22:15–21	Matt. 22:15–21

EXEGESIS

First Lesson: Isa. 45:1–7. Scholars have agreed that chaps. 40—55 of Isaiah must be attributed to an anonymous prophet ("Second Isaiah") living with his people in Babylonian exile in the latter half of the sixth century B.C. Israel had not only lost its identity as a political power, but had also lost its hope that that identity could be restored. Israel interpreted the Babylonian exile as the fulfillment of earlier prophecies that it would suffer God's judgment because of its sins. But now this prophet is given a new word from the Lord to proclaim: a word of hope, a promise, a gospel of salvation (see 40:1–8).

In 45:1–7 specifically, the prophet reports an oracle of God to Cyrus II, the king of Persia under whose leadership that nation fast rose to political dominance in the Mediterranean world. The Cyrus oracle proper comes in 45:2–4, and Yahweh's self-predication stands in 45:5–7. Most striking is the description of the Persian king as God's anointed (v. 1), a title previously employed only for the kings of Israel. This prophet sees in Cyrus an agent, alongside Israel itself, of God's purpose (cf. 44:28), and he seems to perceive that the strengthened position of Persia among the nations will mean the ultimate fall of once-mighty Babylon (for example, chap. 47). Babylon did indeed fall to Cyrus in 539 B.C., some few years after the pronouncement of this oracle.

The imagery of enthronement pervades these verses: God anoints Cyrus and holds him by the right hand (v. 1), and finally he girds him with the robes of power (v. 5). These acts all played a part in the enthronement ritual for Israel's own monarchs, and yet Cyrus remains an alien king. Twice it is emphasized that he does not even know Israel's God (vv. 4, 5), and the prophet does not apply the title "servant (of God)" to Cyrus as he does to Israel itself (for example, v. 4). Cyrus's destiny is not to be converted. Rather, the prophet portrays the king's commission as specific and limited: to relieve the suffering of God's oppressed people (v. 4). He envisions as the end result of this that all peoples shall come to know that Yahweh alone is God (vv. 5–7).

Second Lesson: 1 Thess. 1:1–5a. 1 Thessalonians, probably the earliest of Paul's surviving letters, was most likely written from Corinth about A.D. 50. Paul had founded a congregation in Thessalonica only shortly before this. The purpose of this letter was to remind the Thessalonians of the gospel they had received from him, to encourage them in their Christian faith and life, and to deal with some specific questions they had had to face since he had been away.

The first verse of the present lesson comprises the salutation of the letter. In every Pauline letter except Galatians the salutation is fol-

lowed by a paragraph of thanksgiving in which the apostle thanks God
for the faith and life of the congregation being addressed. The remain-
der of this lesson (vv. 2–5a) is drawn from this thanksgiving section
which extends, overall, at least through 1:10.

First, Paul wants the Thessalonians to remember with him how
their conversion had been manifested in their faith, love, and hope
(v. 3). This is a favorite Pauline triad, and it occurs again in this letter
(5:8) as well as in Rom. 5:1–5; 1 Cor. 13:13; and Gal. 5:5–6. The latter
passage is especially important for understanding the rather surprising expression, "*work* of faith": Faith's "work" is love.

Second, Paul reminds his readers that they are God's beloved and
have been chosen by God (v. 4). These are the terms Jews ordinarily
applied to themselves as God's elect people, but here Paul is applying them to a congregation composed largely of gentile converts
to Christ.

Third, Paul affirms that the evidence of their election was the way
the gospel had come among them: with the power of the Holy Spirit
(v. 5; cf. 2:13). For Paul, the gospel is not just a message about God,
Christ, and faith; it is itself the power of God present for salvation
where it is received by faith (Rom. 1:16). Similar things are said about
how the gospel came to Corinth (1 Cor. 2:1–5).

Gospel: Matt. 22:15–21. This story about paying taxes to Rome is
present in Mark 12:13–17 and Luke 20:20–26 as well. There are only
minor variations in the three accounts, and here one is as likely as
anywhere to be in touch with an actual incident in Jesus' life. In all
three Gospels it is offered as evidence of how Jesus' opponents
sought to entrap and discredit him.

The question put to Jesus seems straightforward enough: "Is it
lawful to pay taxes to Caesar, or not?" (v. 17). This had been an
urgent issue in Palestine since A.D. 6 when the Jews' Roman over-
lords had imposed a poll tax. The Zealots, a Jewish revolutionary
group, refused to pay it, while some Jews, led by the Herodian royal
house, openly collaborated with Rome. The vast majority of Jews
were somewhere in between these two extremes: nominally com-
pliant, but restive under Roman rule, often to the point of secret
opposition. If Jesus counseled payment of the tax, he would have

been denounced as a Roman collaborator and thus alienated from the poor and oppressed to whom his preaching and ministry had been directed. But, if he said that the tax should not be paid, he would have been regarded as a Zealot and condemned as a subversive.

Jesus responds to this challenge by asking to be shown a denarius (v. 19), a small silver coin of Roman issue. On one side it bore a portrait of the reigning emperor crowned with a laurel wreath (the sign of divinity), and an inscription: "Tiberius Caesar, majestic son of the majestic God, and High Priest." Jesus calls attention to these (vv. 20–21a) before he gives his answer to the question: "Render therefore to Caesar the things that are Caesar's, and to God the things that are God's" (v. 21b).

Jesus' response does not consist in the simple yes or no answer his opponents had sought to force from him. Yes, he says, Caesar can claim taxes from you, for the very coins you carry belong to him. But the emphasis falls on the second part of his reply, in which he comments on something his opponents have not had in mind: One also stands under the claim of God. This striking juxtaposition of references to Caesar and God relativizes and limits the scope of the meaning of Caesar's power. There is an implicit warning here to give Caesar *no more* than what belongs to him. Also implicit is the affirmation that ultimately everything belongs to God—not just some token of God's power, but one's whole existence. This accords with Jesus' fundamental message about God's kingdom: it is an eternal rule of justice and love (not limited, like Caesar's, to time and space), and it claims no less than the whole person for obedience to God's will.

HOMILETICAL INTERPRETATION

In combination, the texts for this day suggest two central themes. The lections from Isaiah and Matthew focus on the life of God's people in the world, and raise the more specific question of the relation between the Christian community and the state. The lections from Isaiah and 1 Thessalonians together point to the choosing activity of God (election) and to some of the characteristics of both the act of choosing and the life which follows upon it.

The prophet makes it clear that Yahweh is involved in the affairs of nations. As God worked through Babylon to punish Israel for its sins, he now works through the political power of Cyrus of Persia to relieve Israel's suffering. Thus human social and political life are not independent of God. Not only is Yahweh interested in such life, but he actually works through it. The Second Lesson and Gospel make it clear that God's people are also involved in the affairs of nations. Paul's designation of the "church of the Thessalonians" is a vivid reminder that his readers exist in a specific time and place, that they are in the world and are part of its circumstances. The question asked of Jesus, in spite of its trickery, reflects an actual and urgent contemporary situation. Jesus' answer indicates his awareness that the political and social life of his questioners and hearers is both real and pressing.

The question thus posed by the lectionary texts is this: If God is at work in the political and social life which forms the historical context of his people, how should his people relate to that life? More specifically, in terms of the Gospel text, how should God's people view and enact the relationship between God and Caesar? Obviously this question has been answered in a variety of ways in the past and is still being diversely answered in the present. How one responds to the question no doubt depends in part on theological formulations and political commitments which exceed the limits of these texts. Nonetheless, the assigned lections provide some general guidance for the discussion.

God's people are to recognize the rightful claims of governing authorities. Jesus' answer to the Pharisees and Herodians in no way forbids the payment of tribute (taxes). Indeed, the implication seems to be that it is a matter of duty to respond to Caesar's legitimate demands. Jesus' words distinguish between Caesar and God, but they do not isolate Caesar and God from one another. It may be too much to say that paying taxes is a service to God. It is not too much, however, to say that God is at work in and through those to whom taxes are paid (Cyrus, for example). Acknowledgment of this fact urges more than the payment of tribute by God's people. It urges interest in, and concern for, the total political and social life of which they are a part.

Caesar's power is both relativized and limited by God's power

(Cyrus, after all, is only an agent). Caesar cannot legitimately demand either total obedience or commitment of the "whole person." While response to God is not in conflict with the duties of earthly citizenship, such response involves another and greater rule and claim. All things rightfully belong to God, while only some things rightfully belong to Caesar. This means that Caesar should never be given more than what belongs to him. It also means that one's service to God is not fulfilled simply by service to the state or within the political-social arena. It further means that God's people continuously live in a tension between the two claims.

Sometimes a tension between the claims of God and the claims of Caesar occurs because they are in conflict. In such moments, discerning the rightful claim is often not as difficult as summoning the courage to articulate it and to act upon it (as in questions of human rights, for example). More often, however, the tension occurs because it is not at all clear in specific circumstances what properly belongs to whom, nor what is the best way to respond to God's claims in and through, rather than over against, those of Caesar. Our texts (particularly the Matthean passage) recognize this latter tension but provide no answer. God's people are left to determine the ways in which they will relate the claims of God and Caesar. God's people are also left to determine the manner of their response to the state (as Paul Tillich suggests, by "silent influence," by prophetic "critical judgment," or by the royal function of political activity). By its silence, the Matthean passage may suggest that living in the tension is as important as discerning the correct relation and making the correct response.

God chooses people and nations to be his servants and agents. Israel, Cyrus, and the Christians at Thessalonica were all chosen. Cyrus in particular seems to have been a strange choice—he probably never did know that he was chosen. Yet God's choices always seem strange. He chooses the oppressed, the alien, and the ungodly to carry his name and to do his work.

We also have been chosen and there are some of us who may find that fact very unsettling. To be chosen means to be set apart, to be individualized, and we're not certain we want that. We prefer to lose ourselves in the crowd, to be like everyone else. It isn't easy to be the center of attention. We know that and we're not sure we want to be there. In part, our uneasiness is wholly appropriate. Sometimes those who are chosen forget that they are only agents. They take delegated position and authority into themselves, as though they were choosers instead of the chosen. They begin to think that they alone are worthwhile, even though they were chosen because of their lack of worth. They become oppressors.

The Second Lesson speaks to our discomfort. There is no way to avoid the individualizing power of choice. We have been set aside; as Paul and the Thessalonian Christians became a center of attention (2:14–16), so have we. But we are individualized by virtue of those very things which will keep us from perverting our chosenness: the work of faith, the labor of love, and the steadfastness of hope. These are the signs of our election. They are not of our own doing—they are by the power of the gospel. The work of faith is love. And it is a labor, not simply an emotion. It means actual deeds of sacrifice, and it clarifies the fact that our chosenness is connected to self-giving service. The steadfastness of hope points to our future in the One who chose us and the One whose power works through the gospel to both elect and empower. We are pilgrims whose position and authority are derivative. Our hope is not in ourselves.

What has already been implied by the use of terms like agent and labor of love can be elaborated further. Cyrus was anointed for the relief of suffering Israelites. Along the way, the Persian nation became increasingly powerful under Cyrus's leadership and Cyrus described himself as having become "king of Babylon and king of the countries." But the prophet insists that all of this happened only because the Lord grasped Cyrus's right hand. The prophet further insists that none of it was for Cyrus (except perhaps as Cyrus might come to acknowledge the source of his victories). Cyrus was chosen and empowered for the sake of Israel. His own destiny was not the object of God's work. In like manner, Israel was chosen and delivered in this instance, for the sake of the world rather than for itself: "that men may know . . . that there is none besides me . . . ." As we have been chosen by God apart from our worthiness or lack of it, so have we been chosen for an end beyond ourselves. In short, the Church exists for the sake of the world.

The Twenty-third Sunday after Pentecost

Lutheran	Roman Catholic	Episcopal	Pres/UCC/Chr	Meth/COCU
Lev. 19:1–2, 15–18	Exod. 22:21–27	Exod. 22:21–27	Exod. 22:21–27	Exod. 22:21–27
1 Thess. 1: 5b–10	1 Thess. 1:5c–10	1 Thess. 2:1–8	1 Thess. 1:2–10	1 Thess. 1:5b— 2:8
Matt. 22:34–40 (41–46)	Matt. 22:34–40	Matt. 22:34–46	Matt. 22:34–40	Matt. 22:34–46

EXEGESIS

First Lesson: Exod. 22:21–27. In its present form the Book of Exodus is a compilation of various traditions which had developed over a long period of time. These traditions deal with Israel's deliverance from Egypt (1:1—15:21), some of its wilderness wanderings (15:22—18:27), and the covenant received by Israel at Sinai (chaps. 19—40). Within the latter section scholars have discerned the presence of a group of laws and ordinances sometimes referred to as the Book of the Covenant. These laws extend from 20:22 through 23:33 and are themselves of two main types. Most of those in the first part of the collection deal with civil case law, but from 22:18 on they are more often in the form of direct imperatives (apodictic), and deal largely with questions of ritual practice and moral behavior. The present lesson has been drawn from this second section, a collection of covenant statutes that seems to have originated very early in Israel's life, even before the rise of the monarchy. The statutes in vv. 21–27 all treat the matter of oppression. The disadvantaged must not be wronged—neither the stranger in the land (v. 21; cf. 23:9), nor the widowed and the orphaned (v. 22), nor the poor (vv. 25–26). This kind of concern is apparent throughout Israel's legal codes (for example, Lev. 19:33–34; Deut. 14:28–29) as well as in the teaching of her prophets (for example, Amos 4:1; Isa. 1:17; Jer. 7:5–7; Ezek. 22:7; Zech. 7:10; Mal. 3:5), and it is still alive in the teaching of the early church (for example, Rom. 12:13b; Heb. 13:2; 3 John 5; 1 Tim. 5:3, 16; James 1:27).

In one instance (v. 24) divine punishment is threatened against any who would take advantage of the weak and the helpless, but the chief appeal in this passage is to Yahweh's nature as a compassionate God. This is emphasized by the unexpected appearance of the first person singular, beginning in v. 23, unusual in this collection of laws: Yahweh himself stands behind the laws, attentive and responsive to the needs of the oppressed. The compassion with which God responds to his people's cries (v. 27b) should also govern the way they behave toward one another.

Second Lesson: 1 Thess. 1:5b—2:8. This lesson is drawn from two different sections of 1 Thessalonians, the introductory thanksgiving (1:2–10; see the exegesis of 1:1–5a for the Twenty-second Sunday after Pentecost) and the first main section of the body of the letter (2:1–16). However, these two sections are closely related. In 1:5b–10 Paul reminds his readers how the gospel had been preached and received in their city. The first section of the letter proper then elaborates on this topic.

According to Acts 17:1–9, Paul's original mission in Thessalonica had aroused the hostility of some of the Jews of that city. They denounced the Christians as political subversives, charged them with having turned the world upside down, and brought them before the local magistrates (Acts 17:6–7). This may be the affliction to which Paul refers in our text, 1:6. By their patient endurance and their suffering, Paul says, the Thessalonian Christians have shown themselves to be imitators—both of the apostles and of Christ (cf. 1 Cor. 4:16; 11:1; Phil. 3:17, etc.). Whereas later the Thessalonian Christians are said to have followed the example of the Judean churches in suffering (2:14), in the present passage Paul writes of the Thessalonians themselves having become an example for believers everywhere (1:7–8). Suffering in, with, and for Christ can be a powerful witness to the gospel. Paul saw this in the case of the Thessalonians, and he experienced it more than once in his own life (see especially Phil. 1:12–18). It is not by accident that the Greek word for a witness *(martys)* later became the church's technical designation for those who bore their witness through suffering and death (martyrs).

In 1:9–10 one probably hears an echo of the way the earliest Christian missionary preaching had been formulated. 1 Cor. 2:2 is a more typically Pauline summary of the gospel, but there is nothing contradictory of Paul's views in the present verses: There is but one God whose Son, Jesus Christ, has been raised from the dead and will return to save us from the coming wrath. This particular formulation is appropriate here because, as one learns from later chapters, the topic of the Lord's return is one on which the Thessalonians needed special help (see 4:13—5:11, especially 5:9–10).

The opening section of the letter (2:1ff.) extends the thought to Paul's own apostolic conduct. In his day many charlatan teachers wandered from city to city hawking faddish philosophies only for their personal gain. In 2:1ff. (as in 2 Cor. 2:17; 4:2) Paul is distinguishing his motives, aims, and conduct from theirs. Suffering (on his suffering in Philippi see Acts 16:19–24; cf. Phil. 1:30), and not self-interest, is the mark of the Christian apostolate. (See also 1 Cor. 4:8–13; 2 Cor. 4:7–12; 6:4–10; 11:23–29; 12:5–10. On 2:7–8 see exegesis for the Twenty-fourth Sunday after Pentecost.)

Gospel: Matt. 22:34–46. As this evangelist portrays it, from the time Jesus first set foot in Jerusalem (21:1) the Jewish leaders in that city sought to discredit him by their hostile questions (see 21:23–27; 22:15–22, 23–33). The two incidents which comprise the present lesson belong to this series of controversy stories. Since they depict Jesus' disputes with the Pharisees specifically, they prepare the reader for the sharply formulated denunciations of the Pharisees which follow immediately in chap. 23.

The first scene (22:34–40; parallels in Mark 12:28–34; Luke 10:25–28) shows a Pharisaic expert on the law challenging Jesus to identify the greatest commandment of all. This is a hostile question (v. 35; contrast Mark 12:28); the questioner really wants to know whether Jesus will accept all parts of the law as equally binding. Jesus' response (vv. 37–39) is to identify two commandments, not just one, as the greatest: to love God (Deut. 6:5) and (of equal importance) to love the neighbor (Lev. 19:18). There are other Matthean summaries of the law in 7:12; 9:13a; 12:7; 23:33, but none is accorded the degree of importance assigned here to this one.

This double commandment must have had a firm place in the traditions taken over by the evangelist, and it is not impossible to believe that it goes back to Jesus himself. There are similar rabbinic summaries, however, and the commandment to love one's enemies (formulated by this evangelist in 5:43–47) is more distinctive and more apt to bring us into touch with Jesus' own teaching. The distinctive element in the present passage, attributable to the evangelist himself, comes in v. 40: "all the law and the prophets" (a Matthean phrase, 5:17; 7:12) *depend* on these two commandments. The evangelist apparently means, not just that all general moral principles may be derived from a slender scriptural base (a common rabbinic theme), but that these two commandments are the key to the interpretation of all the others. According to this evangelist, Christianity and Judaism are divided precisely on the matter of the interpretation of the law (note, for example, his formulation of the antitheses, 5:21–47), and it is significant that in this Gospel alone (contrast Mark 12:32; Luke 10:28) Jesus' questioner does not accept Jesus' response.

In the next scene (22:41–46; parallels in Mark 12:35–37a; Luke 20:41–44) it is Jesus who puts a question to the Pharisees: If the Messiah is really David's son, as they say (v. 42), how can David call the Messiah "Lord" (vv. 43–44, citing Ps. 110:1 as David's)? This puzzle is not resolved, either here (v. 45) or in the parallel versions; but for the present evangelist the important point is that the Pharisees had been bested by Jesus, and that they no longer dared to question him (v. 46).

HOMILETICAL INTERPRETATION

One clear theme emerging from the texts for this day is that of the law and its role in relation to the love and service of God. The homiletical possibilities of this theme have been ably explored by Father Bruce Vawter in *Pentecost 3* in series A of Proclamation 1 ([Philadelphia: Fortress Press, 1975], pp. 26–29) and need not be repeated here. A second, or corollary, emphasis is on the love of neighbor, particularly as that love is lived out in a social context. The lections provide the preacher with an opportunity to describe neighborly love in some concreteness, in regard to its substance, its motive, and its enabling power.

The First Lesson urges us to interpret the Gospel's love of neighbor in a social direction. Negatively, it pushes us to see that oppression (wronging the disadvantaged) in any form is an act of non-love. Positively, it pushes us to speak of love in terms of those who are oppressed.

It is important that we see the widows, orphans, and poor of Exodus in their full social context. The personal loss (of husband or parents) or personal deprivation (loss or lack of money) conveyed by such terms is clear. But the social dimension of such a status is often obscured. Widows and orphans are not simply those who have sustained a loss. Rather, they are those who because of their loss have no representation in the decision making of the community. Poor people are not simply those who have no money. Rather, they are those who because of their pennilessness have no share in the power of the society of which they are a part. The widows and orphans and poor are those without social leverage, as surely as are "strangers." They are therefore representatives of all in any age who are excluded, impotent, and disinherited. They are those confined to imprisoning institutions, those considered of little account because they are physically or mentally disadvantaged, those deprived of a liberating education. They are the nobodies, the ones whose opinions never have to be asked, the ones who are effectively rendered invisible.

The Covenant Code clearly demands that such disadvantaged persons not be wronged, and the Exodus passage graphically outlines some of the things of which such wronging or oppression might consist. But oppression is not simply a matter of wronging the disadvantaged. In terms of their societal life, the disadvantaged are oppressed by the very fact of their status as disadvantaged. Oppression is not just a matter of doing the disinherited some further wrong. It has to do with the very fact of their disinheritance.

To love an oppressed neighbor surely means not to take advantage of his voiceless, powerless condition. But it means far more than that. And it means even more than acting in kindness. It means raising up those who have been put down and including those who have been left out. It means making sure that the unseen become visible, that the voiceless find speech, that the powerless are given power. There is no doubt that this is a radical love. It attacks the well-kept notion that only the competent and successful are worthy of inclusion and authority. It questions, and therefore threatens, economic systems and political structures. It requires acknowledgment that we who are favored (and if we're reading or writing this book, we are) are part of the problem because the favored do tend to see the existing order as good and legitimate. It demands that we listen carefully to the oppressed. As James Cone urges, the oppressor cannot even decide what is Christian behavior.

The texts provide several interlocking reasons why God's people should love the neighbor, and more precisely, the neighbor who is oppressed. One reason is clearly stated in Exodus. The God with whom the people are in covenant is a compassionate God (in this he differs from the idols mentioned in 1 Thessalonians). He hears the cries of the wronged, and he works both to right the wrongs committed and to punish the doers of the wrong. Because God is compassionate, his people should also be compassionate (in much the same way perhaps as Paul speaks of "imitating"—see exegesis). It is never a matter, of course, of watching what God does for others and then following suit. As people of the covenant, the ones called upon to have compassion are precisely those whose own cries of oppression have been heard and answered. They are to treat one another in the way that God has treated them.

Jesus' words in Matthew insist that the command to love God and the command to love the neighbor are of equal importance. Not only are they both binding, but they are integrally related. One cannot love God without loving the neighbor, nor can one love the neighbor without thereby loving God. (This relationship is indicated in Exodus by the fact that God enters the scene as soon as the neighbor is harmed.) To be in covenant with God is to be in covenant with one another (the "my people" of Exod. 22:25). To oppress the neighbor is to deny the Covenant and the God who made it.

While the foregoing can easily be interpreted christologically, there are more specific things that can be said for those who are "in

Christ." Those who are baptized into the death of Christ are baptized into the one who was himself oppressed and took upon himself the vast oppression of the world. He was oppressed both by his disadvantage and by his being wronged in that disadvantage (dehumanized and victimized). For the Christian to oppress a neighbor is to deny his own existence as a Christian; it is to deny the Christ into whom he has been incorporated.

More than that, however, the one who is baptized into the death of Christ is also baptized into his resurrection (the early missionary preaching echoed in Paul). The oppressed One has been exalted and the power of oppression has thereby been broken. Those who are in Christ are free to live lives of non-oppressing love. One's worth, dignity, and acceptance are not dependent upon those things which feed oppression: self-love and personal protection, self-emulation and personal success, self-aggrandizement and accumulation of good, and so forth. As Paul and the Thessalonians were enabled in Christ to live beyond self-interest (which includes patient endurance and suffering), so are all Christians. Oppression has become irrelevant. It simply has nothing to do with who we are.

Those who are baptized into the death and resurrection of Christ also await his return (again, the echo of the early missionary preaching). That return is of the day rather than of the night; it is of love rather than of oppression. Because of the exaltation of the One oppressed, the Christian knows that God's vision of justice and wholeness will be realized. "We can wait expectantly and not fearfully, because we do not doubt that God's purposes for the world will win out. The Church is left free to risk for *shalom* because we are sure of its coming." (Walter Brueggemann, *Living Toward a Vision* [Philadelphia: United Church Press, 1976], p. 120).

As God's people called to love, we often find ourselves immobilized in the face of worldwide oppression. The oppression is too vast, too structural, too unyielding to individual or small group action. We seem keenly aware of world problems and seem to have an acute sense of the immensity of the church's mission. But while such attentiveness is necessary, it sometimes blinds us to specific people living near at hand for whom specific action could make all the difference. While we think and talk about the huge problems of our

times, we should also seek to free even a couple of nearby people
(our "neighbors") from the bonds of oppression. Our love can be
effective.

The Twenty-fourth Sunday after Pentecost

Lutheran	Roman Catholic	Episcopal	Pres/UCC/Chr	Meth/COCU
Amos 5:18–24	Mal. 1:14b—2:2b	Mic. 3:5–12	Mal. 2:1–10	Mal. 1:14b—2:10
1 Thess. 4: 13–14 (15–18)	1 Thess. 2:7b–9, 13	1 Thess. 2:9–13, 17–20	1 Thess. 2:7–13	1 Thess. 2:7–13, 17–20
Matt. 25:1–13	Matt. 23:1–12	Matt. 23:1–12	Matt. 23:1–12	Matt. 23:1–12

EXEGESIS

First Lesson: Mal. 2:1–10. The prophetic oracles in the canonical
Book of Malachi date from the last half of the fifth century B.C. and
reflect conditions which obtained in Jerusalem under Persian rule. At
some later date these oracles were added to the Book of the Twelve
Prophets as a separate collection, introduced as it now is by 1:1. Many
interpreters believe that Malachi is not intended as a proper name in
1:1, but should be translated literally, "my messenger." Others hold
that the editor of the oracles constituted the name for this prophet on
the basis of 3:1. In either case, the prophet himself remains anonymous. Whoever he is, he is deeply concerned about the deterioration
of the moral and religious life of his people, and he does not hesitate
to speak, like the prophets of old, of God's judgment which will
come upon Israel because it has neglected its responsibilities (for
example, 3:1–5).

The oracles in Malachi are readily divisible, by virtue of their
structure and content, into six sections of varying lengths, and except
for the last verse, this lesson is derived from the section addressed to
the priests (1:6—2:9). They have been denounced generally for not
having honored God (1:6), and they have been criticized in particular

for their indifference to the need for offering sacrifices in the prescribed way (see especially 1:7–8, 13–14). In 2:1–3 they are warned
that this conduct does not escape God's notice and will be punished,
and in 2:4–6 they are reminded of the terms according to which the
Levitical priesthood had been established (see Deut. 18:1–8; 33:8–
11). Along with the cultic responsibilities of the priesthood, which had
already been emphasized, the prophet now mentions the responsibilities for moral leadership and instruction (2:7). In this, too, Israel's priests should have followed in the way of Levi (2:8; cf. v. 6),
but since they have not, they will be despised and abased among their
own people (2:9).

The last verse of this lesson (2:10) is actually the first verse of a new
section of oracles and must be read in the light of 2:11–16. Here the
prophet denounces Israelite men who marry foreign wives and
thereby introduce alien belief and practices into Israel. V. 10 is not
speaking of the universal fatherhood of God, but is speaking of the
covenant people, Israel, alone: they are one holy community under
one God, and marriages contracted with outsiders profane that community by compromising its integrity and obscuring its identity.

Second Lesson: 1 Thess. 2:7–13. In 2:1ff. Paul is urging his Thessalonian converts to remember how he and his associates had conducted themselves when they brought the gospel to them. The Thessalonians could hardly have forgotten that in the literal sense, since
Paul had left their city only a few months earlier. His reminder is
designed to emphasize that his present letter is as sincere as what he
had preached then, and that they should accept the appeals which will
follow (4:1—5:22) just as earnestly as they have already accepted
his gospel.

Vv. 7–8 go closely with 2:1–6, in which the apostle has sharply
distinguished the motives and aims of his missionary practice from
those of the charlatan street preachers of his day (see exegesis for the
Twenty-third Sunday after Pentecost). Now he emphasizes the dis-
tinctiveness of his apostolic work by depicting himself as having been
no less bound to the Thessalonians than a nursing mother is to her
suckling children, both in the sharing of self and in genuine affection.

He uses the same image, although for a different purpose, in 1 Cor. 3:1–2. The point is virtually the same in 2 Cor. 12:14b–15 where, referring more generally to the love of parents for their children, he describes his ministry as a "spending and being spent" for the souls of his hearers.

Paul's readers are reminded further that they had received the gospel free of charge (vv. 9–10). The apostle was a craftsman (cf. Acts 18:3) and was largely self-supporting, not only in Thessalonica, but elsewhere (for example, Corinth, 1 Cor. 9:3–7, 12–18). He was willing to receive aid from his churches, apparently, only after he had moved on to new fields of service, and not while he was still with them (see, for example, 2 Cor. 11:7–9).

The maternal imagery of vv. 7–8 is matched by paternal imagery in vv. 11–12. Here Paul likens his apostolic role to that of a father who is concerned to teach his children how to walk in the ways of God (cf. 1 Cor. 4:14–21). To "walk" (RSV: "lead a life") worthy of one's calling (v. 12) means to please God (4:1) by applying oneself to his will. It is clear that Paul is preparing here for appeals that will come in chaps. 4 and 5 of this letter.

V. 13 represents a renewal of the original thanksgiving of 1:2, and essentially repeats the point of 1:5a: that Paul's gospel is not just human wisdom (cf. 1 Cor. 1:17–25; 2:1–5), but God's own word. But now he places more emphasis on the Thessalonians' having recognized and received it as such, and on the fact that it is a word that actually "works" among them for their salvation (cf. the prophet's conception of God's word, Isa. 55:10–11, as well as Rom. 1:16; Phil. 1:6; 2:13).

Gospel: Matt. 23:1–12. In chaps. 21 and 22 the evangelist has portrayed the developing conspiracy of the religious leaders of Jerusalem against Jesus. Having repeatedly failed to entrap him by their hostile questions, they must finally fall silent before him (22:46). Now in chap. 23, the evangelist shows Jesus pronouncing a series of "woes" on the Pharisees (23:13–36). Today's Gospel consists of the verses which precede the woes proper. They may themselves be divided into two sections, corresponding to the two groups Jesus is represented as addressing here (see v. 1). Vv. 2–7 seem to be directed to the crowd, and vv. 8–12 to Jesus' disciples. While there may be some echoes of Jesus' own teaching here, those are difficult to recover. Therefore, this passage must be interpreted primarily with reference to the situation that obtained in the evangelist's own day, sometime in the last two decades of the first century. There was a widening gulf between the church and the synagogue, and within the church itself there was a growing need for spiritual, moral, and ecclesiastical discipline.

In vv. 2–7 the increasing hostility between Jews and Christians is apparent. Here the Pharisees (the Jews of this evangelist's own day) are denounced as hypocritical and vain. It is surprising to find their authority as teachers as well as the content of their teaching affirmed in vv. 2–3, because this does not correspond with the evangelist's own view (see, for example, 15:1–9; 16:12). These two verses must represent a source which had come down to the evangelist from a time when Christians were still seeking to live by the law. The criticisms in vv. 4–7 are more severe.

The counsels of vv. 8–12 pertain to life within the Christian community itself. Here Jesus' disciples (the Christian leaders of this evangelist's day) are cautioned not to make pretentious claims for themselves, because they are all brethren under the fatherhood of God and the lordship of Christ (vv. 8–10). Paul, who was not hesitant to present himself as the "father" of his congregation (see preceding exegesis of 1 Thess. 2:7–13), nevertheless makes much the same point in 1 Cor. 3:5–23 (with reference to apostles) and 1 Cor. 12:4ff. (with reference to the Christian community as a whole. See also Matt. 7:13–23.).

In vv. 11–12 the evangelist has brought together two separate sayings which recur often in the Jesus traditions. The first (v. 11) defines greatness in terms of service. It has been used also in 20:26 (parallels in Mark 10:43–44; Luke 22:26) and seems to lie behind 18:1–5 as well (note the parallels in Mark 9:35; Luke 9:48b). The point of the second saying (v. 12), that the proud will be brought low and the humble will be exalted, is often found in the wisdom literature (for example, Job 22:29; Prov. 29:23), and is equally at home in the synoptic tradition (see also Matt. 18:4; Luke 14:11; 18:14). By placing these sayings after vv. 8–10 the evangelist has provided his warnings against seeking honorific titles with a general theological foundation.

HOMILETICAL INTERPRETATION

Two themes are suggested by the lections for this Sunday. The primary theme is that of leadership in the church. It focuses attention on the professional ministry. A related theme is that of life in the Christian community. It focuses attention on the nonprofessional ministry (the laity). Both themes are important emphases of the Pentecost season. The assigned texts may provide opportunity to say some new things about these recurring subjects.

The lections for this day furnish an excellent occasion for the professional minister to explain his or her ministry to the gathered community. While such an exposition could be made in a general way (this is what ministry is), it would certainly be more meaningful if it could be made as specific as possible (this is what *my* ministry is). Needless to say, such a specific elucidation demands careful reflection and honest appraisal. Toward such, the texts offer a means of personal and professional exploration. But in order to be specific, the preacher must locate himself or herself in the generalities of the texts, and in the homiletical interpretation which follows.

St. Paul suggests that the care which pastors are to offer their people is both gentle (like a suckling nurse) and exhortative (like a father with his children). It's a delight that Paul uses both female and male imagery to describe the apostolic care given by himself and Silvanus and Timothy. While his description follows certain sexual stereotypes (affection and authority, for example), it nonetheless points to a fullness of care offered by whole persons. Pastors, in this sense, are to be both nurses and fathers. And perhaps there is not as much difference between gentleness and exhortation as common language usage makes it appear. To exhort means to encourage and to animate as well as to warn or caution.

It does not seem too much to say that to give pastoral care is to nourish, to encourage, and to advise the members of one's congregation. Such care is to be given continuously. Paul, for example, was as sincerely affectionate toward the Thessalonians in what he wrote to them as in what he said and did in their presence. Affection has its place not only in the hospital room and in the funeral home; it is also appropriate to the pulpit and to the committee meeting. Such care is also to be given consistently. Both the OT and Gospel texts warn religious leaders against imposing burdens on others from which they consider themselves exempt. This indeed suggests that pastors are to offer as much care to others as they do to themselves. But it might also suggest that pastors show as much care to themselves and their families as they do to others. Affection and encouragement are to be applied all the way around. The pastor is not to nurse others and then exhort himself or herself (preach grace, for example, but live out his or her ministry as law).

Underlying the giving of both affection and exhortation in pastoral care is a sharing of the self (1 Thess. 2:8). Such sharing highlights perhaps the vulnerability of the pastor, as well as the identification of the pastor with his or her people. The pastor is not set apart as a dogmatic advice-giver. He or she is a fellow pilgrim (an example *of* the congregation as well as *to* the congregation). The pastor experiences the human struggle in his or her own soul. The pastor's inspiration does not come alone from what has been heard or read, but comes also from the visions which arise during personal pilgrimage. The pastor is one who reaches out to other travelers and in so doing opens himself or herself to misunderstanding, opposition, and even rejection as well as to acceptance and exhilaration.

The sharing of oneself is a key not only to affectionate pastoral care, but also to the task of preaching. Indeed, it is the personal element in preaching which points to its essential mystery: the word of God through the medium of human life and language. ("The Word of God, in order to be audible from its past, must itself go forth as human speech . . . ." according to Karl Rahner.) And yet it is the personal, fellow pilgrim, aspect of preaching that creates one of its greatest tensions. The fellow-pilgrim preacher is also messenger. And there is a quality of "outside-ness" about every messenger (otherwise there would be no message). A pastor "breaks in." This is a true description of the way calls and pastoral changes are made. It is also a true description of the preaching ministry, a ministry which involves both comfort and challenge, both good news and bad. The word attacks human idolatries, human indifference and neglect, human presumptions and self-sufficiencies. And that attacking word is spoken by the preacher to the same people for whom he or she shows continual and consistent affection. (There are times, and this Sunday may be one of them, when it might be helpful to share this tension with a congregation.)

It is in the middle of pastoral tensions that the vulnerable minister is encouraged not to forget the power of the Word (the First and Second Lessons urge hearers and readers to remember). A preacher's sufficiency is never in himself or herself. The word of God is at work (1 Thess. 2:13). Certainly this word has strong opposition. There is the kind of insanity in which people seem to be more interested in putting down than raising up, in burdening than easing, in stifling than in letting grow, in living under rules than under gift. There is widespread ignorance of the fact that accumulation and ownership are a dead end, that there are communities larger than one's own small circle, that there is a need to be grateful and challenged and expanded in both space and vision. And yet we can testify with St. Paul and the Thessalonians to the gospel's power and work. Luther said ". . . it is impossible that the Word of God should return to him void." Even where the Word is not altogether preached, and even where faith may be very small and feeble, the Word evokes faith. And there is our sufficiency.

The prophet reminds us that the community of God's people has its own identity and integrity. The covenant people to whom Malachi spoke constituted a community identified by its cultus and by its instruction. Both priests and people were denounced for turning aside from the way and thus obscuring who they were as the people of God. Today the community of God's people is identified by the centrality of word and sacrament within it. The integrity of the community depends upon its guarding of that centrality in its thought and in its life.

The word of God comes to the community as a message to be believed. It is a word directed personally to the one who hears it, appealing to his or her faith. The Christian community is those people who have confidence in the news that comes (accepting it "not as the word of men but as what it really is, the word of God," 1 Thess.

2:13). Faith is that which accepts God's promise; it is a vital, deliberate trust in God's grace.

Perhaps part of the need in Matthew's church for spiritual, moral and ecclesiastical discipline (see exegesis) is reflected in the gospel's warning against presumptuous behavior. Members of the community are not to set themselves up in positions which elevate them above the others. All are brethren (v. 8). Honorific titles have no place. Humility and service (servanthood) are central marks of the community. While Matthew's situation was different than ours (prior to the development of special offices), his warning is hardly irrelevant. The church is not free from arrogance, nor from the whiff of fame and greatness which smells so sweet. Is there perhaps a pecking order in your congregation, or in your denomination?

The Twenty-fifth Sunday after Pentecost

Lutheran	Roman Catholic	Episcopal	Pres/UCC/Chr	Meth/COCU
Hos. 11:1–4, 8–9	Wisd. 6:13–17	Amos 5:18–24	Song of Sol. 3:1–5	Jer. 26:1–6
1 Thess. 5:1–11	1 Thess. 4:13–18 or 1 Thess. 4:13–14	1 Thess. 4:13–14	1 Thess. 4:13–18	1 Thess. 3: 7–13
Matt. 25:14–30	Matt. 25:1–13	Matt. 25:1–13	Matt. 25:1–13	Matt. 24:1–14

EXEGESIS

First Lesson: Hos. 11:1–4, 8–9. Hosea lived and prophesied in the northern kingdom during the eighth century B.C. It is uncertain whether the prophet lived to see the fall of the northern kingdom to the Assyrians in 722, but he may have. Hosea's prophetic oracles (chaps. 4—14) speak mainly of the judgment which Yahweh will visit upon his people because of their unfaithfulness. It is from these that the present lesson has been taken.

Even though they have not been included as such in this lesson, vv. 5–7 need to be taken into account as well as vv. 1–4 and 8–9. Some of the force of vv. 8–9 is lost when vv. 5–7 are omitted from consideration. In vv. 1–4 the prophet gives a moving sketch of the long history of Yahweh's love and care for his people and of their indifference to it and repeated idolatry. The inevitable and disastrous consequences of their unfaithfulness are presented in vv. 5–6, and Yahweh's lament is summarized in v. 7. But then in vv. 8–9 there comes the word of grace: Yahweh has never yet given Israel up, and he never will (see also v. 11; v. 10 may be an interpolation, and v. 12 goes with chap. 12).

V. 1 recalls God's deliverance of his people from Egypt at the Exodus, and vv. 2–4 characterize their time of wandering in the wilderness as generally a period of wanton disregard for Yahweh's love. The imagery here is of a father's love for his son (v. 1), teaching him to walk, healing his hurts (v. 3) and nurturing his existence (v. 4). The reference in v. 4 is probably not to easing "the yoke on their jaws" (RSV) but, as in most recent English versions, to the lifting up of Israel like a little child to the father's cheek (for example, NEB, JB, TEV).

It is precisely Hosea's use of parental imagery for God that allows him to portray Yahweh as he does in vv. 8–9. Yahweh is still the speaker, but now, in an abrupt change from the preceding verses, Israel is addressed directly (no longer him, v. 1, but you, v. 8). And now, moved by a father's love for his child, God repents of his anger (see, for example, NEB translation of v. 8) and resolves that he will never again (as in vv. 5–7) think of letting Israel be led to destruction. Here the prophet is affirming that the righteousness and holiness of God are never isolated from his love. He is with his people, not to destroy them, but to uphold and to redeem (v. 9).

Second Lesson: 1 Thess. 5:1–11. In the last part of this letter (4:1—5:22) Paul is issuing various kinds of appeals designed to confirm the Thessalonians in their faith. The counsels of 4:13—5:11 all pertain to the matter of Christ's expected return at the eschaton. In 5:1–11, specifically, the apostle is urging wakefulness and sobriety in prospect of the Lord's coming again.

Vv. 1–3 make it clear that the members of Paul's congregation in Thessalonica share the general Christian expectation that Christ will return suddenly and without any particular advance signs (cf. Matt. 24:36, 42–44; Luke 12:39–40; 2 Pet. 3:10; Rev. 3:3; 16:15). The warning against a false sense of security (v. 3) echoes a slogan also criticized in Jer. 6:14; 8:11 and Ezek. 13:10, and the picture of a swift, inescapable destruction is present as well in Matt. 24:39; Luke 21:34–35.

The heart of this passage comes in vv. 4–8 where, as he does so often, the apostle combines an indicative with an imperative. The indicative stands in vv. 4–5: Believers already belong to the Day that is coming (see v. 2). The imagery here is different, but the thought is the same as that in Phil. 3:20–21 and Rom. 8:14–25 (cf. also Rom. 12:1–2). But the imperative follows from this (vv. 6–8): Their belonging to God requires that they serve him where they are right now. As in 1:3 (and elsewhere) Paul defines the Christian's responsibility in terms of faith, love, and hope (v. 8), in this case using imagery derived from Isa. 59:17 (see also Wisd. of Sol. 5:18 and Eph. 6:13–17). Rom. 13:11–14 is closely parallel to these verses and shows how Paul uses the prospect of the Lord's return to support the kind of concrete ethical exhortations one finds in Rom. 12:3ff.

In vv. 9–10 the "indicative" of Christian existence is stressed once again, but now in a formulation which employs the traditional language of the church's missionary preaching (v. 9 is parallel to 1:9–10) and of its creedal statements (v. 10, Christ's death "for us"; cf. Rom. 5:6–11; 1 Cor. 15:3–5; 2 Cor. 5:14–15, etc.). The affirmation that believers belong to the Lord whether they wake or sleep (v. 10) would have been particularly relevant for the Thessalonians (see 4:13–18 and the exegesis for the Twenty-sixth Sunday after Pentecost). Beyond that, however, it is one of Paul's most fundamental theological convictions; see also Rom. 14:7–9.

Whereas vv. 9–10 are an affirmation of the faith Paul and his readers share, in v. 11 the apostle affirms the readers themselves, even as he urges them to persevere in their affirmation of one another and in the strengthening of the life and witness of their congregation as a whole.

Gospel: Matt. 25:14–30. Three stages of development are discernible in this parable of the talents (parallel Luke 19:12–27), but there is a fundamental continuity of meaning that runs through all three levels.

Where it stands in Matthew, this is one of the parables about the

Lord's return (24:32—25:46) which are designed to instruct and exhort believers about their responsibilities in the meantime. The evangelist specifically links this parable to the admonition of 25:13 to watch for the Lord's return. *"For,"* he now goes on in v. 14, the situation is like that of the man with the talents. This evangelist would have us think of the lord of the house as the Lord (Christ), of his departure from his own country as Christ's ascension, of the servants as Christians left behind in the world, of the enormous amount of money entrusted to the servants (one talent = 10,000 denarii!) as the blessings of God, and of the master's eventual return as Christ's coming again at the Last Judgment.

That the master came home only "after a long time" (v. 19) reflects the church's experience of the delay in Christ's returning, and is another Matthean touch. So, too, are the references in vv. 21, 24 about entering into the joy of the Lord (into his kingdom) and the final, dire warning about the fate of those who are not faithful while the Lord is away (v. 30; cf. 8:12; 13:42, 50; 22:13; 24:51). The lesson this evangelist wants his readers to gain from this parable is clear. How long before the Lord returns is hard to say, but when he comes, they will be held responsible for the way they have led their lives in his absence. Have they been actively at work for him or, like the servant who hid the one talent, have they cared only about their own security? Have they been willing to risk the loss of everything in order to serve their Lord (= others; see 25:31–46)?

At some earlier point in the transmission of this parable, the originally independent saying of v. 29 (found also in 13:12, in Mark 4:25 and the Gospel of Thomas, Log. 41, as well as in Luke 19:26) was joined to it, along with the comment (v. 28) that the one talent of the irresponsible servant was given to the servant who had accomplished the most. Here the point is that when God's gifts are hoarded, they are lost, but when they are employed in his service they abound.

The original parable, then, perhaps concluded with v. 27 and would not have been an allegory of Christ's ascension and return in judgment. It would have focused exclusively on one point, perhaps best epitomized by the saying of Mark 8:35: "Whoever would save his life will lose it; and whoever loses his life . . . will save it."

HOMILETICAL INTERPRETATION

The texts for this Sunday invite us to reflect upon the identity of
God and upon our own identity in relation to him. But the invitation is
to far more than some kind of mental assessment or abstract analysis.
It is an invitation to participate, to enter fully into the dramatic
activity that occurs between the one called God and his people. The
images and stories of the lections resist our turning God, or ourselves,
or the relationship between us, into impersonal ideas. They invite us
to an encounter.

The invitation to encounter is given immediately in the prophet's
marvelous imaging of God as a father in action. It has been pointed
out, for example, that the Greek image of the father was quite different from that of the ancient Hebrew. While the Hebrew image conveyed the personal activity of the father as guardian, the Greek image
pictured the father as the seminal source of life. Guardian and source:
the one intensely personal, the other an impersonal idea. For
the Hebrew prophet, God is certainly no mere idea or concept. He
is a living and personal God who encounters his people in dramatic
activity.

It is obvious that the image of father is not the only image used in the
OT to utter or disclose God. It is also obvious that such an image has
its limitations. The prophet is limited by his own patriarchal society.
Father-imagery expressed more powerfully for him the protective
and caring parent than did mother-imagery. This limitation may be a
severe one in certain areas and congregations today. The preacher
may be well advised to speak of parent rather than of father. It is
necessary to avoid the implication that God is most like the male head
of the household. In addition, the father image is limited by our own
experience of fathers and parents. All human beings are deficient in
important respects and cannot be relied upon absolutely. Not all
fathers are loving and protective. And even the best fathers are not
loving and protective all of the time or in every way.

But in spite of its limitations, the prophet's image of God as father is
a marvelous one. It conveys the activity of God toward his children
(Israel, the church, Jesus) as reliable and readily available protection

and care. More than that, it conveys the passionate feelings that God
has toward his children. Love, anger, disappointment, ambivalence
are all present. God is neither detached nor unaffected. He is a God
who is "totally immersed in our struggles and emotions and messy,
frustrated lives" (Edmund A. Steimle, *From Death to Birth* [Phila-
delphia: Fortress Press, 1973], p. 25). But even more than that, the
prophet's use of the father image enables him to convey something of
the great mystery of personality in God. God suffers and is bewildered
in the face of the lovelessness of his people. At one and the same time
he is both angry and forbearing toward his disobedient children. His
holiness is of annihilating power, yet the power of his love prevails
(". . . this power at the heart of the divine being prevails not only over
the unworthiness of its object, but also over the demand of its own
righteous anger for judgment," says Walther Eichrodt in *Theology of
the Old Testament,* vol. 1 [Philadelphia: Westminster Press, 1961],
p. 281). The prophet clearly senses the struggle behind the words "I
will not come to destroy" (Hos. 11:9) and the words "God has
not destined us for wrath" (1 Thess. 5:9). Our God is passionately
"for us."

All three lections affirm that it is God who initiates the action
between himself and his children. It was God who called Israel out of
Egypt and who taught, healed, and nurtured his "Son." It was God
who made Paul and the Thessalonian Christians "sons of light and
sons of the day." It was Christ who called together his servants, the
church, and "entrusted to them his property." It is important to see
that whatever imperatives claim the lives of God's people, those
imperatives always follow upon an indicative. The activity of God
always precedes the responding activity of his children.

The Matthean text points specifically to the fact that the God who
initiates action also gives gifts to his people (in this case, an enormous
amount of money). However we may wish to define these gifts, they
are those which belong to a people called out of bondage, to a people
called from darkness to light, and to a people called to productive
servanthood (for example, Israel's prosperity; the Thessalonians'
faith, love, and hope; the servants' "talents"). All three texts point to
the necessity of a proper use of the gifts given. Israel is to acknowledge God as the gift-giver; the Thessalonians are to encourage one

another and build one another up; the servant-Christians are to risk loss for the sake of their master.

The Second Lesson and Gospel emphasize the future-orientation of those who belong to God. God is active not only in what has already occurred, but he is active also in that which is yet to come (referred to in the Matthean allegory as the return of Christ, and in the Thessalonian passage as the coming "Day of the Lord"). The present is qualified by the future as well as by the past. Such a future-orientation underlines three things. First, those who belong to God are secure in him; "whether we wake or sleep we . . . live with him." Second, the state of belonging to God is not a static condition. It does not involve simply a life of remembering what has gone before. It involves a life of soberness and wakefulness toward that which is yet to be. It involves a life of expectation and of change. Third, the gifts of God are to be used in the active doing of his will. The gift-holders are motivated by the "coming Day" to which they already belong. It may be important to specify for some congregations that "wakefulness" and "expectancy" do not mean being preoccupied with the time or manner of the Lord's return. St. Paul insists that "the Day" is not a matter for idle curiosity. The important thing is the use of the gifts right now—in light of the coming "Day of the Lord."

It is interesting that none of the excuses offered (or possible) by the one-talent man is acceptable. "I am timid and no good at taking risks." "You are a hard master—you don't sow but you want to reap—and you frighten me." "I am modest; I don't have much to give and I know it." "You didn't give me any instructions—and you know my imagination is limited." While all may be true, none is accepted. God wants faithfulness, and that means trusting the giver of the gift by putting it to use—indeed, by risking it. When Paul tells the Thessalonians to encourage one another, perhaps he had something like this in mind. The best friend may not be the one who tells us to "take it easy," or who warns us that "that won't work," or who tells us to watch ourselves and not "work too hard." Such advice often succeeds only in riddling our morale and contaminating us with another's fear. The best friend may be the one who encourages us to reckless adventure, in the security of our belonging to God, and who astonishes us with a call to boldness. The end result of faithfulness in the parable (the two- and five-talent men) is not rest. The further gift is more work: "I will set you over much." And perhaps the very productivity in the parable is meant to encourage us. Using the gifts does make a difference.

The Twenty-sixth Sunday after Pentecost

Lutheran	Roman Catholic	Episcopal	Pres/UCC/Chr	Meth/COCU
Mal. 2:1–2, 4–10	Prov. 31:10–13, 19–20, 30–31	Zeph. 1:7, 12–18	Prov. 31:10–13, 19–20, 30–31	Zeph. 1:7, 12–18 or Song of Sol. 3:1–5
1 Thess. 2:8–13	1 Thess. 5:1–6	1 Thess. 5:1–10	1 Thess. 5:1–6	1 Thess. 4: 13–18
Matt. 23:1–12	Matt. 25:14–30 or Matt. 24:14–15, 19–20	Matt. 25:14–15, 19–29	Matt. 25:14–30	Matt. 25:1–13

EXEGESIS

First Lesson: Zeph. 1:7, 12–18. Zephaniah prophesied in Judah during Josiah's reign (1:1), sometime between 640 and 609 B.C. His invective against the syncretistic religious practices of the people, and even of the leaders, of Jerusalem (1:4, 5, 8) shows that he was active before the religious reforms instituted by Josiah in 621. During this period Assyrian power was rapidly declining (Ninevah, its capital, fell in 612 to the Babylonians and Medes) and there was general international unrest and political turmoil. Judah itself was beset by a profound moral malaise and was boldly neglectful of its own religious faith (see 1:9–12). Even the priests and public officials of Jerusalem were indifferent to their responsibilities (1:4–6, 8; 3:3–4), and the nation as a whole was without shame (2:1; 3:5). In this setting Zephaniah thundered again the warnings of Amos and Isaiah about the judgment with which "the Day of the Lord" would come.

Today's lesson is from the first, and certainly genuine, cycle of oracles (1:2–18). Some interpreters believe that vv. 2–6 and 8–13 originally stood together because they contain the particulars for which Judah will be punished: its idolatry, its unrighteousness and its presumptuous self-confidence. Vv. 7, 14–18, on the other hand, describe the Day of the Lord itself. This whole section, plus vv. 12–13 from the other section, constitutes the present lesson. Three points about this material are especially noteworthy.

First, there is the characterization of the people of Judah in v. 12. Smugly complacent in their drunken debauchery, they dismiss the relevance of God to their lives with the slogan, "Yahweh will do neither good nor harm." They do not deny the existence of God, but his meaning.

Second, Zephaniah has gone further than any of his prophetic predecessors in portraying the terrible consequences of this moral and religious indifference. The medieval hymn, "Day of wrath! O day of mourning!" *(Dies irae)* is based specifically on 1:15–16.

Finally, however, not even Zephaniah is a prophet only of doom. Even if the later promises of deliverance (3:14–20) are not attributable to him, the exhortations of 2:1–3 are. These are closely attached to the oracles of 1:2–18 and seem to presume that for those who humbly seek the Lord and his righteousness, there is still hope for deliverance from the impending disaster.

Second Lesson: 1 Thess. 4:13–18. In this paragraph Paul is addressing a problem which has come up in Thessalonica during the few months he has been away. The apostle's preaching there had included an affirmation that the Lord would return (see 1:10), and from comments he makes elsewhere it seems evident that he anticipated only a relatively short interim before that would occur (for example, 1 Cor. 7:29a; Rom. 13:11b–12a), presumably during his own lifetime and that of his converts. But in Thessalonica, it appears, at least one of the new believers has died, and Paul has learned that the congregation is deeply grieving the loss.

The way Paul introduces the topic in v. 13 may suggest that he himself has not had to face this problem until now. Does the hope that Christians share encompass those who do not live to see Christ come again? Paul's basic response to this comes in v. 14. It is opened with a creedal affirmation, certainly familiar to his readers: "We believe that Jesus died and rose again." Because that is so, Paul assures them, when Jesus comes again God will also raise those who have died in the Lord.

Vv. 15–17a elaborate the point. To enforce his assurances about the dead Paul emphasizes that they will be gathered up to the Lord first, even before the living (vv. 15, 16b–17). Later, in a letter to the Corinthians, he will defend this belief in the general resurrection at some length, and will predicate it, as he has here already, on the reality of Christ's own resurrection (1 Cor. 15). The vivid portrayal of Christ's descent from heaven, heralded by an archangel's call and the sound of a trumpet (v. 16a) is unique in Paul's letters, but these details as well as others are present in the Jewish apocalyptic tradition to which the earliest church was indebted (cf. Matt. 24:30–31 and the parallels).

The affirmation of v. 17b and the exhortation of v. 18 refer back to the whole of vv. 13–17a. It is clear that the apostle's main point here, as in Rom. 8:38–39, is that "neither death nor [anything else] will be able to separate us from the love of God in Christ Jesus our Lord": "we shall always be with the Lord" (v. 17b; cf. 5:10; Rom. 14:7–9). It is also clear (v. 18) that Paul wants the faith, love, and hope he once saw in Thessalonica (see 1:3) to be active now in the congregation, healing and supporting those who grieve.

Gospel: Matt. 25:1–13. This parable stands only in Matthew (but cf. Luke 12:35–36) and, like the one that follows (see the exegesis for the Twenty-fifth Sunday after Pentecost), concerns the return of the Lord at the eschaton. If an original parable of Jesus lies behind it, as some believe, what it was and what it meant can no longer be determined. However, the meaning it had for the later church and its use in this Gospel are more easily identified.

The parable is introduced (v. 1a) as being about "the kingdom of heaven" (a typical Matthean phrase). "Then" refers to the coming of the Son of man, mentioned several times in the preceding chapter (24:30–31, 39–44, 50). The scene is set in vv. 1b–4. Ten maidens set out with oil lamps to form a festal procession for a bride and her bridegroom. Five of the maidens are called wise because they took extra oil for their lamps, while the others are called foolish because they did not.

The heart of the parable comes in vv. 5–12. The bridegroom is delayed so long that the maidens fall asleep, the wise ones as well as the foolish (v. 5). When he does arrive, the foolish maidens realize they will need more oil for their lamps (vv. 6–7). Those with extra for themselves dare not share lest no one will have enough for the procession, so the foolish maidens must leave to buy more (vv. 8–9). When they return, the procession has finished and they find themselves shut out of the marriage banquet (vv. 10–11). They have not fulfilled their responsibilities, and thus their pleas to be let in are to no avail (v. 12; cf. Luke 13:25).

The key to the meaning of the parable is the reference to the bridegroom's delay in coming (v. 5). The church would read this as a parable of Christ's delay in returning, a delay in the dawning of the kingdom of heaven. The message of the parable is that the church must take this delay into account and be prepared for it. The faithful are to be like the wise maidens who took extra oil, not like the foolish maidens who persisted in the belief that the time was short before the wedding feast began.

The admonition of v. 13 is hardly an original component of the parable. Its admonition to be watchful, since one does not know when the day will come, is compatible with the message of preparedness, but misses the essential reason for the need to be prepared: not because the time of the Lord's return is unknown, but because it will surely be delayed.

HOMILETICAL INTERPRETATION

A central theme of the lections for this Sunday is the coming "Day of Wrath," the divine judgment. Some of the theological and sermonic possibilities for the development of this theme have been helpfully described by Father Bruce Vawter in *Pentecost 3* in series A of Proclamation 1 ([Philadelphia: Fortress Press, 1975], pp. 32–35). There is no need to duplicate those suggestions here. Instead a second but related theme will be explored. The focus will be on the fact that the coming day of judgment has been delayed. Not only does such an emphasis pick up on a situation reflected in the assigned texts, but it seems an appropriate accent as the Christian community moves toward the season of Advent. The church finds itself in the position of trying to maintain a keen sense of expectancy for the Lord's return, while gearing itself for a prolonged wait. Each of the texts casts some light on what it means for the church to exist in the period of delay.

It is extremely difficult to maintain much, if any, sense of expectancy during a prolonged period of waiting. Disappointment is often followed by anger, and anger is often followed by indifference. Whatever the particular sequence of their experience, Zephaniah's audience exhibits classic signs of indifference toward "the Day of the Lord." They no longer reckon with divine action in their lives. God has become irrelevant. The slogan that "the Lord will not do good, nor will he do ill" is chanted with lives decayed by moral sickness and corrupted by religious neglect. The prophet's invective is particularly sharp, and it may be that he overstated the situation to the point of caricature. It may also be that the complacency which shamed Zephaniah's nation (even uncaricatured) was far more severe than anything which infects the church today—although perhaps not society in general. But the temptation to think that God is inactive and to react accordingly is always present. There is good reason why prophets and apostles urged even God's people to remain alert and watchful. Because the day doesn't come quickly, we imagine that it won't come at all, or that its coming is of little significance to our daily lives.

An additional effect of the Lord's delay is that people may miss his coming in the present. Delay in this case is mistaken for absence. Most of the people of Judah and Jerusalem missed Yahweh's coming in the oracles of Zephaniah. Most of those who heard Jesus' message of the dawning kingdom missed God's presence in it. And certainly many failed to see the coming of God in the church's preaching of Jesus Messiah, God's Son. In no way does the "not yet" aspect of the Kingdom of God negate the "already" dimension of that kingdom. God is present in the words of his messengers. He comes in the comforting activities of the Thessalonian Christians. He is present in the excitement and preparation of those who await the marriage feast (the sacramental community). In the period of delay the presence of God may be hidden, but it is nonetheless real.

V. 13 of Matthew 25, while not an original component of the parable of the ten maidens might suggest that God's presence in the period of delay is as startling in its "coming" as is the final day. The bridegroom arrives at midnight—an arbitrary time perhaps, but a time when sight is not clear and figures are hidden in shadows. Less figuratively, no one really expected "God—born of peasant stock walking around incognito as Mary's son! Spending his time with call girls and racketeers" (see Edmund Steimle's fine sermon on the Matthean lection in *From Death to Birth* [Philadelphia: Fortress Press, 1973], pp. 59–65). God's presence in the world cannot be limited to the sacramental community. He is also present ("hidden") in the "midnight" people and communities of the world. He is present in a young man who thunders against his own people, for example, and he is present, and most clearly, in the rejected One of Judah. He is present in all those who are victims of the indifferent, of those who "fill their master's house with violence and fraud" (Zeph. 1:8).

The Matthean parable, in its allegorized form, makes it clear that the church's responsibility never ends. The church must take Christ's delay into account and be prepared for it (see exegesis). Part of what such preparation means is suggested by Zeph. 2:3: "Seek the Lord, all you humble of the land, who do his commands; seek righteousness, seek humility. . . ." Such a response is also suggested by Matthew's Gospel in its call to piety and faithful service (for example, 10:41–42 and 25:21). God's commandments are still valid for those who are in Christ. The baptized are *in* the law even though they are not *under* it. The period of prolonged waiting is a time when Christians live free from the law's threat, but do not live free from sin. They still need to exercise themselves in that law which stands as a rule for godly life and behavior. The wise in Matthew's story are those who keep the commandments and the foolish are those who don't. The church, represented by the ten, will not escape judgment—our responsibility never ends. A final decision is yet to be made. The door can be shut. It is in this knowledge that Christians commend themselves always to the grace of God.

The church's time of waiting is also a time of hope. It is a time when Christians wait expectantly for that which has been promised. And that which has been promised is resurrection through Jesus Christ. Paul's response to the Thessalonians' problem concerning those who die during the delay has far-reaching significance. It centers all consolation squarely on the resurrection. Indeed, any hope for the dead or for the living is firmly grounded in the fact that "Jesus died and rose again" and in the fact that "we shall always be with the Lord." Life beyond death is a matter of miracle rather than of survival. We live in expectation of that miracle. The apocalyptic imagery that Paul uses points to the cosmic proportions of the resurrection. Resurrection hope encompasses not only individuals but all of humankind, the "alive" and the "sleeping." Christians, therefore, do not hope just for themselves. Paul points to the fact that hope is not simply some kind of protective device (as the "helmet" of hope in Thess. 5:8 might suggest). It is a power, an active comfort which effectively quiets grief. Its power comes from its grounding in the resurrection of Christ and its promise. In the period of prolonged waiting the Christian church is the bearer of this gift-giving message of hope.

The parable of the ten maidens reminds us that in the time of waiting the church is a mixture of wise and foolish people. There are several possible responses to this fact. One response is simply to acknowledge it, leaving any and all determination of foolish and wise to the Day of Judgment and to the Lord. A second response is to assume that while the church catholic is a mixture, any particular congregation is made up of all wise or of all foolish people and to treat them as such. A third response is to determine which people have oil and which people don't. Such determination could be followed by the enforcement of stricter discipline, and even by doors shut to the disobedient or to the uncommitted. A fourth response is to recognize that not only each congregation but each Christian is a mixture of wise and foolish. It could stress discipline but leave any final determination up to the Lord. It could acknowledge the mixture in both persons and groups and encourage mutual confession and support.

Christ the King
The Last Sunday after Pentecost

Lutheran	Roman Catholic	Episcopal	Pres/UCC/Chr	Meth/COCU
Ezek. 34:11–16, 23–24	Ezek. 34:11–12, 15–17	Ezek. 34:11–17	Ezek. 34:11–17	Ezek. 34:11–17, 23–24
1 Cor. 15:20–28	1 Cor. 15:20–26a, 28	1 Cor. 15:20–28	1 Cor. 15:20–28	1 Cor. 15:20–28
Matt. 25:31–46	Matt. 25:31–46	Matt. 25:31–46	Matt. 25:31–46	Matt. 25:31–46

EXEGESIS

First Lesson: Ezek. 34:11–16, 23–24. Three types of prophetic oracles appear in the Book of Ezekiel. There are oracles of judgment against Israel in chaps. 1—24, oracles against foreign nations in chaps. 25—32, and oracles concerning Israel's salvation in chaps. 33—48. Scholars are agreed that this book in its canonical form represents the careful work of a final editor, and that some of the oracles must be regarded as later additions dating from that time or earlier. Those which comprise today's lesson, however, seem to be Ezekiel's own.

Ezekiel's ministry spanned the years from the first deportation of exiles to Babylon in 597 B.C. to (and including) the destruction of Jerusalem by the Babylonians in 587. The catastrophe of 587 would have seemed an impressive fulfillment of Ezekiel's earlier prophecies of destruction (chaps. 1—24), and it marked a significant turning point in his ministry. Now his message changes to one of hope and his oracles become promises of salvation. It is from these oracles that the present lesson is drawn. Chaps. 34—37 have as their subject the restoration of Israel and the moral renewal of its life, and within this section chap. 34 (along with 37:24–28) has as its special theme the shepherds of Israel.

Ezekiel was not the first to refer to Israel's rulers and leaders as shepherds (see, for example, 1 Kings 22:17), and his sharp invective against Israel's past leaders as shepherds who cared more for themselves than for their sheep (34:2–10) may be dependent upon the similarly worded criticisms of Jeremiah (Jer. 23:1–6; cf. 10:21; 24:34–38). In place of these pseudo-shepherds, who have caused the flock of Israel to be "scattered over all the face of the earth" (v. 6 RSV), Yahweh himself will be the shepherd (vv. 11–12). The promise is that now their God will gather them from exile and return them to their own land, the pastures of Israel (v. 13). The exiles are assured that Yahweh's shepherding of the restored nation will be the opposite of that of their past rulers (vv. 14–16 reverse the description of vv. 3–6): Yahweh will return the strays to the fold, tend the weak and the injured, feed and care for them all, ruling not with force and harshness (v. 4), but with justice (v. 16). In vv. 23–24 the promise is extended to include the restoration of the Davidic dynasty, with the earthly prince as God's agent for the people's welfare (cf. 37:24–28); but Yahweh remains their Savior and Lord (v. 24a).

The image of Yahweh as the shepherd of his people is frequent in the OT (for example, Pss. 23:1; 74:1; 95:7; Isa. 40:11; 49:9–10; Jer. 31:10). In the NT one should note above all John 10:1–18 where Jesus, the true shepherd, is contrasted with the false shepherd who cares nothing for the sheep. Here there is a direct echo of the imagery of Ezekiel 34.

Second Lesson: 1 Cor. 15:20–28. One of Paul's chief concerns in 1 Corinthians is to correct the view that salvation is fulfilled already in the believer's present life of faith (see, for example, 4:8ff.). One practical result of this mistaken notion has been the Corinthians' preoccupation with their possession of spiritual gifts, and their flaunting of these as evidence that their life now transcends the temporal and mundane (chaps. 12—14; now they speak with the "tongues of angels," 13:1). To counter this Paul forcefully reiterates his preaching of the cross (for example, 1:17–25; 2:1–5), indicates how his life as an apostle is conformed to that gospel (for example, 4:9–13), and emphasizes in various ways how the lives of all believers should be conformed to it (for example, 4:6–7, 14–21; 6:19; 8:11–13).

The discussion in chap. 15 must be viewed against the background just sketched. At least some Corinthians deny that there will be any general resurrection of the dead (v. 12), perhaps contending, like some later Christians, that one's present new life in Christ is already the fulfillment of that hope (see 2 Tim. 2:17–18). Paul argues, however, that to abandon this hope is to deny what is most fundamental for faith. The Corinthians themselves affirm the creed that speaks of Christ's death and resurrection (vv. 1–5). If now they deny the hope of a future resurrection with Christ, they deny Christ's resurrection, Paul's preaching, and their own faith (vv. 13–19).

Vv. 20–28 elaborate this argument by rehearsing the stages of the anticipated eschatological drama. It is true, says Paul, that Christ brings resurrection from the death all have died in Adam (vv. 20–21; cf. vv. 45–50 and Rom. 5:12–21). But the future tense in v. 22 ("in Christ *shall* all be made alive") is crucial, as it is also in Rom. 6:5, 8. This is made clear in v. 23: Christ's resurrection is the "first fruits" of the resurrection of all believers (cf. v. 20), but theirs does not occur until Christ has come again. In vv. 24–28 Paul identifies the subsequent stages of the eschatological drama, emphasizing in v. 26 that death is "the last enemy to be destroyed." This point, again, seems directed specifically against the triumphalist theology of the Corinthians.

The final statement of the paragraph (v. 28) is of fundamental importance for understanding Paul's theology: Ultimately, Christ will himself "be subjected" to God. Paul's preaching is radically *theo*logical. It is the preaching of God's love made real in Christ's death (Rom. 5:6–11), of God's power for salvation (Rom. 1:16). It was by God's grace that Paul was called as an apostle (1 Cor. 15:10; Gal. 1:15–16) and it is only by the strength God supplies that he is adequate for the task (2 Cor. 3:5–6). Just as all things come from God (1 Cor. 11:12b; cf. 4:7b, c), so finally all things belong to him: all apostles and all believers, all time and space, all life and death, and even Christ himself (1 Cor. 3:22–23). That precludes every presumptuous religious claim (1 Cor. 3:21a).

Gospel: Matt. 25:31–46. This parable of the Last Judgment is the final one in the series of eschatological parables which had begun in 24:32. There is no parallel passage in the other Gospels, and it is unlikely that a parable of the historical Jesus is recoverable here. The passage must be interpreted in accordance with the meaning it has for this evangelist. He has not only placed it at a crucial juncture in his Gospel, concluding the final block of teaching material (chaps. 21—25) and preceding the narratives of Jesus' death and resurrection (chaps. 26—28). He has also let it serve as a vivid and memorable summary of what is required to be a follower of Christ.

Vv. 31–33 set the scene on Judgment Day (other Matthean portrayals of this are 7:21–23; 13:36–43) which, according to this evangelist, will not come until all the nations of the world have been evangelized (see 28:19; 24:14). This judgment is thus of *believers,* and that accords with the evangelist's conviction that there are both good and evil in the kingdom (= the church, for example, 13:41). The imagery employed in vv. 32–33 is derived from Ezek. 34:17.

The judgment itself (vv. 34–45) is narrated in two parts. In vv. 34–40 the King summons the righteous into their inheritance (vv. 34–36), they express their surprise (vv. 37–39), and their righteousness is identified as their service of the needy (v. 40). In vv. 41–45 the King banishes the wicked to destruction (vv. 41–43), they express their surprise (vv. 44), and their wickedness is identified with their neglect of the needy (v. 45). The conclusion, v. 46, adds the points about eternal punishment and eternal life, but otherwise detracts from the impact of the parable proper and is probably secondary to it.

Some of the elements in this parable are familiar enough from the OT and the traditions of apocalyptic and rabbinic Judaism, not only the details of the judgment scene as such, but also the idea that true religion means to care for the poor and the oppressed (for example, Isa. 58:6–8; Sir. 7:32–36; note also today's lesson from Ezek. 34). What is distinctive about this parable is, first, its identification of the Son of man of Jewish apocalyptic thought (v. 31) with Christ the "King" (vv. 34, 40) and "Lord" (vv. 37, 44), and second, its contention that Christ is met in the needy neighbor and served as that neighbor is served (v. 40). The evangelist who has given us this parable is the same one who has emphasized that only those who practice a "higher righteousness" will enter the heavenly kingdom (see 5:20), and the parable is an illustration of what that higher righteousness is all about. This parable may also help us understand why the evangelist has previously been so deliberate about equating the two commandments to love God and to love the neighbor (22:37–39): There is no higher righteousness than that which expresses itself in loving and serving the neighbor, because precisely in that service (as even the righteous learn, to their surprise) one is serving the Lord Christ himself.

HOMILETICAL INTERPRETATION

The festival of Christ the King ends the liturgical year. Originally introduced in 1925 by Pope Pius XI, the celebration (set for the last Sunday in October) was primarily intended as a recognition of Christ's sovereignty over the nations, and thus provided a special emphasis on social action. By its current placement on the last Sunday after Pentecost, the festival now emphasizes the eschatological context of Christ's rule. It looks back to the Ascension, and it looks ahead to the appearing in glory of the King of Kings. The texts for this Sunday enable the preacher to explore some of the many meanings attached to the assertion that "Christ reigns" (or, as we regularly confess, "He ascended into heaven, and is seated at the right hand of the Father. He will come again to judge the living and the dead").

The lections for this day clearly indicate that it is Christ who is the King. The prophet points to Christ's rule by way of promise, at least as his writings have been interpreted by the church. The promise of "one shepherd, my servant David" (Ezek. 34:23) has been fulfilled in Jesus, the true and great shepherd (John 10:1–8; Heb. 13:20). St. Paul directly marks the reign of Christ. It is a reign under which Paul lived, a reign which began with Christ's resurrection and ascension, and which will continue until the Last Day ("the End," 1 Cor. 15:24). The evangelist Matthew points forward to that Last Day, when Christ will "sit on his glorious throne" and separate the nations. While the time frame is somewhat different in each of the texts, they share a central emphasis on the Christ who is King.

The perspective of the festival and of the texts is thus radically christological. The eschatological emphasis makes this particularly clear. At the end of history stands Jesus Christ, and toward this end everything moves—not only individual life but the life of all nations and of all humanity. Under his feet—the promised one—all enemies will be subdued. He alone qualifies as the maker of absolutely valid judgments. One thing signified by this fact is that everything depends upon Christ for its ultimate salvation. Trust placed in oneself, in one's nation, even in the most effective of international agencies, is trust misplaced. Power, authority, and status finally belong to none of these. They cannot bear the weight of our hope.

The perspective of this festival can also be seen as radically *theo*logical (see exegesis). The text from Ezekiel emphasizes the fact that it is Yahweh himself who will be the shepherd to Israel. The servant David (v. 23) will be prince, but he is indeed "set up." He will rule for the people's welfare, but he will do so as an agent of the God who remains his people's Savior and Lord. Just so, St. Paul insists that all things belong to God, even Christ himself. While Christ is the fully adequate representative of God, Christ's reign will be of limited duration. When Christ's work is completed (at the End) God will relate directly to his restored world ("be everything to everyone"). God will once again be the head of all creation; his kingdom will be fully established. Perhaps the purpose of this thrust is not so much to make Christ subordinate as it is to proclaim the effectiveness and sufficiency of his reign. Christ alone fulfills God's purpose for his creation. There is no other agent through whom God accomplishes his work of redemption. Christ alone subjects the world to himself and thus to God. There is none other, for example, who rules over death.

The dominant tone of this festival must be one of joy for the Christian congregation. The texts point us toward a future that is the glorious fulfillment of our hopes and of God's promises. What lies ahead is a time beyond exile and alienation, beyond hunger and hurt, beyond manipulation and neglect, beyond loss and loneliness (Ezekiel). It is a time of total victory, when all of our enemies will have been beaten once and for all—sin, death, despair, anxiety (1 Corinthians). It is a time when the "blessed" will inherit the kingdom prepared "from the foundation of the world" (Matthew). "The will of God from all eternity is life and health and peace, the well-being and perfecting of all his creatures." (Emil Brunner in a sermon on Matt. 25:31–46 in *The Great Invitation and Other Sermons* [Philadelphia: The Westminster Press, 1955], p. 152.)

The themes of separation and judgment in the Gospel text must be taken seriously, but should not be permitted to muffle the note of joy sounded at this celebration. Emphasis in the Matthean passage can be put on that which awaits the righteous. Indeed, such an emphasis can stress the fact that God's judgment in Christ justifies. It establishes the justice spoken of by Ezekiel—a justice which feeds, binds, strengthens, fattens, and protects. Surely one of the key meanings of Christ's Kingship is located in the assertion that Christ not only judges and pardons, but that he also holds all things and all people within the firm grasp of his love's redeeming purpose. His love is sovereign as well as holy.

While the joyful future is fully promised and therefore secured, it is still yet to come. The royal care associated with Christ's complete reign is already given to the church (Christians are nourished, healed, "justified"). But the church's present is not yet the time of hope's fulfillment (see exegesis of 1 Cor. 15). Some in the Corinthian church mistakenly thought that the future and its gifts were already theirs. It led them to a triumphalism which was a presumptuous denial of the cross. Christ, and not the Corinthians or we, is the "first fruits." The time of the church is a time of sensed victory, but it is also a time of warfare. The inimical powers are no longer on the throne now occupied by Christ, but they have not yet admitted defeat and still act as though they rule. Death, for example, has been overcome in principle, but it is still real and it still threatens. The present is a time of waiting in faith. "As it is, we do not yet see everything in subjection to him" (Heb. 2:8). The enemy is not to be underestimated even though final victory is guaranteed.

The present time of the church is also a time for doing. And what the church is to do is to treat all people as they would treat Christ himself and as they have been treated by Christ. Indeed, that is exactly the case—Christ *is* cared for or neglected when the neighbor is. Because of this, there is no higher righteousness than that which expresses itself in loving and serving the neighbor. What matters is whether or not we are merciful or unmerciful toward those with whom we have dealings. This is the way of the cross rather than the way of triumphalism. It is a recognition that Christ reigns, but not completely. The neighbor still needs our care.

One of the most comforting aspects of the Matthean text is that Christ alone knows the good works of all people. We need to be reminded that all we need to know is the good work of Christ. Our progress in the faith is veiled. We have no need of marking the steps or of counting the deeds. As Bonhoeffer says, "We can do no more than hearken to his commandment, carry on and rely on his grace, walk in his commandments, and—sin." In the end time we shall be astonished. We will realize that it is not our works that remain. What remains is the work which God has accomplished "without any effort of will and intention" on our part. (Dietrich Bonhoeffer, *The Cost of Discipleship* [New York: The Macmillan Company, 1963], p. 335.)

There are those who point out that it may be an error to equate "the least of these" in the Matthean story solely, or even at all, with the neighbor who is in need. They indicate that those who are "the least" must not be separated from those who are "my brethren" (Matt. 25:40). Inasmuch as brethren is a term used by Matthew to signify the disciples, it is suggested and sometimes insisted that the present passage has more to do with the treatment of Christ's disciples than with a caring response to the victims of hunger and dehumanization. If such an interpretation is followed, the fact that Christ is King is highlighted in a dramatic way. The nations of the world to whom the disciples are sent will be judged on the basis of their acceptance or rejection of the church's proclamation. Certainly a part of that proclamation is the command to care for the needy, but that proclamation is also the delightful announcement of God's grace and favor acquired through the merits of Christ. It is the proclamation that "Jesus is Lord." On the one hand, this proclamation specifies the absolute centrality of Christ. It is he who stands at the end of history, and it is upon him that everything depends for its ultimate salvation. On the other hand, this proclamation assumes the powerful missionary compulsion under which the church lives. The gospel is meant for all nations. The church exists globally to testify to God's claim upon his world and to present a living picture of what redemption can mean for life.

PENGUIN BOOKS

A LANDING ON THE SUN

Michael Frayn was born in 1933. He began his career as a reporter on the *Guardian*, then became a columnist first for the *Guardian* and later for the *Observer*. He has made a series of personal films for BBC television and has written nine stage plays, including *Noises Off* and *Benefactors*, along with an original screenplay, *Clockwise*; he has produced a number of translations and has published a volume of philosophy as well as six novels. *Now You Know*, his most recent novel, is available from Viking.

Michael Frayn

A Landing on the Sun

PENGUIN BOOKS

PENGUIN BOOKS
Published by the Penguin Group
Penguin Books USA Inc., 375 Hudson Street, New York, New York
10014, U.S.A.
Penguin Books Ltd, 27 Wrights Lane, London W8 5TZ, England
Penguin Books Australia Ltd, Ringwood, Victoria, Australia
Penguin Books Canada Ltd, 10 Alcorn Avenue, Toronto, Ontario,
Canada M4V 3B2
Penguin Books (N.Z.) Ltd, 182–190 Wairau Road, Auckland 10, New
Zealand

Penguin Books Ltd, Registered Offices: Harmondsworth, Middlesex,
England

First published in Great Britain by Penguin Books Ltd. 1991
First published in the United States of America by Viking Penguin,
a division of Penguin Books USA Inc., 1992
Published in Penguin Books 1993

1 3 5 7 9 10 8 6 4 2

PUBLISHER'S NOTE
This is a work of fiction. Names, characters, places, and incidents
either are the product of the author's imagination or are used
fictitiously, and any resemblance to actual persons, living or dead,
events, or locales is entirely coincidental.

THE LIBRARY OF CONGRESS HAS CATALOGUED THE HARDCOVER AS FOLLOWS:
Frayn, Michael.
A landing on the sun / Michael Frayn.
p. cm.
ISBN 0-670-83932-9 (hc.)
ISBN 0 14 01.7700 0 (pbk.)
I. Title
PR6056.R3L36 1992
823´914—dc20 91–37594

Printed in the United States of America

A Landing on the Sun

1

On the desk in front of me lie two human hands. They are alive, but perfectly still. One of them is sitting, poised like a crab about to scuttle, the fingers steadying a fresh Government-issue folder. The other is holding a grey Government-issue ballpoint above the label on the cover, as motionless as a lizard, waiting to strike down into the space next to the word *Subject*.

These hands, and the crisp white shirtsleeves that lead away from them, are the only signs of me in the room.

Slid neatly back to make room for the empty folder are the two full ones I am also working on, labelled in the small neat letters characteristic of this grey pen and these two pink hands. *Subject*: Annual Assessment of Departmental Efficiency, Proposed Procedure and Timetable; *Subject*: Joint CO/Treasury Overview Meeting, Sunningdale. Beyond the desk is a plain maroon carpet. At the edge of the carpet are a filing cabinet and a hatstand and two upright chairs. From a hanger on the hatstand hangs the jacket of a pale grey summer suit. A net curtain stirs at the window, diffusing the sharpness of the outside world. Which is in any case an airwell, with more net curtains at the windows on the other side.

There's nothing personal about this place. That's why I feel so much at home here.

Sometimes I glimpse a figure moving behind the net curtains on the other side of the airwell. Sometimes through the wall I hear phones ringing and muffled voices answering them. 'Bartlett,' they say, briefly and flatly, with neither pride nor shame. Or 'Kyle' or 'Milmo' or 'Gedge'.

Sometimes my own phone rings, and the voice that answers it is here inside the room, emerging from somewhere about the point where my two shirtsleeves meet. Because of course I have my voice in here with me, as well as my hands. I'd forgotten that. 'Jessel,' it says, flatly and truthfully. Then nothing for a bit, then perhaps 'Yes' or 'No', or, 'Before Cabinet on Thursday . . . At ministerial level . . . As a matter of urgency . . .' And then, when I put the phone down again, it resumes its full natural flow, inside my head instead of outside, as perfectly articulate and well-modulated as only a voice inside one's head has a chance to be.

My hands are going to write a single word on the outside of the empty folder, in the space for *Subject*. I know what the word is, of course. When it appears I shall be launched into my next piece of work. This is the short moment of stillness before the journey starts.

My hand moves. 'Summerchild', it writes, in the familiar script. Left hand moves down the label to the heading *Security Classification*. Right hand puts down the pen and moves to the top drawer of the desk. It takes out a blue tag printed with the words 'Staff in confidence' and sticks it into the space on the label.

A small sound is audible in the room. I recognize it as a sigh, but have no recollection of authorizing its publication.

Monday. Another week, another file.

2

Summerchild. Yes. And at once there is something a little awkward in the room, a little uneasy, a little personal. The outside world has suddenly got a foothold here. The world of muddle and incoherence, of being seventeen, of home, of unidentified feelings, of unresolved questions.

As soon as Ken Hurren mentioned the word in his office this morning, when he asked me to take the task on, I felt a secret dismay.

'It's one of those old chestnuts that crops up from time to time,' he said. 'All the supposedly mysterious deaths of people connected with defence. Summerchild is usually one of the cases that gets cited. Innocent Civil Servant, apparently no defence involvement, body found on MOD property.'

He waited to see if I was going to frown and drag some faint recollection out of my own memory, but I said nothing. Summerchild was in fact found on the pavement on the other side of Whitehall. But, yes, it was in front of the Ministry of Defence, and he'd jumped out of one of the windows.

'I think it was some time in the seventies,' said Ken. 'I imagine you were still at school.'

He smiled, in the somewhat sanctimoniously paternal style he has adopted since he became deputy head of the Division. I smiled back. It was in 1974. The summer of 1974. The end of June, to be precise. I'd just left school. Ken, I imagine in my turn, had just left university.

'Anyway, look it up and minute me about it, will you?

3

Apparently the television people are showing interest in the case. Or so I'm informed. I gather they're going to tell us he was working on some secret defence project, after all. There's also supposed to be a mysterious disappearing colleague and some kind of Russian connection. It sounds nonsense to me, but I'd like to have a brief résumé of the affair to hand, just in case there's a sudden panic at Number Ten.'

Defence – disappearance – *case*. My slight personal acquaintance with the subject of all this discouraging impersonal solemnity seemed slightly ridiculous. So I continued to say nothing. I merely asked why it was a matter for us in the Cabinet Office. The answer was even more unsettling – that this was the department he'd worked in. I hadn't realized that I'd followed so closely in his footsteps. He worked in Whitehall, that's all I'd known at the time. It seemed a full enough account. I'm not sure that I was aware, at the age of seventeen or eighteen, of any sub-divisions within that single blanched palace of administration, that great white hall of bumbledom. But it was to this very building that he departed each morning, from an office much like this that he returned each night. I can just see, through the net curtains of the office opposite, someone leaning back from his desk, the phone to his ear. That could be him. He'd be – what – in his fifties now if he'd lived, a Deputy Secretary, perhaps a Second Permanent Secretary with his own division. 'Summerchild,' he could be saying, briefly and flatly, as if there never had been a *case*, as if he had no more unexplained attributes than anyone else.

He wouldn't have been on this airwell at the time, though. According to Ken he worked in the old Government Commission, which was tucked away in the back somewhere, until the present Government wound it up and the Cabinet Office took over its functions. Together, of course, with responsibility for any legacy it left of mysteries and embarrassments.

'It shouldn't take you long,' said Ken. I suppose my reluctance was more visible than it should have been. 'I know you've got one or two other things on. End of the week, perhaps?'

4

He should have referred it to Management and Personnel over in Great George Street and let the Security Division sort it out. But he wants to keep it in his own hands. He wants to be ready with something his own people have prepared, as soon as the alarm goes up from the Secretary of the Cabinet. I suppose these two blind crabs of mine should be grateful for the variety that my work involves. They should be pleased to turn for a moment from the Annual Assessment, which even they find a little dull, to some piece of historical research. You'd think they'd be intrigued at a chance to play detectives. But they don't give much sign of it. I suspect even they find something distasteful in the prospect. Perhaps it's simply because they don't really know how to go about it. They've spent their professional life dealing with general classes of person, with samples and percentages of classes, not with individuals. They're trained to collate evidence about the present, and project it into the future, not to find out what happened fifteen years ago to some one particular person, least of all one with whom I had a slight personal acquaintance.

I move the folder to one side and take a pad of ruled Government paper. I write slowly as I think:

1. George Street, for S's personal dossier.
2. Registry, for any reference.
3. Westminster Coroner's Court, for papers of inquest.

I start telephoning. As I do so I gaze at Kyle (or Gedge, or Henning) on the other side of the airwell. He is running his hand through his thin grey hair. I suddenly remember Summerchild's hair. It was fine and coppery, standing up around his head like the burning bush, or a single over-arching eyebrow raised in perpetual surprise. No one in any of the offices around *this* airwell has red hair or freckles. Nor for the moment can I think of anyone else in the entire Administrative Grade of the Civil Service who does. I believe there are no red-headed Civil Servants. How curious.

5

I remember that one of the Assistant Secretaries in the Home Affairs Secretariat is an old Government Commission man. John Killick. I dial his number and on the other side of the airwell Kyle picks up his phone. 'Killick,' says Kyle. So that's Killick! Or is it the merest coincidence that Kyle is sitting back in his chair, with the receiver to his ear, stroking the bald patch on the back of his head as I explain my business? Killick has no recollection of any work in the department on defence, or of anyone mysteriously disappearing. So far as he can remember Summerchild was working on a comparison of incomes inside and outside the Civil Service. He was doing it with Michael Treacher, who is now teaching government somewhere in Canada. Killick hangs up. A moment later so does Kyle.

I go to Registry, thinking about Summerchild. I remember the first time I saw him, appearing out of the winter darkness in that unmade-up lane outside his house in Greenwich. I was standing there talking to his daughter, Millie. Or not talking to her. This would have been after a rehearsal of the local schools orchestra, some time early in that last year of his life. I imagine I was holding my trombone case, kicking at the loose pebbles in the roadway. Millie would have been fiddling awkwardly with the thick brush of ginger hair – coarser than her father's, and even redder – that sprang away all round her face, while her cello case, which I had carried back for her, was no doubt propped up against one of the crumbling and gateless brick pillars in front of their house, like a portly little old man too out of breath to speak. At some point during this silent debate Summerchild came walking up the lane. Not that he was Summerchild then, of course. He was *Mr* Summerchild – an entirely different creature. To me, at any rate. To Millie, presumably, he had the appearance and nature of *Daddy*. He was on his way home – characteristically late, I realize, now that I keep the same office hours – from the back blocks of the building where I am now sitting. He stopped and carefully put down his briefcase. He smiled at Millie. She smiled at him. He nodded to me. I nodded to him.

He sighed and gazed at the cello. He seemed to have some fellow-feeling with its weariness. We stood there, all four of us, in silence for what seemed a very long time. The fine red-gold of his hair was like an angel's aureole against the street lamp. I had the feeling that if I hadn't been present he might have risked uttering a few words to Millie. She was rather younger than me and known to be as brilliant as her hair. He must have wanted to know what triumphs she had to report. I don't suppose he was pleased to find an ageing trombonist hanging around outside his gate, distracting his daughter from her future.

Eventually he sighed again, picked up his bag and went on up the steps into his house. No, he must have said something first, now I come to think about it, because I can remember very distinctly the way he spoke. The words seemed to have been dragged up one by one from the depths of himself, like prisoners loaded with chains, and released to the world only with great reluctance. What words they were, though, I have no recollection. Perhaps if I could remember them the whole mystery would be solved.

I saw him a few times more after that, in the months that followed, coming slowly up the lane from the station, as Millie and I stood at the gate. I heard the same sigh, and no doubt the same gravelled reluctance of speech, though I can't remember anything he said. I now detect in them not only tiredness and disapprobation. With hindsight, and also with my regular weekly exposure to the full taxonomy of psychic pathology, I diagnose a somewhat depressive turn of mind. How much more depressed he would have been, if he could have seen the silent trombonist in years to come, ensconced in his offices, sifting the sparse and scattered remains of his life. Whilst poor Millie, far from playing cello concertos at the Festival Hall, or leading archaeological expeditions to Asia Minor, or whatever she was expected to be doing by this time, is . . . I don't know. What *is* she doing now? Still living with her mother, I think, in that unmade-up lane. I must make inquiries.

She left the orchestra after her father died. I don't think I ever saw her again.

By this time I am in Registry and Mrs Tamm is silently laying the results of her research in front of me. I like Mrs Tamm's silence almost as much as I like the impersonality of my room. In so far as she possibly can, she lets this great dull store of words speak for themselves, without addition to their number. She is silently waiting for me now to understand the nature of what she is offering me. It is a ledger, the size and solidity of an old-fashioned accounts book, with broken corners and an air of belonging to that grey period which is too far gone to be new but not yet far enough off to be old. She gives me time to read the label on the front cover – Government Commission Press Department, 1974 – then opens it and slowly turns the pages, so that I can see it is a cuttings book, in which the Commission's Press Officer has pasted the results of his labours, the stories inspired by all his briefings, handouts and leaks. Mrs Tamm turns to the middle of the book. There, alone on the page, is a very short cutting of a different sort. 'Death fall', says the headline.

'Thank you,' I say to Mrs Tamm. She goes silently back to her work.

According to the handwritten inscription over the cutting it is from *The Times*, page three, on June 25th.

The body of a man found yesterday in Spring Gardens, SW1, was identified last night as that of Mr S J L Summerchild (39), a Civil Servant. Police said that Mr Summerchild appeared to have died as the result of a fall. Foul play is not suspected.

I find this a little surprising. An inch on page three? In my memory there were prominent headlines and a sudden flurry of importance. There were newspaper reporters standing in the lane where he had lived, waiting all day for someone to come out of the house. And what's this about Spring Gardens? Where are Spring Gardens? He was found outside the Ministry of Defence, in Horseguards Avenue. That's surely what all the fuss was about.

I turn the page. We are back into grey acres about Civil Service decentralization, for which the Commission seems to have been responsible. But other accounts of Summerchild's death must have been appearing in the newspapers somewhere, because a little further on there is another cutting from *The Times*. This one is dated two days later, June 27th. It is from page one, at least seven column-inches long, and it is pouring cold water on reports of a more sensational nature. 'Whitehall body: "no spy link"', says the headline, and beneath it, 'From our Political Staff'.

Reports that Mr Stephen Summerchild, the Civil Servant whose body was found in Whitehall earlier this week, had connections with espionage were being firmly discounted at Westminster yesterday.

The official line is that it remains Government policy never to comment on allegations of this nature. But unofficially the suggestion was authoritatively pooh-poohed.

Mr Summerchild, it was pointed out, was employed in the Government Commission, the department set up by Harold Wilson in 1965 to coordinate the workings of the various ministries. Whitehall sources believe he is much more likely to have been concerned with such humdrum matters as integrating inter-departmental communications to prepare the ground for Civil Service computerization.

Speculation was sparked off because Mr Summerchild's body was discovered on Ministry of Defence property – a yard in Spring Gardens, at the back of the Admiralty. A Ministry of Defence spokesman said yesterday that he appeared to have fallen from one of the offices on the third floor, but declined to surmise why he was visiting the Admiralty.

Mr Summerchild lived in Greenwich with his wife and seventeen-year-old daughter. Mrs Summerchild was not available last night for comment, but neighbours described him as a reserved man who was devoted to his family, and who had a passion for music. He occasionally played the violin in local musical events.

One neighbour said: 'He was not the kind of man you associate with James Bond activities.'

I am curiously disconcerted by the wrongness of my memory about where the body was found. There was something horribly appropriate, it seemed to me, about the idea of a man being dashed to death, like a sacrifice to the god of war, at the base of that great white tomb in Horseguards Avenue. But round the back of the Admiralty, put out in the yard like a dead cat . . .

Why the Admiralty, of all places? There's something neither here nor there about it, neither plain enough nor mysterious enough, neither explicable nor inexplicable. Though if he took his own life, as everyone has always supposed, and as we are still likely to be supposing after the present rumours have been scotched – if *the balance of his mind was disturbed*, that curious disruption which accompanies a man's election to end his life, but never any other procedure, no matter how eccentric or irrational – then reasons are not to be looked for.

I turn the pages of the cuttings book. Proposed changes in Civil Service terms of employment, the problems of interface between Whitehall and the European bureaucracy in Brussels, leaders from the *Guardian* and the *Telegraph* about decentralization . . . Nothing more about Summerchild until July 5th, when there is a two-column report of the inquest, headed 'Open verdict on death fall man'. The story has slipped back to page two, though, I notice. I shall be getting the full papers from the Coroner's office eventually, and I run a rather cursory eye over the brief details here.

Mr F K A Tite, Summerchild's Permanent Secretary, gave evidence in person, I see. Somewhat surprising. I wonder if the Secretary of the Cabinet would go into the box if I were found outside the Ministry of Agriculture. Wouldn't have described Summerchild as depressed, he says . . . Had perhaps seemed somewhat preoccupied . . . No idea of reason for this . . . Didn't know why Summerchild should have gone to the Admiralty on the morning of June 24th, but his work was related to conditions of employment in the Civil Service and involved liaison with other departments, so nothing particularly surprising about it . . .

Then Mrs Summerchild . . . And as soon as I read the name I see her standing there in the witness box, self-contained, precise, unknowable. Her head is lowered defensively, so that one's impression of her is greying hair, with watchful eyes lurking in the shadows beneath. She is observing the Coroner now with that same surreptitious brooding care with which she had once watched Millie and me from her kitchen window, as we stood talking, or not talking, at the gate. She measures out her guarded replies to him in neat, carefully checked words, as once she had suggested, from the top of the steps outside their front door, that Millie might like to invite me in for a few minutes. Her husband had been very involved in his work, she tells the Coroner. Had never discussed it at home. Had been working late. Very late? – Sometimes. – Had seemed at all depressed or anxious? – Had seemed tired. – Anything unusual about his manner when he had left for work on the morning of the 24th? – Not that she had noted.

The pathologist: Injuries consistent with a fall from an upper storey. Had been dead no more than an hour when he was found . . .

An Admiralty clerical worker: Had found the body at about 9.50 am, when taking office waste out to the yard for collection. Was lying beside dustbins and boxes of waste paper, just inside the locked gates to the yard.

A Ministry of Defence security officer: No record of Summerchild entering the building. No one in the offices overlooking Spring Gardens with any recollection of seeing him . . .

A police witness: Difficult to establish exactly where Summerchild had fallen from, because of subsequent rain. There was a window open on the third floor, but marks consistent with the rubber-soled shoes he was wearing suggested that it was from the parapet in front of the four dormer windows in the roof. If this was so, then the most probable point of impact was approximately 50 feet away from where the body had been found. – Could the body have been moved? – Possibly. But it had been raining and the surface of the yard had been washed clear of any traces. – Could he have survived the fall and dragged himself to the position where he was found? – This seemed the most likely explanation.

Then, after the inquest, nothing more, until I notice a slip of paper projecting from the book much further on, which turns out to be another of Mrs Tamm's silent helpfulnesses. It marks a cutting from the *Times* Parliamentary Report, November 20th, Prime Minister's Questions. 'Mr C S Jones (Lab), Leicester NW – Will the Government now publish the report on which Mr S J L Summerchild is known to have been working at the time of his death? – The report has already been published as Cmnd. 4078.' I look up, aware that Mrs Tamm has placed some document silently beside the cuttings book. It is Cmnd. 4078 – *Comparability: The Effect of Differentials in Reward on Recruitment and Wastage Rates in Four Selected Sectors of Government and Manufacturing Industry.* I turn the pages. Cost-of-living allowances . . . Expressing job satisfaction as a numerical index . . . Table VII . . . Annexe C . . . I don't need to read it through to know that there will be no mystification here, no hint of distress or depression, no trace of weariness or unusual hair colour, no premonition of ruptured aorta or broken ribs.

This is as far as I can get with my researches for now, because after lunch I have to go to the Treasury, with my colleague Jane Showell, for a meeting of the joint working party on Sunningdale; not even death takes precedence over the Treasury. But while Tony Lesser is once again listing the Treasury's objections to the topics Jane and I have proposed for discussion papers, a picture suddenly comes into my mind, with the most painful vividness, of Summerchild dragging himself across the hard wet ground, on the morning of June 24th 1974, to the locked gates of that yard behind the Admiralty. It is as if the words had suddenly come to life inside my head. 'Could he have dragged himself . . .?' *Dragged himself*. The syllables are raw and cold in my nostrils, like the wetness of the ground I am pressed against. They scrape me down from head to foot – my torn clothes, my hands, my broken knees, the nose on my face. They hurt inside me like the split sacs and shattered bones. Could he have dragged himself . . .? He could. He did. He is now doing so.

A silence has fallen in the room, I realize. Tony Lesser has stopped speaking. He is looking at me with a slight frown, disconcerted by something about me, ready to be embarrassed. Jane has looked up from her papers. So has Lyell, the other Treasury man. They are on the point of asking if I am all right. I have an instant of panic – what has my face been doing? Then I remember what it's been doing: nothing that they could see, because it's hidden behind my beard. My strange and wonderful beard! My dense and well-trimmed hedge against the inquiring world. I stroke it gratefully as I raise a counter-objection to Lesser's counter-proposals. Their question dissolves, unasked; the moment passes.

When the meeting is over Jane and I walk back towards our own department, past the sightseers waiting outside the security barriers at the end of Downing Street. The June warmth has become slightly oppressive and I feel a continuing sense of strangeness, of standing slightly outside myself. We are talking about the meeting. As we reach the door of the Cabinet Office she says, 'I think that was all right, wasn't it?' I stop. 'I mean the meeting,' she says, looking at me with a sudden trace of anxiety. I tell her I'm going to take a walk and I continue up Whitehall on my own, leaving her gazing after me. She thinks she is a little worried about me. I think she is a little irritated at needing to be worried.

I don't know quite which way to go; I'm not in the habit of taking strolls in the middle of the day. I push through the tourists and into the Horse Guards. I walk out on to the great parade-ground beyond, where the grandstands left over from Trooping the Colour are still displacing the more usual arrangements for Trooping the Parked Cars. When I get to the road, with St James's Park beyond, as fresh and green as an early summer salad, I stop and turn. I am looking at the most magnificent townscape in London. My world, seen from the outside.

From here it appears to be not the central generating plant of ministerial power but some vast open-air theatre. The Parade is the stage and the great offices of state that enclose it on three sides are the décor. On my right, as I look at it, are the five lofty plane trees which shade the back gardens of Downing Street. Then, in the corner, the Cabinet Office, with the elegant classical façade of Kent's old Treasury flanked by its nineteenth-century annexes. Somewhere in the heart of the further annexe my empty office awaits me. Somewhere in the annexe on this side, where the Government Commission pursued its sober tasks, Summerchild lived out his working life.

I start to think for some reason about the idea of being all right. The meeting was all right. Summerchild was not all right. What about me? Am I all right, as they were on the point of asking? What is this *all right*? It suddenly seems as peculiar a notion as the balance of one's mind. I try to visualize the balance of my own mind. In one pan the Unknown Substance. In the other the neat little brass weights, geometrically round and gleaming, maintaining the scale in perfect equilibrium.

I continue with my survey of the world I inhabit. Next to the Cabinet Office is the Scottish Office. Then the back of the Horse Guards. Everything is quiet and contained. No one is stepping out of any of the windows. No one is even leaning out of a window. No one, on this warm summer afternoon, is so much as visible at a window. There is no sign of human life. Everything is *all right*.

I continue to turn. And there, all along the lefthand side of the Parade, is the grandest building of them all – the Admiralty. Its long colonnaded frontage basks in the after-noon sunlight. The green copper cupolas and complex wire-less aerials on the roof reach importantly into the blue of the sky. Now I know where my walk is taking me.

14

I go past the creeper-covered bunker at the end of the façade and follow it round into the Mall, until I am facing Admiralty Arch. Between the Arch and the back of the Admiralty proper runs a small unnamed side-street which I must have passed a hundred times without really noticing. It has a curiously defensive nature, I realize as I walk down it. The roadway is closed to traffic by a turnpike, then, underneath a kind of Bridge of Sighs connecting the main block with the buildings attached to the Arch, it is closed again by a set of ornamental gates – and then closed for a third time by another turnpike. Beyond this second turnpike it ends in a T-junction with another small street. I walk up to the lefthand end of this street, where it emerges in Trafalgar Square, and check the name: Spring Gardens. I retrace my steps and walk up the righthand arm of the T, where the roadway is closed by a second set of iron gates. Beyond them is a courtyard surrounded on three sides by the rear walls of office buildings, like a miniature version of Horse Guards Parade. The wall on the left seems to be the back of a bank, the wall on the right and the one at the back of the yard belong to the Admiralty. There is a parapet along the roof of this third wall, with four dormer windows beyond it. From somewhere along that parapet, on a wet June morning nearly fifteen years ago, Summerchild fell. Across that tarmacadam towards these gates he crawled. And among bins and rubbish like the ones in front of me now he stopped crawling, and died, and lay unnoticed.

The gates are padlocked. I rest my head against the bars and gaze through them as into a cage. In the warm afternoon shade the scene says nothing to me. The ground itself is not as harsh as the words I felt beneath me for that one curious moment at the Treasury.

For an hour he lay here and no one saw him. I look up at the windows. The end wall is three floors high, with dormer windows in the attic above, and each floor has four windows on it. The righthand wall is three floors high, with ten windows on each floor. Forty-six windows. In all of them

15

hang net curtains. In none of them is there anyone to be seen. Forty-six windows, and not a soul looking out. I begin to appreciate for the first time, as I stand here on the outside looking in, how very reserved is the world in which we work.

Another picture of Summerchild comes into my mind, another encounter in the darkness of the unmade-up lane. But this time the scene is back-to-front. This time I am the one walking along the lane and he is the one standing outside the gate. He is carrying his violin case, for some reason, and he is standing absolutely still, gazing at something with great absorption. It is not the lights of London, visible over the roofs of the houses on the lower side of the lane. It is his own house. He hears my step on the rough stones of the roadway, glances at me, then walks silently up to his front door and lets himself in. I suppose I was on my way to call for Millie, but I walk on past the house instead, obscurely ashamed to have caught her father unawares. What was absorbing him so deeply, I realize as I go by, was the sight of his own living-room, with the curtains innocently open, and his wife and Millie moving silently about the bright world inside.

I walk back to the Cabinet Office. I do not like the task I have been given. I am now standing outside a gate, outside a window, looking into a life that does not belong to me, and I should rather look away. There are no great secrets here, I am sure of that, only intimate awkwardnesses, only small sad discrepancies in that little grey heap of Unknown Substance on the balance-pan.

I get back to my office and set to work with the phone. It is a frustrating business. Whichever way I try to come at the Unknown Substance it remains just beyond my grasp. Sir Francis Tite (as he now is) is alive, but is said to be senile. I can't get my hands on the inquest papers until the end of the week. Worst of all, Management and Personnel say there's no trace of Summerchild's dossier at Great George Street. According to the register it was last signed in on September 5th 1974. There is no record of its being signed out again.

This could mean that something sinister has happened to it. It could equally well mean that it has simply been mislaid.

My one success is with Michael Treacher, who Killick said was working on the comparability report with Summerchild. I track him down to the University of Saskatchewan and just catch him at home before he leaves for work. Back from the great plains of Central Canada comes the brief response, as crisp and neutral as if from the other side of the airwell, 'Treacher.'

I explain my business. 'How curious,' says Treacher. 'Someone called about this the other day. Also from the Cabinet Office.'

'Really?' I say. I suppose this was the television company.

'Yes, we had quite a little chat about the place. I couldn't help asking him if the waitresses in the Cabinet Office canteen still wear those terrible green overalls.'

I can't quite understand this.

'There aren't any waitresses in the Cabinet Office canteen,' I say stupidly.

'Thank you,' says Treacher. 'I'm sorry to play tricks. Your supposed colleague was perfectly happy with the idea of green waitresses. Yes, I did work with Stephen Summerchild on the comparability report. At one stage. I had to finish it on my own, of course.'

'You mean, after his death?'

'No, after Tite took him off it.'

I feel a faint stirring somewhere inside me. A sudden alertness, a touch of adrenalin in the blood. A small discrepancy has appeared, a faint crack in the ordinariness of things. So Tite's evidence at the inquest was not strictly accurate. I formulate a carefully unsurprised question.

'When was that?'

'I can't remember. This is 1974 we're talking about, isn't it? Heath went some time in March, I think. I recall it as being immediately after Wilson came into office. It was probably something to do with the change of Government. Tite wanted him for the special unit he was setting up.'

A special unit? The crack is widening by the moment.

'This unit,' I say cautiously. 'Can you tell me anything about it?'

'Not really,' says Treacher. 'Something confidential, I assume. I don't think many people knew about it. I noticed Tite didn't say anything about it at the inquest.'

'I noticed that,' I say. 'Summerchild didn't tell you anything about it himself?'

'Stephen?' Treacher laughs. 'I'm not sure Stephen ever told anyone anything about anything. He was a terrible depressive, you know. It was often quite difficult to get two words together out of him.'

'You've no idea what this unit was doing?'

'I saw him in the canteen once or twice after he'd left comparability,' says Treacher. 'I suppose he must have said something.'

I wait.

'But what it was I can't remember. I just recall that I got a bit of a shock when I heard they found him on MOD property. Because I had the definite impression that this was the area he was working in.'

'Defence?' I feel a reluctance to pronounce the word.

'Or something connected with it,' says Treacher. His tone changes. 'Do they still have cabinet pudding in the canteen?'

I don't think there's anything behind the question this time but nostalgia. But even nostalgia can misremember; I don't think they've ever served cabinet pudding in the Cabinet Office.

'It's mostly apples and yoghurt these days,' I tell him.

After I have put the phone down I sit gazing at Kyle on the opposite side of the airwell. He is also replacing his receiver and turning to gaze thoughtfully out of the window. I get the impression he has had some rather unwelcome news.

Defence, then. I was wrong. A world of secrets and mysteries. And all of them to do with the dull task of bringing people to their deaths.

3

I could quite reasonably give up at this point, I think. I could – perhaps should – go back to Ken Hurren tomorrow morning and tell him that there may after all be some question of security involved. I think he would then be obliged to pass it across to Great George Street, and I could honourably retire to the dull comfortable depths of the Annual Assessment.

But what sticks in my head, ridiculously, is the cabinet pudding. Maybe they *were* still eating cabinet pudding in those days. The Treachers and the Summerchilds are the older generation. 1974, yes. Heath. Wilson. I'd forgotten what was happening in the world until Treacher pronounced those ancient incantations from my childhood. The miners' strike and the three-day week. Cold and darkness. I remember the grey excitement of walking to rehearsals through the blacked-out streets, of playing 'Mars the Bringer of War' by candlelight, in overcoats and scarves. Yes, and I remember the tanks moving down Whitehall; or at any rate I remember the picture I had of them in my head as Tilly Tilling, in the middle of a history class, suddenly began to tell us about the military putsch that was coming. I remember the shake in his voice, the vengeance.

I realize with a shock that those tanks are moving down this same peaceful street I'm now walking along. Because by this time I'm halfway up Whitehall on my way home. I've stayed at my desk until half past seven, writing up the minutes of our meeting at the Treasury – even doing a little preparation for a series of consultations I have to begin tomorrow in connection with the Annual Assessment. Warm shadows have lengthened across the road and the tourists have gone. In the side-streets running down towards the river theatregoers are looking for parking-spaces, but on the pavements there's no one but a few belated bureaucrats like myself, heading for trains and Tubes. No tanks. The tanks never came.

I like this street. I like all these noncommittal grey frontages, some unobtrusively elegant, some cautiously flamboyant, that give so little away about the thought that teems behind them. I hope I look a little like a Government building myself. A quiet façade, perhaps with a touch of distinction. Pale grey summer suit, ready-made but a perfect fit; neat hair already beginning to match the suit; and, what pleases me most, this trim matching beard to bridge most of the gap between suit and hair. I run the tips of my fingers over this beard at difficult moments and am reassured by its fibrous smoothness as much as my son used to be, when he was a little younger, by the feel of his old piece of blanket. I know that my thoughts and feelings are as safe as Cabinet Office minutes behind this beard. My whole personality is decently concealed. I don't think anyone would even realize I was a Civil Servant. A little idiosyncratic, I think, my appearance – but without going to the slightly absurd lengths of ginger hair and freckles.

I am indeed a walking department of state. Because on the inside – yes, I have my airwells, I have work going forward behind the net curtains. Evidence is being collected – these buildings, this traffic. A never-ending report is being written – here it is. This report is being minuted in the margin – I'm doing it now. 'The first sign of madness,' joke people who have been caught talking to themselves, confident of course that it is not. A late sign of sanity, in my view, if you do it as I do it, silently, the lips entirely still, the net curtains drawn. After all, to think is to speak. To think clearly is to organize one's speech into sentences and paragraphs; sentences and paragraphs into sections and chapters; sections and chapters into a coherent draft report, ready for submission. And to speak silently is to speak without asking for other people's time or sympathy; without wounding their sensibilities or undermining their faith; without breaching confidentiality or the Official Secrets Act. To speak to oneself is to speak without constraint, to draft a minute which will be laid before a minister who will never read it.

I have timed my departure from the Cabinet Office to leave seven minutes to walk to Charing Cross, and then another two (no more!) before my train leaves — if, of course, it happens to be running. Seven minutes is what it takes me at this time in the evening; eight, sometimes nine, coming the opposite way in the morning, to allow for waits at the two pedestrian crossings and the crowds coming out of the station. But that's fast walking, as anyone else in the Cabinet Office who travels by way of Charing Cross would confirm. It must have taken Summerchild at least an extra minute in each direction; as I recall it from those evenings fifteen years ago, he walked at a much more reflective pace, as if slowed by some inner weight. I wonder if he left two minutes in hand, like me, to get from the barrier to a compartment level with the Greenwich exit, or three, or five, or whether he liked to arrive at the very last moment and leave a slight uncertainty in the air. He must have caught this same train many times, and all the others before and after, as I have. He must have been on one or other of them every night, in weather much like this, all through that last summer of his life.

The train starts, and thunders slowly over the bridge across the river. The Government buildings along the Embankment drop away behind us, and here I am in another world, another life. South London. Every evening Summerchild looked down from these same arches on to this same exhausted tangle of brickwork. He saw this warehouse . . . this grimy market . . . this factory . . . Inside his head, beneath the odd blaze of hair, behind the reckless display of freckles, the same low horizon unrolled, the same milk-crate stacks of

Council flats came up out of the east, like this, slowly turned, just so, and fell away into the west, like that . . . I stopped seeing those flats years ago. It's not me seeing them now – it's Summerchild. Only of course he never saw them, either. I am giving him eyes he never had. I am drafting the minutes he never drafted. For a moment even the voice I am drafting them in changes. The light, detached tones inside my head grow low and reluctant, as if I were switching the tape-recorder to a slower speed.

And now here I am getting off the train at Greenwich, as Summerchild did, instead of the next station down the line, as Jessel does. I do it without premeditation, as naturally and wearily as if I did it every night. I am – how did my neighbours describe me? – a reserved man who is devoted to his family, with a passion for music. I walk slowly through the tunnel beneath the line, one of a dozen returning commuters, cross over the road with ten of them, make my way through the gnarled little streets beyond the redundant town hall with eight of the ten, and begin to climb the scarp of the South London hills with the remaining five. Halfway up the hill I turn off, and now I am on my own.

I am in a little lane that runs across the front of the hillside, with a kind of broken roadway underfoot which disintegrates as I follow it into gravel studded with outcrops of manhole. I haven't walked along here for years – not, it occurs to me, for fourteen years. And yet I know it almost better than my own street. I find the name in my head, as if it had always been there: Hyde Hill Lane. I am moving slowly now, as slowly as Summerchild moved when he came out of the darkness on that winter's night. I pass the lock-up garages and the grease-blackened signs that indicate some small motor repair workshops. On my left the ground drops away through uncertain undergrowth into back gardens and a view of rooftops. On my right there is a sudden and implausible terrace of little bow-fronted villas from the early thirties, still waiting for this left-over country lane to grow up and get itself surfaced and turned into a bypass. But it has

22

not grown up. It has escaped from time and place and municipal control. It has the lost intensity of a dream.

Now here on the left London is beginning to appear beyond the rooftops, lying wide and blue and docile at my feet. I look at it for a moment, tracing out my journey from Westminster. I turn away from it. I know precisely what I shall see, on the other side of the lane, looking out to London over my shoulder. And there indeed they are – an odd little cluster of houses built a century and a half ago, in a jumbled assortment of all the styles available at the time. They have the same wistful air as the terrace further back, as if they too had once entertained hopes of the lane going somewhere in life. The Summerchilds lived in the third one along, with the peeling woodwork and the neglected grey rendering. I believe Millie and her mother still do. I realize that I am standing just as Summerchild stood that other night, when I saw him gazing with such intensity into his own life. Now one of the tall windows on the front room stands open to the warm evening air, but there is nothing to be made out in the darkness of the room beyond.

For a moment I think I might walk up the steps and ring the bell. I imagine the door opening and a woman with a ginger fuzz of hair, painfully familiar, painfully changed, standing on the threshold, frowning in puzzlement. 'Brian . . . Brian Jessel . . . I got off the train at Greenwich – it was a fine evening – I was just walking . . . I was just wondering . . . You know – what you were doing, how you were . . . Whether you could tell me anything about . . . well . . . No, that's not the point. But I was thinking about you only today, as it happened, because . . . well, for no very good reason.'

It's impossible. I continue up the lane and return to the world of surfaced roads and pavements. I am no longer the late Stephen Summerchild, a reserved man who is devoted to his family, with a passion for music. I am the living Brian Jessel, a reserved man who is devoted to his family, with, yes, certainly, something of an interest in music. An interest in music that I had rather forgotten about until the thought of

Millie in the lane reminded me. I cross the park, as I crossed it so many times in the past, and regain the modest Edwardian streets beyond Maze Hill. I lift my key towards the lock on my own front door, with all my usual sudden rush of fears and anxieties. But before I can turn it, the door opens. Cheryl has been standing inside the front room, looking out of the window, waiting for me.

'I'm sorry . . .' I begin, as I usually do.

'No, it's just that my sister's going out,' she says, as she picks up the various plastic carrier bags already waiting in the hall. Sometimes she brings her children with her, which I don't much like, and sometimes she leaves them with her sister, which I like even less, because for her to have her two children minded for her so that she can mind my one is simply crazy. The whole arrangement with Cheryl is hopeless. And if her husband comes back, as he is apparently hinting he might, or if she moves, or gets a job, as she is always threatening to do if he doesn't, or if my colleagues in the DSS find out that I am paying her, then even this hopeless arrangement will come to an end and I shall be back to the agencies and the advertisements, back to the interviews and the references, back to strangers in the house.

'He had a little accident at school today.'

My heart stops. 'An accident?'

'I knew something was wrong – when I got there he wouldn't look at me. Mrs Lewis had got his shorts in a bag. I washed them out – they're on the line.'

Oh, yes, an *accident*. The front door closes. I go upstairs and softly look round the door of my son's bedroom. He is asleep, of course. As always. And, as always, I feel the usual wave of uncontrollable anguish at the sight of him. He is lying on top of the covers, as he often is, with his head at the bottom of the bed and his feet on the pillow. There are sharp-edged pieces of Lego mixed up with the bedding and an old cardboard box lying across his chest. I carefully clear as much of the debris as I can. But there is something about the way he is lying that makes my chest tighten with despair. His life is as muddled as his bed. The home in which we both live is a nonsense, and a nonsense from which I can see no way of ever extracting us.

I go downstairs, a reserved man, devoted to his family, and get the remains of the family joint I cooked for my mother-in-law and Timmy and myself yesterday out of the refrigerator. It looks hard and dark, and I can find no fresh vegetables to go with it. Everything inside this house is personal. Everything was chosen by me, worn by me, cooked by me, repaired by me. This is why I am not at home here.

I will go to see Ken Hurren first thing tomorrow morning and tell him that Summerchild was working on defence. When I think of him sighing in the lane on the other side of the Park he seems far too close to home, far too much a part of all the difficult things in life. I don't want the mess spreading back into my working world. Then tomorrow evening I'll get home in time to see my son awake, in time to cook a meal, in time to get to grips with things.

4

There are fourteen references to defence in the index of the old Government Commission files in Registry, and I have now wasted the first hour and a half of my working day checking through them all.

I have not changed my decision to disburden myself of the task. I am merely rounding my contribution off, by finding – or, as I hope, by failing to find – some recorded trace of Summerchild's work. I think I settled upon this last gesture as my train stopped at Greenwich this morning. I had been the last to get on at the previous station, so I was standing with my back wedged against the window. At Greenwich the door opened behind me and someone else forced his way in. He did it reluctantly, with a weary sigh, and I knew, as he pulled the door to behind him, and pressed his chest into my back, that he had hair like a forest of ginger exclamation marks. And as we swayed on towards Charing Cross together, this densely corporeal ghost and I, the weariness of his sigh and the redness of his hair passed into me, and I was Summerchild again, on his way into our mutual office. I suddenly wanted to see the work I was doing laid out in front of me. Or at any rate to see its absence. If it had been removed from the files, like myself and my career, I could lay myself to rest and forget myself.

File after dusty file Mrs Tamm lays in front of me. Some of them contain printed reports, some sheaves of handwritten minutes held together by Treasury tags. Looking for something that you don't expect to find is a demoralizing task, and succeeding in finding nothing offers only a dreary satisfaction. Defence requirements and regional planning procedures . . . Changes in the presentation of defence estimates . . . There are no great mysteries. There is no sign of the existence of any special unit. But at any rate I can finally dust my hands and put my jacket on with a clear conscience. Nowhere did I expect to get and nowhere have I duly got.

But what's this? Mrs Tamm is silently putting another stack of files in front of me. 'War Games . . . War Graves . . . War, Second World, Official History of . . .' I look at her in surprise and she shrugs gracelessly, as if she were refusing to take responsibility for her indolence rather than her zeal. She's right, I realize – the word 'defence' may not have formed part of the unit's name. But then, if Defence could be War, it could be Military, or NATO. could be Army or Armed Forces or Armaments. My heart sinks; the great indefiniteness of the world is spreading through the files like damp. I find myself sighing, as Summerchild might have sighed. Mrs Tamm turns on her heel and goes back to her desk. My sigh has evidently offended her. I take my jacket off again and sit down to look through the War files . . .

I have scarcely reached 'War Damage, Limitations of Government Liability for', when I realize Mrs Tamm is standing in front of me again. I look up and smile at her, to undo the effect of my sigh. She looks away – out of the window, disclaiming any interest in my efforts. I look down at what she has brought me. This time it is a single index card. 'Strategy', it says at the top. Yes, why not? But if Strategy then Tactics. Or Logistics. Or Ballistics . . . I run my eye down the headings on the card with a growing sense of hopelessness. Strategy Air, Strategy Asia (inc. SEATO) . . . I must stop now, before my whole day is wasted . . . Strategy Naval, Strategy NATO, Strategy Nuclear . . .

Suddenly my eye leaps to four words in brackets at the bottom of the column: '(See also Strategy Unit)'.

For a second or two I stare at the words quite blankly.

Then a kind of warmth runs through my veins. Two shots of adrenalin through my blood in as many days – this task may have lasting ill-effects on my health. I have searched the grey Atlantic wastes for some sign of the wreckage, expecting to find nothing, and there suddenly, very small among the waves, is *something*. Not much. Two words, in brackets.

I glance up at Mrs Tamm. 'I've looked,' she says flatly, before I can ask. 'There's nothing.' But for her to speak at all suggests that the discovery may have released some few small drops of adrenalin into her blood, too.

There is apparently a storeroom, however, where some of the Government Commission's old papers have been dumped to await recycling. So now here I am – Mrs Tamm won't leave her desk - not heading back to my own room and my labours on the great Assessment, but in the back parts of the building where I have never been before, picking my way blindly along the twisting *ad hoc* corridors, up and down odd arbitrary stairs, in the faint hope of (seeing also). Up two steps here – then right - then down seven steps, ducking my head all the time to avoid the slope of the ceiling ... This is what the strategists in the Strategy Unit would call a Debatable Land – a territory on the frontier between different empires which has changed hands back and forth over the years. Once this was a series of separate houses, with walls isolating level from level, with lackeys running up and down the poky backstairs, and tweeny-maids freezing in the little attic bedrooms. Before the Treasury was rehoused at the end of Whitehall its junior clerks were scratching here at their ledgers. The ledgers went; storekeepers moved in. Dull demijohns of ink were ranged behind these doors, grosses of brown wooden penholders and grey steel nibs. When the war came the stationery was moved out and obscure intelligence projects were pursued and filed and forgotten in these rooms. The Government Commission was established here in triumph, and sank here into obscurity. Summerchild knew his way round the corridors. Up these stairs – or down those – the (Strategy Unit) lurked inside its protective brackets. Now we in the Cabinet Office have colonized the territory in our turn and made it our backyard. I try an unmarked door and it opens to reveal . . . yes, stationery again. Not ink and nibs, but typewriter cartridges and continuous-feed computer paper . . . The label on the key Mrs Tamm has given me is crumpled and blank. What I'm looking for is a locked, unmarked door on the fourth floor up a flight of stairs. Which of these levels counts as the fourth floor? Am I up a flight of stairs or down a flight of stairs? I try another door. It opens and a young man with a bald head looks up, too startled to speak, from a desk draped in yards of printout. I am the first human being he has seen since he was posted to this backwater.

I bend to look under a low archway in a dark corner and find a narrow spiral staircase, designed to accommodate only very small and undernourished skivvies. I squeeze my way up and try my key in the battered, irregular door at the top. It turns, and the door judders open upon a little room under the eaves, with windows that look out over rooftops and the open sky. It appears to be a storeroom for the canteen rather than the Registry, though – all I can see is a confusion of brown cardboard boxes blazoned Vim and Heinz and Tate & Lyle. I lift the flaps on one of them. The tomato ketchup it once contained has gone. In its place is compacted human thought – a dense mass of paper, some of it in files, some of it in envelopes and parcels, a lot of it loose, all of it covered in typescript or print or handwriting.

I take off the jacket of my pale grey summer suit. But where shall I put it? There is no furniture in the room. I lay it neatly over a Sarson's Malt Vinegar box. I roll up the sleeves of my crisp white shirt, because old thought is dusty stuff. I pick up some of the papers that have escaped from their boxes, pages of unidentified figures that are meaningless in their isolation, and use them as a duster to clean the top of a solidly filled Quaker Oats box and make a chair for myself. Then I open up the next nearest box, labelled Squeez-Ee Washing-up Liquid. Now, can I (see also) the slightest trace of a (Strategy Unit) . . .?

29

The very subjects written on the front of some of the files are dead. Mixed Manning and the Multilateral Force, NEDO and NEDC, ROR and ROS . . . Who now still cares about Mixed Manning? Who even knows what the Multilateral Force was, or could differentiate between NEDO and NEDC? Thought, I reflect as I pull slices of it out and push them back, is as fundamental a constituent of the world as baked beans or demerara sugar. And thoughts that were thought a long time ago are as dead as old Squeez-Ee detergent bottles, and as slow to biodegrade. I think about the half-drafted minute lying on my own desk, on a lower floor in the front of this same building, about the arrangements for Sunningdale. My minute is alive with still undischarged function, taut with unresolved tension between the Treasury's demands and ours, subtly fragrant with the personalities of the different officials whose views have shaped it. The work of the coming year will be its fruit. Then in a few weeks' time it will have been outstripped by the very events which it is shaping. It will be as dead as the Squeez-Ee files. Thought is like the honeysuckle around my front door. The newly green and sweetly blossoming tendrils reach ever further towards the sun and become dead underbrush through their very life and growth. My minute will be burnt, or composted, or trodden down into mulch, into humus, into peat, into soft coal, into hard. Maybe, on the underground conveyors in some as yet undug mine, the shiny blackness will split and reveal, like the shape of a leaf, the last faint outline of my life and work. . .

Ten past twelve, and still no sign of the leaf-shape I'm looking for . . . Seven minutes to one . . . Seven minutes *past* one . . . I've got to go. I must clean myself up and get some lunch – I have a meeting on grading with various people up the road in the Civil Service Commission at quarter past two . . . Must just look in this last box . . . This is ridiculous – I'm not going to have time for lunch if I don't go now . . . Nothing . . . Nothing . . . Nothing . . . Three minutes past two. I get to my feet, my stomach aching from emptiness, my whole body cramped from bending over, my hands too dirty to roll down my sleeves . . . I pick up my jacket with the back of my hand and open the door, then realize that there is still one box I haven't looked in − the Quaker Oats box that I was sitting on. Four minutes past two . . . I open the lid and reveal a discouraging mass of loose papers. I pull out a handful at random . . . Nothing . . . A second handful . . . And there, hand-written at the top of a letter: *Strategy Unit − Establishment*. And at the bottom: *S Summerchild*.

It appears to be about matters of accommodation and staffing. It is dated March 11th 1974 and addressed to a Dr Serafin, with copies to Mr Tite and the Establishments Division. But I can't take in anything between the name of the subject at the top and the name of the sender at the bottom. All I am conscious of, as I stand there with the page in my hand, is that here at last are the two terms of my inquiry, Strategy and Summerchild, united by the same sheet of paper. And written in Summerchild's own hand. It is as if, out of nowhere, his voice had spoken in the room, as it once did in the lane. His writing is larger than mine, I note, and as fine as his hair. The curves have a grace about them; above and below the line the g's and d's trail away in the wind like pennants. I have an impression of *dreaminess*.

Five minutes past two . . . I cram the minute halfway back into the stack of papers in the Quaker Oats box to mark where it came from and pick up the box. I can't bear to let it out of my hands − I shall have to carry it with me to my appointment at the Commission . . . I shall have to run with it! It weighs a ton . . . I'll get dust all over my white shirt . . . What am I going to do with it while I run into the lavatories to wash my hands . . .?

I put it back on the floor. It will have to wait for me, like a newly opened birthday present while you go off to school. I rush out of the room, turn the key in the lock . . . and what's this? Agh! Head! Against ceiling − low − forgot! Now what? Stairs − down − small − spiral − I remember now − cascading upwards under my helpless heels.

5

Strategy Unit – Establishment at the top; *S Summerchild* at the bottom.

I have lain awake all night waiting to get back to these words and I have now read them a dozen times. I am back in the little room at the top of the spiral staircase on Wednesday morning and I am sitting on the Squeez-Ee box, with the minute in front of me, going through the remaining contents of the Quaker Oats archive, page by dusty page.

I have also read the handwritten text between the top and bottom a dozen times:

With reference to our meeting on March 7th: on the assumption that the Unit's terms of reference will be agreed in some form broadly consonant with the one you indicated, I have drawn up proposals on the attached annexes under the following headings:

A: Accommodation.
B: Staffing.
C: Bodies from whom submissions should be sought.
D: Forms in which evidence should be taken.
E: Possible methods of reporting.
F: Designation.

With regard to this last point. I have had to find a provisional title for the venture to use in my various requisitions for staff, accommodation, etc. As you will see from the heading to this minute, I have decided that for the time being we are 'the Strategy Unit'. The (very guarded!) formulation 'unit' does not in any way preclude us from becoming a committee, a commission, a staff, a section, or anything else you may choose once it has been decided what form we are going to take. The (equally guarded!) term 'strategy' is also purely provisional. Taken together, the words I hope conceal more than they reveal, and will serve only until such time as the precise formulation of your terms of reference enables you to select more apposite nomenclature. (In Annexe F I have listed fourteen different permutations of form and function for you to consider.)

I suggest that we delay announcing our existence to the press until we have a name and clearly stated function. Communications with the press, in my experience, are best kept short and simple. They should not be couched in such a way as to encourage speculation or lead to further inquiry – or indeed arouse any other form of interest.

The single page has obviously been torn away from the Treasury tag that once attached it to its fellows and there is no sign of the promised annexes. Nor have I found them anywhere else in the box so far ... I should be in Ken Hurren's office, not here – I should be turning over my findings to Security. There can be no possible excuse for any further delay. I should *have been* in Ken Hurren's office and now be back in my own, absorbed once again in assessing the department's performance, noting perhaps the promptness with which I myself had channelled work to the appropriate division.

But I am held by the sound of Summerchild's voice. Up to now I have heard only the few reluctant words in the lane. But here he is, in full measured flood. Not to me, of course – but this is part of the fascination. He is turned away from me, oblivious of my existence, addressing someone in the shadows of humour – 'conceal more than they reveal' – which perhaps sorts with the reluctance and the sigh. But those rather racy exclamation marks are a surprise. So is the familiarity of calling us 'us'. I don't think I should have risked anything quite so rakish.

Then we come to the form of the communication. The deferential tone, and the fact that it's couched as a letter rather than as a minute, suggest that it was directed to someone outside the Civil Service. There is no address on it, but I imagine Dr Serafin was an academic. A younger man, I think – younger than Summerchild himself; there is a firmness behind Summerchild's deference which suggests that he is addressing someone not too senior – certainly one who has not yet served in the world of Royal Commissions and advisory units. But plainly a man who has made his mark in the world, if he is already being sent for. I have for some reason a picture of a rather youthful military historian. He should be quite easy to trace.

More pale humour in the final dictum about the press. Also, I think, a slight desire to shock, to cut something of a figure as a worldly and cynical administrator. Yes, in his own quiet way Summerchild is presenting himself to an audience.

The announcement to the press, presumably, was never made. Did the Unit never in fact settle on a simple enough statement of its function to entrust to journalists? What this function was I'm even less clear about myself after reading Summerchild's letter. The term 'strategy' is 'purely provisional'. The words 'Strategy Unit', he says, 'conceal more than they reveal'. Yet this is the term which the addressee was eventually persuaded to confirm, rather than any of the fourteen more 'evocative' designations in the missing Annexe F.

The date should tell me something. Summerchild and Serafin had met, presumably for the first time, on March 7th. This, as various minutes in these boxes have reminded me, was two days after Harold Wilson entered Number Ten. The State of Emergency declared by Heath was still in force. I keep coming across internal memoranda about which offices are to have their heating turned off during the morning and which during the afternoon. There is a circular about the functioning of the lifts during power-cuts, and another about cooperation with the military in the event of troops being called in to guard Government buildings. The setting up of the 'Strategy Unit' must have been one of the new Government's very first acts. Could the 'strategy' have concerned the exercise of the Government's emergency powers? Is this why it was so secret? I still have the grinding rumble of Tilly Tilling's tanks in my mind.

'Dear Dr Serafin'. The fine, romantic handwriting suddenly leaps out at me again from the surrounding porridge of the Quaker Oats archive. This letter is dated March 12th.

Strategy Unit – Accommodation

With reference to your letter dated March 11th, I note your disinclination to pursue the addresses in Croydon and Kilburn and fully sympathize with your feelings. I felt I should include them in the list if only so that you could see the limited choice at present available. The advent of a new Government, I am afraid, always results in a rash of new advisory bodies and a consequent pressure upon accommodation. It is, as my colleague in the Establishment Division remarked, shaking his head sagely, when I made application to him, 'a difficult time to be setting up home'.

I have therefore arranged for us to view the premises in Northumberland Avenue the day after tomorrow, on your next visit to London. They are at any rate central and have I believe served for various committees of inquiry, etcetera, before.

There is again something about the tone of this minute that strikes me. Perfectly correct, entirely urbane – yet there is a hint of the personal in it, something almost – I don't know – avuncular. I am beginning to see, I think, with some professional interest and sympathy, how Summerchild is dealing with this clever young outsider. He has assembled a list of self-evidently unacceptable addresses for the Unit's accommodation from which the reassuring words 'Northumberland Avenue' have been grasped with relief. But I wonder if Northumberland Avenue is really where he intends the Unit to end up. I know those offices in Northumberland Avenue – I have been involved in submitting evidence to two separate Royal Commissions there – and I do not believe this proposed tour of inspection is going to be a very joyous occasion. I must assume Summerchild knows the premises, too. I picture the two of them (and I must suppose Summerchild pictures it himself) walking across Whitehall together, and up Great Scotland Yard, through the thin March sunlight, warmed by the faint hope of summer; then plunging into the frowsty Edwardian gloom, where neither sunlight nor hope of summer ever penetrate. I see (and Summerchild sees) the young provincial historian becoming even more silent and preoccupied than Summerchild himself as they look at the worn carpets and unoccupied chairs. Summerchild taps on the hardboard divisions to demonstrate their solidity and stops at once when they ring hollow. He cranes hopefully up at windows, to demonstrate that you can see the sky if you lean far enough back, and shows Dr Serafin how there is lavatory accommodation available in the basement, only three floors down. He has more than likely planned the expedition for the half of the day when it is not Northumberland Avenue's turn for heating.

I see them walking back up Great Scotland Yard afterwards, with the historian lost in thought and Summerchild asking him solicitously if he would like to view the Croydon or Kilburn premises after all. Summerchild is, I think, shepherding his chairman slowly towards where he would be safest – inside the Government Commission building, sharing the Cabinet Office canteen with all the rest of them, under Francis Tite's eye. I believe the rooms have already been set aside. Does Dr Serafin know about them yet? Does he realize that he is part of Tite's plans – as I now dimly begin to perceive – to revive the flagging fortunes of the Government Commission?

Because this, I think, is what's happening here. The Government Commission, set up by Labour in 1965 to circumvent the rest of the Civil Service, has been quietly declining under the Conservatives; Heath has made his own arrangements to the same end, by setting up the Central Policy Review Staff, which has been housed by the Cabinet Office next door. Now Labour is back – and word has immediately gone round Whitehall that Wilson is setting up his own Policy Unit inside Number Ten. So now the Government Commission has rivals literally on either side of it; it is outflanked to left as well as to right. But, within hours of Wilson's entering Number Ten on March 5th, Tite has struck back. Some time that same day, or the following one, the new Prime Minister has entrusted some study of strategy, or some strategic study of something else, to an outside expert – and by the 7th, as we know from Summerchild's first letter, Wilson has somehow been persuaded to staff and service this new operation through the Government Commission. Indeed, Summerchild has already had his first meeting with Serafin, and been accepted as Secretary of the operation. By the 11th Summerchild has given the new formation a temporary designation, which will prove to be permanent, and has provided a wealth of possible addresses, colleagues and procedures. By the 14th Serafin is being steered back across Whitehall, out of the pale sunshine, and in through the threatening corridors of the Cabinet Office towards these peaceful quarters at the rear, where rooms have already been quietly set aside for him. I am always amused by the idea that outsiders have of Whitehall as being slow-moving; we are like a snake, whose coils seem to be lying motionless even as they flow past your eyes and are gone. But even by Whitehall standards Tite is moving fast. He must have been a rather remarkable Permanent Secretary – I should like to know more about him. I suspect I am going to. His fate, and the fate of his department, is going to be closely bound to the new Unit. And when Summerchild fell from the back of the Admiralty, I am beginning to think, the prospects of Tite and his department must have fallen with him.

I am intrigued to watch Summerchild at work, too. This is Millie's father, coming up Hyde Hill Lane of an evening so wearily, with so little to say for himself; yet here he is sliding through the grass with such snake-like speed and resourcefulness. Now I am wondering about the other lists that he annexed to his letter, of suggested colleagues, procedures and methods. Will they go the same way as the list of accommodation? Will Serafin show his independence of mind and his refusal to be controlled by his Civil Servants and reject them all, item by item, so that he ends up discovering for himself the colleagues, procedures and methods that Summerchild has already selected for him?

First the accommodation, though. How, exactly, is he going to let Serafin stumble upon the rooms that are waiting, as I imagine, somewhere rather close to where I am now sitting?

'Dear Dr Serafin. . .' Another letter in Summerchild's handwriting, dated March 15th. This is – yes – the day after the visit to Northumberland Avenue. *Strategy Unit – Accommodation*, it begins, once again.

With reference to your letter of yesterday's date, I note your severe reservations about the rooms in Northumberland Avenue. I should perhaps remind you that they would normally be somewhat warmer than they were during our inspection, at any rate during one half of the working day . . .

Just as I thought!

Nevertheless, I take your point, and will naturally do my best to secure the alternatives you saw inside our own building . . .

And he's done it! But *how?*

. . . I must apologize if I gave the impression of trying to keep these from you, as you (perhaps jokingly) suggested. To the best of my recollection I mentioned their existence as soon as you had expressed dissatisfaction with Northumberland Avenue. I had not done so before merely because I had not thought of them in this context; I had supposed that you might prefer to be at some slight remove from the nefarious influences of the department . . .

The man had style. No wonder he was weary by the time he walked up to his front door at the end of each day.

I have a suspicion that somehow the heating was on by the time they reached their new destination. But what was it that Summerchild said to make Dr Serafin so keen to see these other premises in the first place?

. . . I must also apologize if I seemed to be trying to put you off them. I simply thought I should warn you that they were effectively in a garret . . .

He told him they were in a garret. That was the word of warning that made Serafin insist on seeing them. Because at once he pictured something familiar and intimate – something like his own rooms overlooking some quiet college court. Here he is, the brightest young Fellow of King's or All Souls, being led round in an invisible collar and chain by my freckled colleague. 'Effectively in a garret'. How brilliant. Summerchild would have mentioned it by way of defending Northumberland Avenue, perhaps while they were still walking back along Great Scotland Yard. At least it wasn't a *garret*, he would have said, which was the only other thing they'd been offered. I imagine they walked in silence for some way after that; putting a new idea into someone's imagination, even if that imagination belongs to the cleverest young Fellow of the very grandest college, is like turning on the television – it takes a little time for the set to warm up. 'A garret?' says Serafin finally, as they cross the end of Scotland Place. 'What sort of garret?' Summerchild shrugs. 'Just a garret.' If Serafin is astute he asks what you can see out of the windows. Summerchild runs his hand through the glinting aureole around his head, trying to remember. 'Roofs, mostly, I think,' he says reluctantly. 'Roofs and chimneys.' 'I think I should like to have a look at it,' says Serafin very politely, 'if I might.' And Summerchild bows his head. He can see that Dr Serafin is going to be a very firm chairman. 'I'd better lead the way,' he says grudgingly. 'It's rather a hike.'

Because of course if they are in a garret they are somewhere very close indeed to where I am sitting now on my Squeez-Ee box.

> ... Perhaps I should stress, once again, that I am here to help, not to hinder. I have therefore asked Establishment if the room on the fourth floor can be cleared of stores and made available for our clerical staff, and if, as you requested, desks and other facilities for our own use can be got up into the smaller room at the top of the spiral staircase ...

So it was this very room. Of course. I can hear the two of them on the narrow stair outside, Summerchild placing his feet with ostentatious care on each step, bending his head rather further than is strictly necessary under the low ceiling, while Serafin demonstrates his effortless familiarity with such picturesque difficulties. The key turns stiffly in the lock. The door judders open, and Summerchild looks doubtfully in at me and the old grocery boxes. He stands back while Serafin comes into the centre of the room and slowly revolves on his heel. 'I suppose we could clean it up a bit,' says Summerchild reluctantly. 'We could ... put up some shelves.' And yes, there *were* shelves. Now I look I can see the rows of holes in the walls on either side of the old chimney-breast where they were fixed.

Serafin gazes at the irregular geometry of the walls, and the quaintly sloping ceiling. He opens the little door half-hidden in a corner and finds ... what? I open the little door myself. Inside is a tiny sink and draining-board, with a gas-ring and an ancient grey kettle. It's like the scout's room in an Oxford college. Beyond is another door, which opens to reveal an ancient lavatory. All the necessities of life are up here. You could shut yourself away in this garret all day and never come down. Serafin emerges from the minuscule domestic offices and crosses to one of the two windows. I follow him and peer over his shoulder.

We are looking northwards. In the foreground are the chimney-stacks of the Cabinet Office – complex pillars of weathered grey London stock brick rising like the high Alps from the blue slate foothills of the roof. Beyond them is another range, which must be the Scottish Office, and then, on the horizon, the fine spider's web of antennae on the roof of the Admiralty. Serafin moves to the other window. I follow him. This one is looking west, straight down into the garden of Number Ten. I can see part of Horse Guards Parade – almost see myself standing there the other afternoon, looking up at these windows, still ignorant of what I was looking at. Beyond the Parade is the green sea of treetops in the Park, and then the Palace. The Royal Standard is flying. The sky is piled with sunlit June cumulus.

Serafin knows now why Summerchild was so reluctant to let him see this place and so anxious to make him settle for the dingy remoteness of Northumberland Avenue. It is because this garret is at the very heart of Government. From here you are looking into the rear windows of Whitehall. If the Prime Minister is walking in his garden on a summer's morning you could push up the rickety sash – like this – and call down to him. This is the very last place where they would want some outsider installing himself and pursuing his researches.

Summerchild is indeed looking more dubious than ever. 'I think you may find that some of your less youthful associates have difficulty with the stairs,' he says. At once I can see Annexe B, Summerchild's list of possible members of the Unit, as clearly as if it had just come out of the porridge oats box. It comprises industrialists very close to retiring age, and senior army officers who have passed it. I believe I can read the names of a few redundant colonial administrators. Serafin, too, is thinking about Annexe B. He knows, just as well as Summerchild does, that these are big men who once rowed for their colleges. They will crack their heads on the low door frame and be forced to stand bent forwards beneath the slope of the ceiling in attitudes of unsuitable humility.

As a matter of fact, I believe that Summerchild is playing not one game here but two. Even as he uses the accommodation in Annexe A to manoeuvre Serafin into discovering for himself the waiting garret, so he is using the garret to manoeuvre him into rejecting all the proposed associates in Annexe B. Once Serafin has insisted on installing himself in the garret – against all reasonable advice – he is going to discover that the kind of staff he needs will be young and agile, with a good knowledge of the backstairs of Government buildings and an ability to duck their heads and remain inclined slightly forwards for long periods of time. In short, one or two of the bright young Principals and Under-Secretaries in the department. When Serafin presses him, Summerchild will try to suggest a few names.

All this is as yet in the future; Serafin is still working out how he is going to insist on occupying the garret, in the teeth of Summerchild's objections. There is no sense of triumph yet in Summerchild. In his head, as in mine, the unending private minute is being written and I can read it, I discover, almost as clearly as my own. Nothing in it suggests even that he is aware of pursuing some covert stratagem in the battle. He does not know he is taking part in a battle. He is not a devious or deceitful man, and he has no ambition to be an actor. He believes that things are as they seem to Dr Serafin; that he is putting up proposals which are as sound as his judgement and experience can make them, that he is withdrawing them in deference to Serafin's objections, and that he will be forced to formulate alternative proposals which cannot be known to him yet because they will take their rise from views Serafin has still not expressed. It is a cause for chagrin, not satisfaction, that Serafin has rejected all his advice. He is suppressing this chagrin, of course – and he could scarcely be suppressing it if he weren't feeling it.

How strange, though, that the report running inside my own head can quote so freely and copiously from the report running inside Summerchild's. I'm not sure that this has ever happened to me before. I can't help putting myself in his place, of course, as he looks for ways to contain someone we both regard as an outsider. I can't help reading between the lines of his letters to Serafin. If there were any of Serafin's replies here then I might have rather more insight into his side of the story ... Yes, that's odd. The half-dozen letters from Summerchild that I have found scattered through the porridge oats box seem to be replies to letters from Serafin, but not one of Serafin's letters has yet come to light. Here are two more from Summerchild, dated March 18th and 20th ... The question of accommodation seems to be settled, but the Unit apparently still has no agreed terms of reference. Or so I deduce. But where are the letters in which Serafin informed Summerchild of this? Summerchild must have filed them, surely?

Even as this problem forms itself in my head it is superseded by its very simple and obvious solution. The papers scattered through the contents of the Quaker Oats box have not come from the Unit's files. The Unit's files have vanished, like Summerchild's personal file. What I am finding is the remains of another file altogether – one kept by *Serafin*, which contains all the communications he received. This is why I can follow Summerchild's thoughts – because I am standing where *Serafin* stood.

And sitting, of course, more or less where he sat, now that he has moved into his new office. I dust down another box and put it on top of the one I am perching on, to bring it up to the height of a normal chair. Now I can see rooftops outside the windows as well as open sky. I slide my construction across to the windows, and build myself a desk with two more boxes. The light from the western window, overlooking Downing Street, falls across it. Through the window behind me, if I turn round, I look northward towards the array of wires above the Admiralty. So here I am, installed in my new office, beginning another day's work. I open my briefcase and sort through various, what? – books and papers by colleagues, say – looking for my file of letters. There is a tap at the door. 'Come in,' I say. Or do I? I can't actually hear the words. I don't know what my voice sounds like. Whereas, when the door opens, and Summerchild enters, stooped beneath the lintel and diffidently smiling, I can hear him perfectly. 'Good morning,' he says. 'I've been giving a little more thought to the question of our terms of reference. I wonder whether the way to proceed might not be to write our own. That's to say, put up our own draft for approval. Approval, in my experience, is usually somewhat easier to come by than the thing approved.' He lets each word go with some reluctance. His voice is low, as if the machinery producing it were running slow, not fully warmed up. I gesture (I imagine) towards a chair on the other side of my desk and he sits down in an attitude which suggests that he intends to stay for rather more than a minute, and rather less than half an hour. He is carrying a file, I notice. I assume that it contains among other things the letters I have sent to him. Am I looking at this file at all anxiously? Do I already have some suspicion that one day it is going to be removed from the records and scattered, perhaps vanish altogether? What have I said in those letters? What am I saying as we sit here talking about this rather strange difficulty that we find ourselves in? What terms of reference are we suggesting for ourselves?

But I'm Jessel, and I have Jessel's life to lead. I put all the documents I've found into my own Summerchild file. As I pick up my jacket from the Sarson's Malt Vinegar box which I seem to have appointed as coat-rack, I pull the lid up with it. There is a mess of loose papers inside that I have glanced through before. But now one of them catches my eye because I recognize the handwriting. 'Annexe A', it says at the top. It is the missing accommodation list, filed for some reason under vinegar instead of porridge. I was right, I'm pleased to see, about his tactics: the six addresses on it don't include the one I am now in. I'm just about to put it away in my file when I see that there is something else pencilled upside down at the bottom.

It's another list. But this one has no title at the top and it's written in a completely different hand. The letters are small and hurrying and the pencil wasn't sharp. With some difficulty I read:

1. Marmite.

Marmite? *Marmite . . .?* I feel an obscure sense of shame and irritation at finding the word Marmite written on a Government document, even one filed under Sarson's Malt Vinegar. It relates to that other world, the great shabby confusion outside these walls to which I return each evening, to Timmy and Cheryl, to my mother-in-law who comes to help out at the weekends, to everything unresolved and unsatisfactory. I do not believe that Summerchild and his Director were discussing the financial structure of the Marmite company, or the competitiveness of the British savoury spread industry. It does not appear to be written in that tone of voice. I believe this is a shopping list. What are the other items?

2. 2X35L 1X32M.
3. Heels.
4. Syntax.
5. Plectra.

Heels, yes. A reminder to take a pair of shoes to be heeled. I don't know about the other items. Is there a brand of cleaner called Syntax? Plectra sounds like a make of margarine . . . A shopping list, certainly.

But whose? Could Summerchild have given Annexe A to his wife to write on? Impossible. If only because he didn't have it to give – he'd sent it off with his first letter. No, what I am looking at are the first direct signals to reach me from the dark constellation of Serafin.

45

I find them somewhat disconcerting. They are not quite what I should have expected from a man like Serafin.

I put the list away in my file, lock the room and carefully pick my way down the little staircase. Marmite, heels . . . But what was the next item? I take a look in the file as I make my way down to the main entrance. *2X35L 1X32M*. I have a feeling that motor oils and radio parts are sold with this sort of code. Marmite and motor oil? Marmite and transistors? Plectra I have certainly seen on my weekly trips to Safeway . . .

The phone is ringing as I come through the door of my office.

'Jessel.'

'Cryer, Home Office.'

'Cryer' means nothing to me. 'Home Office' means more work. I stand with the phone in my hand, remembering that I have still had no lunch.

'John Killick said you might be interested in anything anyone could remember about Stephen Summerchild.'

The thought of lunch goes. I sit down.

'I didn't know him very well, I'm afraid,' says Cryer. 'In fact I always thought he was in the DTI. It was a great shock to open the paper and discover he was involved in whatever it was. I knew him through the Civil Service Orchestra, you see. He was next desk to me for three or four years. He played the violin.'

I have my pen in hand, poised above the Summerchild pad. But we seem to have reached the end of the story.

'That's all I know about him, really,' says Cryer. 'He wasn't a very forthcoming man. I just thought you might like to know about playing the violin. I've always felt that was a somewhat surprising sidelight.'

'Thank you,' I tell him. 'Yes. That's very helpful.'

I put the phone down and try to remember whether the canteen is still open. But . . . the DTI? Why should anyone look at this silent, red-haired violinist and leap to the conclusion that he was in the Department of Trade and Industry?

I am suddenly consumed with a ridiculous curiosity. I pick up the phone again and dial the Home Office.

'Oh,' says Cryer. 'Because he seemed to be working on that kind of thing.'

'What kind of thing?'

'Well . . . washing-machines.'

Washing-machines? So they did talk. Suddenly, after three or four years of silence, as they stood side by side in some rented school hall, slackening their bows and cleating them away in the lids of their violin cases, they began to talk.

About washing-machines.

'Well, you know,' says Cryer. 'There's an expression for it. The quality of life. It was a bit of a catch-phrase at the time. He said he was concerned with it in some kind of way. I assumed it was something to do with domestic machinery.'

'Thank you,' I say again. But this time I mean it.

Because I saw the words only yesterday. Somewhere, in one of the brown boxes in the little garret room, wedged between National Economic Development Council and Regional Employment Premium, I saw a file labelled just that – Quality of Life. So now I know where to find the rest of the Unit's papers. Now I know what they were doing up there in their garret. Now I know why it was called the Strategy Unit.

The first thing Harold Wilson did when he arrived in office was to set up a Policy Unit inside Number Ten, to work on short-term, day-to-day problems. The second – obviously, now I see it – was to set up a complementary unit to deal with long-term aims. Number Ten had captured the tactical unit; Francis Tite's genius was to carry off the strategic one. Perhaps he had even suggested it. I imagine him reading and re-reading the Labour Party's election manifesto as the results came in. In some forgotten corner of the text he had found some vague pledge that no one else had noticed. I imagine something about 'looking beyond day-to-day considerations at the quality of life we should be working towards for our people'.

So it wasn't defence and the instruments of death that

brought Summerchild to that little yard in Spring Gardens. It was life itself. Or the quality of it. I have only a very hazy idea about what the phrase means, I realize. But then Summerchild didn't know himself to start with, by the sound of it. Washing-machines? I thought it was something to do with – I don't know – sauna baths and golf driving-ranges. Perhaps lead-free petrol, or traffic-free streets. But our ideas change. One day we want champagne; next day it's Alka-Seltzer.

I can't get back to the garret until tomorrow. But by tomorrow evening, I think, I shall know what the quality of life is – shall perhaps even have discovered how it killed Summerchild. I shall know as much of the whole story as I'm ever going to know. The only thing I've time to do today is to run into Registry and look up Dr Serafin.

Nothing in *Who's Who*. I find that slightly surprising. The *Universities Year Book* . . . Yes, Serafin. But another one, 'b. 1963'. I think mine, however brilliant, must have been more than eleven years old when he was appointed to the chairman-ship of a Government advisory body. So Serafin has gone. The career that looked so promising in 1974 has evidently come to a premature end. Has he died, like Summerchild himself? Emigrated to the United States?

Or defected to the Soviet Union . . .

A foolish thought. I can't help noticing, though, that the Serafin in the *Universities Year Book* is called Vladislav and is in Russian studies. I suppose Serafin is a Russian name.

6

Still stroking my son's forehead with my left hand, I reach out into the darkness with my right and fumble for the little clock on his bedside table. For a moment the dial shines in the night and at once Timmy stirs. Quarter past two and he's still not really back to sleep. I must have been sitting here on the edge of his bed, first singing and stroking, then just stroking, for half an hour or so. He was crying again. It's always the same. I wake to hear him crying. I come in and put the bedside light on, and he lies there with his eyes half-open, conscious but immobilized, as if he were under some strange paralysing drug, unable to tell me what the trouble was, unable to nod or smile or shake off his dream.

I suppose it was about his mother. She sometimes comes to me in dreams, too – smiling and calm, as if nothing at all had happened. Once she was holding out a small present done up in coloured wrapping. There was a feeling of Christmas in the air. This is why the night is so terrible. The mind is on its own in the building. It goes wandering through the files unchecked, pulling open the drawers and scattering the papers, writing wild minutes of its own.

One of these unthinkable night-thoughts thinks itself now: it's because of Summerchild that I'm sitting here stroking Timmy's head. If whatever happened to Summerchild that year hadn't happened – if he hadn't been found lying with the garbage in Spring Gardens – if Millie hadn't stopped playing in the orchestra – if I'd gone on seeing her week by

49

week – grown up with her – become easy with her – married her – then Timmy would still have a mother at home. Except that in that case Timmy wouldn't be Timmy, and the thought that there might be no Timmy, that there might be some other person altogether occupying his space in the world, fills me with terror, as if I had looked out of the bedroom window and found the solid earth beneath the house had disappeared. Night-thoughts . . .

But then whatever happened to Summerchild did happen. Back and forth goes my hand, over the softness of my son's forehead and up into the softness of his hair. My wrist aches; my own eyes are closed. Back and forth go my thoughts, over the items on a list, up into the quality of life. I can't quite make out the items on the list, however many times I go over it, or rather I can't make out the rooms on the staircase, or the stairs on my son's forehead. They go round and round, and begin to vibrate frighteningly, so that the whole washing-machine starts to tramp across the kitchen floor, in a growing flood of hot soapy water . . .

Timmy stirs; my hand has stopped moving. Off we go again, over the softness of his forehead, up into the softness of his hair. I'm wide awake now, because I've suddenly seen the formula 2X35L IX32M appear in my brain, like the glowing green digits on the video, and then softly, effortlessly deconstruct itself into elements of meaning. The video becomes a radio, and the L and the M expand gently into Long-wave and Medium-wave. The X's silently detach themselves from the numbers on either side and become multiplication signs. I am looking at two lots of 35 in the long waveband and one lot of 32 in the medium waveband. 35 and 32 what? Metres? Megahertz? I know nothing about radio – but I don't need to, I realize, because, even while I watch, the waves are softly withdrawing from the wavebands, as from a beach at low tide on a calm summer's afternoon, leaving me gazing through the darkness of my son's bedroom at three shirts, two of them size 35 long, one of them size 32 medium.

Shirts. Yes. I'm smiling to myself in the darkness, Timmy –

I wish you could see me. Marmite, heels, three shirts, half a pound of Plectra, and some product called Syntax, which I now envisage as being like a health-food called Bemax that my father used to sprinkle over his breakfast cereal. Serafin puts Syntax on his. It's Syntax that assures Serafin's quality of life.

I gently stop stroking. Timmy stirs and moans. I start stroking again.

But here's a puzzle. Why is one of the shirts a different size? – Because it's for someone else. Here I am, Serafin, writing my shopping list on the first piece of paper that comes to hand and what I'm writing down is two shirts for myself and one for my son. If my son takes a 32 he is full-grown, almost as big as me. Or else – more generously – I am buying one shirt for myself and two for my son. In which case my son has already outgrown me. Or perhaps *none* of the shirts is for me . . . Of course. I have not one son but two. Why am I buying two shirts for one son and only one for the other? Because I have *three* sons, and I am buying them one each. Three young men, all old enough to buy shirts for themselves, and their father's still going out and buying them shirts! Strange. Yes, but I'm not their father, am I. I'm their mother.

I'm a woman. My whole shape changes around me in the darkness, like the radios melting into shirts. My hand softens against the softness of my son's forehead. My hips sit wider and heavier on the bed. And the whole shape of the Strategy Unit changes, too. I now see a certain awkwardness in the way Summerchild sits on the other side of my desk. I see resentment in that courteous smile, hostility in that diffident prose, an element of sheer male aggression in his deft professional manipulation of me. This is why the tone of his communications with me has that slightly patronizing and protective edge. It's not a difference in age; it's a difference in sex.

I slide out of my smooth new womanly skin, and slide in behind the russet freckles and bristles facing me across the office to check this analysis. Yes, the softness I am looking at

51

somehow irks me. I think this woman with the three grown-up sons is not younger than me at all, but almost certainly older. I feel an obscure resentment against her motherliness. I find myself being another son – a good son, courteous and thoughtful, holding doors open, appearing to defer to all her wishes. I smile indulgently as I watch her write a shopping list on a document drawn up in my own hand. My smile is not entirely sincere.

I stroke Timmy's forehead more and more lightly, until I am stroking empty air. This time he doesn't stir; he is off the beach at last, out beyond the shallows, in deep still water. I creep back to my room, leaving both our doors ajar. Whether I get to sleep again myself I find difficult to determine; it's hard to recognize sleep in the dark. Plectra, I discover, is a make of washing-machine, which thunders and shakes and tramps across the office floor, and Sontax is a sleeping-pill called Spantax, which is a Spanish taxi firm called Taxi-max . . .

Whether I was asleep or not, a few hours or minutes later I am undoubtedly awake. The room is full of early sunlight and birdsong, and I know what Syntax is. It's very simple. Syntax is syntax. Syntax is what my friend Kevin Rice, who was at Manchester with me, was always talking about. Syntax and semantics. Syntax and logical form. Kevin was always talking about syntax because he was reading philosophy and this is the kind of thing philosophers talk about. So now I know why it's on my shopping list. When I've bought my sons their shirts I'm going on to a good academic book-shop to get an item for myself – a book called something like *Syntax and Significance: A Cognitive Approach*.

I am a woman, I am a mother of sons, I am a philosopher.

7

Plectra I break as I reach the bottom of the spiral staircase on my way back to my little garret. I am arriving off an early train from Oxford or Cambridge, my mind full of Marmite and shirts. I hear inside my head a dismal metallic howling. It is the noise made by one of my sons playing his electric guitar. He plays it with a plectrum. 'You going up to town, Mum?' he said, as I scribbled my shopping list just before I dashed out of the house to catch my train. 'Get me some plectrums from that shop in Charing Cross Road!' And, even as I hurled the word down on to paper in my headlong rush, I couldn't help correcting his solecism. *Plectra*, I scribbled.

So that's the sort of person I am. Three hulking sons, and a precisely literate mind. I feel a shade disappointed that the small but promising mysteries of the shopping list have yielded up such a homely creature.

I unlock the door of the garret, place my jacket on top of the Sarson's Malt Vinegar box and hunt through the Squeez-Ee box. Yes, here it is – a thick brown file with the careful capitals of the title written in Summerchild's now familiar hand. I feel a ridiculous disappointment. Soon there will be nothing left to know and I shall have to go back to the Annual Assessment.

I take the file over to my improvised seat by the window, by now reluctant to open it. A minor mystery, of course, is how the file has survived intact. Why were its contents not scattered by the same hand that turned the records of the

Strategy Unit out of their covers? I gaze absently out of the window, wondering. Perhaps no one knew this file existed. It was never catalogued; I am the first person outside the Unit ever to know what it was doing . . .

On the other side of Horse Guards Parade a little group of people are clustered around a strange animal with three splayed front legs, two rear legs in trousers and a single eye projecting from the middle of its forehead. Facing this creature, like a matador in front of a bull, is a man who never takes his eye off it for a moment. He gestures at the building behind him, as if trying to distract the animal's attention. The bull lifts its head a little and gazes up at the Admiralty for some moments. Then the trousered rear legs begin to edge step by step to the left, and very slowly and deliberately the animal turns its head. It has forgotten about its opponent; it has become interested in the architecture. It examines the Horse Guards, then the Scottish Office. It's not a dumb, tormented animal at all. As it continues its unhurried survey I begin to feel a grim human intent behind that gaze. I have the impression of an enemy general, scanning our lines through his field-glasses, or a hardened housebreaker, openly searching for a point of entry. It continues to turn, moving now towards the Cabinet Office. The little group of staff-officers accompanying the general turn as well, falling back deferentially to keep out of his line of vision . . . He turns his head a little further and it comes to me that these are the people who are making the programme about Summerchild. With terrible deliberation the camera lifts its single eye towards the roofline. Together with all its accompanying staff it gazes straight at me . . .

I move sharply away from the window, shocked to find myself being looked at, cross with myself to have been caught looking back. I am also alarmed to find the enemy so hard on my heels. Can they really have discovered the secret of the garret room already? I look cautiously out again, standing well back in the shadows . . . The beast is gazing disconsolately at the ground, its architectural studies abandoned. Its rear legs have joined the general staff, who are all in discussion with their backs towards me. Perhaps they were gazing up here quite absently and speculatively, as I did on Monday. Or perhaps this programme isn't about Summerchild at all. It's something educational about government, or the history of the Civil Service.

It reminds me, though, that not all the mysteries are yet solved. The most important one, the one that I started with, remains as opaque as ever: I have still not the slightest idea how or why Summerchild died. Indeed, now that I know about the Marmite and the teenage sons it seems more mysterious than ever.

The Quality of Life, yes. I open the file . . .

Inside is a thick sheaf of dog-eared papers, held together by a Treasury tag in the standard Civil Service manner. The first page is a brief routine memorandum from the Clerical Supervisor in Personnel, dated April 18th 1974, announcing the transfer of a Mrs L Padmore from the Strategy Unit to the Economic Secretariat. But I am getting ahead of myself. The top document in a file, like the top layer in an archaeological site, is the most recent. I want to go through in chronological order, so I turn to the back of the stack and find the lowest deposit, the first record of the new Unit.

It isn't much like any document I've ever seen in a Civil Service file before. It consists of a stack of plain thin copy paper, in the now obsolete quarto size, completely covered in faint, irregular, single-spaced typing. Many of the letters are flying in the air above their fellows, or sinking beneath them, and the orchestra of different characters is dominated by the solo x key. As I turn the pages, the light comes through several dozen small holes where the paper has been punctured by full stops, and through a number of larger windows made by pastry-cutting characters like o. The last line on each page peels away and dives through the bottom of the paper.

There are nine pages. Wedged so tight against the bottom of the last page that I can hardly read it are four handwritten words that make my heart leap: 'Yours sincerely, Elizabeth Serafin'. So this document is my own handiwork. And I *am* a woman. I think of myself rushing out of the house in North Oxford, or the quiet residential streets beyond the University Library in Cambridge, snatching my ancient portable type-writer off my desk as I go, with the voices of boorish boys shouting 'Mum! Don't forget my plectrums!' and the voice of a husband, too, calling after me that we've run out of Marmite. 'Oh, and Elizabeth . . .!' he shouts. So I'm an Elizabeth. I don't know what I think about that.

I turn back to page one. 'March 25th 1974', it begins. Then: 'Dear Prime Minister . . .'

I stop reading. Dear Prime Minister? This is rather a sur-prise. Especially followed by a letter going on for nine densely filled pages. I feel a twinge of sympathetic embarrassment on my late colleague's behalf. So, Dear Prime Minister . . .

The organization which you asked me to set up now exists, at least in embryo. I began work this morning, together with my Secretary, Mr S Summerchild, and a Clerical Officer, Mrs L Padmore, in the premises made available to us by the Govern-ment Commission. My very first act – since one has to begin somewhere – was to decide upon the form in which I would report to you. The one I have chosen is this – brief, informal letters, written from time to time as our work proceeds, in a plain, straightforward style, as it might be to a friend.

I put the file down again and stroke my beard for comfort, the way Timmy used to stroke his little piece of blanket. Where is Summerchild, while all this is going on? At his desk, presumably, in this very room, tormented by the thin chatter of my little portable. The only place for his desk would have been opposite mine, with the light over his left shoulder. I look across at him. What's he doing, while I write my brief, informal, nine-page letter to the Prime Minister? Writ-ing something of his own, no doubt, carefully and silently, by hand, trying to keep his face absolutely expression-less. He will presumably have to sort out all this nonsense later.

Where was I? Yes . . .

. . . as it might be to a friend. I have chosen this form for two reasons. The inquiry you have asked me to undertake is, so far as I can understand, essentially a philosophical one. I believe that philosophical inquiry is, by its very nature, open and untechnical. I also believe that it is very unlikely to produce the kind of answers that can be summarized in a final report. The 'answers' produced by philosophy are the questions that it asks. The final report on a philosphical inquiry is the inquiry itself.

What I must decide next is how this inquiry is to be conducted. But before I can do that I need to establish something even more basic: what it is exactly that I am inquiring into. I have promised to keep these reports brief, but I must make a historical excursion here to establish the background to this absolutely fundamental question.

I have so far received only one explanation of what this advisory unit I am setting up is supposed to be doing. This was in your original phone call to me at home in Oxford, on the evening of March 6th. It would perhaps have been entirely adequate if I had received it in any normal circumstances. But the circumstances were not normal. I must explain that I have no phone in my study, to avoid interruption when I am working, and that I take phone calls in the dining-room . . .

I have to stop again. Poor Summerchild! He sits over there, some twelve feet away from me, vexed no doubt by the babble of the keys, but still unaware of the horror they are spelling out. What is he going to say when he discovers that he is expected to transmit the first report from an advisory unit in the history of goverment to include an account of the Director's domestic arrangements? It's all right for me – I can close my eyes for a moment, and stroke my beard, and make little gasping noises to myself. He is going to have to keep a straight face, and deal with it.

. . . and that I take phone calls in the dining-room, on the other side of the hall. I am perfectly used to carrying pen and paper with me when I go to answer the phone. But when you called I was teaching, and the rule when I am teaching is that one of my sons must answer the phone. I'm afraid that when Alexander tapped on my study door I was in a rather abstracted state. I was listening with half my mind to the essay my pupil was reading and although the ideas he was expressing (about sense-data) were in themselves neither new nor interesting they had set off ideas of my own, as the ideas in undergraduate essays often do — I think of it as one of the uncovenanted benefits of teaching. These ideas were occupying the other half of my brain. So I went to take the call in some confusion — confusion made worse by haste when Alexander told me it was the Prime Minister. I have never been phoned by a Prime Minister before, but I imagine they are not used to being kept waiting. So flustered was I, in fact, that I became entangled with the bicycles in the hall (my sons always keep them there, and other things being equal I usually get past them without too much difficulty), and I arrived in the dining-room even more distraught than I set out from the study.

Worse was to come. I had assumed up to this point that you really wished to speak not to me but to my husband (who is of course E J Maitland, a philosopher whose reputation is rather more likely than mine to attract telephone calls from the great officers of state) and that I was being summoned to the phone merely because he was not there. When the gentleman in your office, however, addressed me not as Mrs Maitland, but by my maiden name, which is the one I write under, I realized that it must indeed be me who was being phoned, whereupon it suddenly seemed (perhaps only by association of ideas) imperative that I had the means of writing to hand. Now, our dining-room had served during the General Election just concluded as the local Labour Party committee-rooms, and there were still various sheets of strawboard balanced on tables and sideboards, covered in the stubs of canvass-returns, with pencils at hand to mark them. Just as I was put through to you I had the idea of reaching out to take one of these pencils and to tear off one of the canvass-returns as a notepad.

All might still have been well had it not been for yet another unfortunate circumstance. Just as I was stretching, the room went black: another power-cut. In the darkness I reached too far and dislodged the sheet of strawboard. It fell forwards and I managed to catch it on my outstretched forearm. I knew that if I let it go it would collapse on to a teapot and mugs still waiting to be cleared from the sideboard, which would confuse the situation still further. On the other hand I felt I could scarcely ask you to wait while I dealt with the strawboard – you were by this time I think just on the verge of a few conventional politenesses about my work, an awkward stage in conversations of this sort which is difficult to endure gracefully but which is even more difficult to interrupt. I have to confess, I'm afraid – and now we have come to the point of this long and circumstantial detour, of a sort which I assure you will not recur in these reports – that under the pressure of the circumstances I did a very foolish thing. I put the receiver down for a moment so that I could take two hands to the strawboard.

If this was foolish, what was unforgivable was not to confess sooner – immediately I had picked the receiver up again. Because by this time you had moved on to explaining what you wanted me to do and I think I had missed some essential point. When I rejoined the conversation you were talking about your 'strikers' and your 'defenders', by which I for a moment thought you meant the miners and their supporters, but which I then understood to be part of an extended football metaphor and to refer respectively to your Policy Unit and your Private Office. You went on to discuss your own role as a 'sweeper' (which I gather from my sons is roughly what I was brought up to call a half-back). As I understand it, you were continuing the same metaphor when you told me that you wanted me to be a kind of groundsman. (Or groundsperson, as you quickly modified it to, though let me assure you – grateful as I am for your awareness of the issues involved – that I have no simplistic sensibilities to be offended in this area.) You said, I think, that you wanted me to 'check the condition of the pitch' and to 'make sure there's a goal somewhere down the other end of the field'. I believed at the time that I more or less grasped the metaphorical implications of this, but after I had put the phone down I found I was not as clear as I should have hoped to be about exactly what was required of me in concrete practical terms. This is when I came to suspect that I had missed something of importance.

I'm afraid that my moment away from the phone also meant that I missed my opportunity to query whether I am really the right person for the job. The last thing I heard you say before I left the receiver to its own devices was something like 'Some of us here have been reading your books ...' I assume that 'some of us' is scarcely likely to include anyone as busy as you must be yourself. 'Have been reading', I realized even as I struggled to find somewhere to stand the strawboard in the darkness, makes a somewhat smaller claim than 'have read', and I scarcely expect that my 'books', to anyone outside the very restricted world of philosophical studies, are going to include the two on Spinoza; all of which suggests a second-hand and partial acquaintance with my only other work, *Natural Man*. This has indeed attracted considerable interest outside the profession. It has been been taken up both by those who see in it an attack upon civilization as an unnatural cage in which man is incarcerated and by those who take it to be a defence of civilization as man's natural home. Had I had the receiver in my hand when some break in the conversation occurred at this point, I should have explained to you that it is in fact neither; it is merely an examination of the various modes of thinking which the phrase implies – an examination which, in the tradition of British philosophical inquiry, seeks merely to study and perhaps oil the conceptual machinery and then to put it back more or less as it was. Though I am, as it happens, an officer of the local Labour Party, this may not suggest the radical intellectual approach that you were perhaps looking for in your 'groundsperson'.

This last point, however, in passing. Here I am in my office, after all, with my embryo staff around me; you may think it a little late in the day to check my credentials. The other question, however, as to what exactly I am supposed to be doing as I sit here, is plainly still a live issue – which is the reason for this intolerably circumstantial disquisition. At first, when I put the phone down in the darkness that evening and returned to my pupil in the study, I was not too worried. I had, after all, been summoned to meet you face to face in

Downing Street the following morning and obviously any difficulties could be sorted out then. But circumstances, as you will recall, intervened at this meeting, too. Our conversation in your study turned out to be considerably shorter than I had anticipated. I drank my coffee and listened while you talked about the Government's commitment to looking at the quality of life you should be working towards for our people (or that *we* should be working towards for *your* people – I am not quite sure whether your use of the words 'we' and 'our' included me or not); but before I could raise the questions that remained in my mind from the night before – let alone my new uncertainty as to what exactly was meant by the expression 'the quality of life' – a young man had come in and murmured something to you about 'the Governor' and 'the Bank'. Whatever it was, it seemed to require all your attention and I understood that I was to go.

As I left, if you remember, you were kind enough to invite me to get in touch with you at once if I had any problems, and as soon as we were outside I suggested to the young man that I should indeed wait and continue our talk at some later point in the morning. Indeed I insisted, against his advice, on waiting, and waited for the best part of two hours, but then could wait no longer. (I had a meeting of an advisory committee at the Bodleian at three, which was likely to be acrimonious and prolonged, and I simply had to buy something for the boys' dinner first.) All my subsequent attempts to find a mutually convenient time to meet have failed – mostly, I have to confess, because my term-time commitments in Oxford made it difficult for me get up to London except at hours when you were in Cabinet, or in the House. By the time term had ended, as you know, the Government was plunged into various difficulties of its own, which naturally took up all your attention.

I am not, perhaps I should make clear, complaining about any of this. I am merely placing on record, as precisely as possible, the conditions that determined the starting-point of our inquiry. New enterprises and institutions are not created *de novo*, out of nothing; they emerge from a fabric of events which is already complex, which has been long in the weaving, and from which they take their characteristic shape and colour.

The small events in my study and dining-room, the large events crowding your office, have already dictated the first necessity of our inquiry: to write our own terms of reference. Before we take on staff and work out our programme we must elucidate what seem to be the key concepts in my instructions to date: 'pitch', 'goal', and 'quality of life'.

In other words, we must decide what we are doing before we start doing it. My next report will, I hope, present draft terms of reference for your approval.

Yours sincerely,

Elizabeth Serafin

Good God. Good *God*! Is this why the Unit and all its works seem to have disappeared from the records – because it was unthinkable that such a document should officially exist? But what happened to it when Serafin finished it? It wasn't submitted to the Prime Minister like this? No, of course not – it was typed out first. Typed out? By Mrs Padmore? (Who I assume is now ensconced in the larger room at the foot of the spiral stairs.) Read, by someone in the Clerical Grade? I'm not given to prudery, but at the thought of some poor woman in the Clerical Grade being allowed to read this ... this ... whatever it is, I feel a flush of pure shame inside my beard. Mrs Padmore, as we know from the memorandum at the front of the file, is going to be transferring to the Economic Secretariat in a few weeks' time. I think it's fairly obvious why.

No. Wait. She didn't give it to Mrs Padmore – she gave it to Summerchild. He sat at his desk, reading it, silently, with every external sign of seriousness. Then ... I look over towards Summerchild's desk. He gets up, holding the thin sheets of paper in front of him, perhaps just a little further away from himself than he normally would, and puts them delicately on the desk in front of me. He says, very gently ... What does he say?

I pull round the next document on the Treasury tag. Yes – it's a page of Government paper in Summerchild's judicious hand, which does not make holes in the paper, or need x-ing out, or fall off the bottom of the page:

> I suggest that we should delay submitting this to Number Ten until you have had a chance to draft the actual terms of reference, as you propose. Then you might care for me to redraft the complete document in more concise form. You may feel, on consideration, that a brief outline would serve your purposes better. Ministers, in my experience, rarely read more than two double-spaced pages. If you feel very strongly that the background to the Unit's formation needs to be set out, I could perhaps draft it in the form of an (again brief) annexe.

Yes. Thank you. *Thank* you, Mr Summerchild. Or perhaps I should start calling you Stephen – I'm nearly as old as you are now. We have been working together for the past three days. Judging by the thickness of the file in front of me we are going to be working together for some little time yet.

I turn over Summerchild's elegant minute and uncover the next document on the file. Single-spaced typing – holes and x's. 'March 27th 1974. Dear Prime Minister, In spite of the most helpful representations and advice from my staff, I have decided to continue submitting my reports to you in the informal way I settled upon initially . . .'

Here we go again. But I'm already late for my Assessment Group meeting. I get up and dust my hands. I could take the file with me, now I've found it . . . It's rather dusty, though . . . I see myself putting it down on the table in front of me at the Assessment Group and the papers slipping loose . . . Someone – Headland, in the Economic Secretariat, probably – frowns at the appearance of the typing and looks more closely. Upside down across the table he reads something about bicycles in the hall and cogitations in the study . . .

On mature consideration I put the file back in the Squeez-Ee box and lock the door on it once again. These papers are never to be taken outside a secure environment.

8

I am sitting in my office after the Assessment Group meeting,
looking at a draft position paper on the assessment of the
assessment process itself that David Poole, in the European
Secretariat, wants the Group to put up to the Secretary of the
Cabinet. But I am also sitting in Dr Serafin's study, with an
essay on sense-data in my hand. I am her pupil, but I cannot
read what I have written, because the lights have just gone
out and the glow of the electric fire has dwindled to nothingness. I am sitting in the darkness, straining to hear my tutor
on the phone in the dining-room on the other side of the hall.
She is talking to the Prime Minister. I have a warm sense of
privilege, I think, in spite of the sudden lack of an audience
for my opinions. This time last year I was sitting with twenty
other people in some dull sixth-form room, being told about
participles or Corn Laws by someone no one had ever heard
of, and here I am, just one year later, on my own in a solidly
built house in North Oxford, a cup of coffee on the floor
beside me, giving my views on sense-data to a well-known
professional philosopher who then has to break off to take
a call from the Prime Minister. What are they saying? All I
can hear is the sound of large, heavy objects falling over
... the telephone being dropped ... someone crashing into
a bicycle.

What I am feeling as I listen to this is a strange movement
in the undergrowth immediately in front of me; a smile
spreading inside my beard ...

The phone goes off like an alarm clock at my elbow. The Prime Minister. . . The draft position paper goes sliding over the edge of the desk into the waste-paper basket as I snatch up the receiver.

'Jessel.'

'Hurren. I wondered where you'd got to with Summerchild.'

Hurren? Oh, *Hurren.* Yes. I think rapidly. Where *have* I got to with Summerchild?

'Making progress,' I tell him. 'It's rather a long story. I'm getting there slowly.'

'Nothing that's going to worry us?'

'Oh, I don't think so.'

I put down the phone. I'm getting *somewhere* slowly. But where? I still haven't the slightest idea. And *isn't* it going to worry us? It's going to worry *me.*

9

What, for example, is Summerchild feeling – what is my colleague Stephen feeling – as he goes home after reading Serafin's appalling letter and writing his exemplary minute? Has his depression deepened? Is this the story that's developing? Is he oppressed by the same obscure shame that I felt when I read the letter? Is he walking even more slowly up the hill from the station this evening, even more wearily along the lane?

The towers of South London glide slowly up out of the east as I think these thoughts, perform their well-rehearsed half-revolve and retire with dignity into the west. The train stops at Greenwich and I find myself getting off and starting on the ritual walk, one of a dozen, as before, one of ten, one of eight, one of five ... Now, I'm climbing the hill. And, no, it's not harder – it's easier. I'm not smiling inside my beard now that I'm Summerchild, naturally, because I've no beard to smile inside. But I have some secret bubble of amusement in me and it's lighter than air. I sail up the hill and along Hyde Hill Lane as if I were a balloon. The evening sun has burst out from cloud over London and flooded the fronts of the houses in the lane with a mature and contented light. I stop for a moment at my gate and look up at the windows of my house. It's not golden June, of course – in 1974 it's still March, and dark, but the curtains of the ground-floor rooms are open and the lights are on. In the kitchen Anne and Millie are laying the table for dinner, talking seriously. How curious that someone with such a short, neatly waved cap of brown hair should be talking to someone with such a fuzz of ginger hair – and talking so seriously, with no sense of disparity! I go up the steps in two effortless bounds and let myself in.

At any rate Summerchild does. I stand at the bottom and watch him. As he disappears through the front door so the neat brown head and the wild red one turn. By the time he reappears in the kitchen Millie is watching him closely and Anne is frowning slightly; they have seen immediately that there is something different about him. He offers no explanation, as they sit down to dinner, and Anne and Millie talk about other things. Perhaps at some point he smiles slightly to himself, so that Millie smiles, too, and says, 'What?' Summerchild shakes his head and says nothing. Anne watches him over the table in that brooding speculative way of hers, as if he were a long-pondered clue in a half-completed crossword. He looks up at her inquiringly and she looks away with another slight frown. Millie glances at each of her parents in turn, then picks up her dessert spoon and studies that instead. She seems to find it a slightly amusing object. The whole atmosphere of the house has changed ... Now dinner is over and they are drifting into the other room at the front of the house. Millie is setting up two music stands and lugging her cello case in from the hall. Stephen is tightening a bow, bouncing it against his forearm to check its tension. Anne is sitting down at the piano, unfolding her spectacles, smoothing the music in front of her. A, she plays, looking over at them patiently, A ... A ... A ... Stephen and Millie are touching bows to strings, then screwing up their faces as they force pegs another fraction of an inch tighter, waiting for a string to break ... They settle ... look at each other interrogatively ... Bows hover above strings, hands above keys ... Then Stephen bobs his head, and –

The front door opens. A woman is coming out of the house.

She comes down the steps in the evening sunshine, with a little dog on a lead. I turn away immediately and move on up the lane. I can feel behind my head the haze of reddish hair going away in the opposite direction. I can feel it turn, too, as Millie realizes who she has just seen.

She'd hardly changed at all. She still looked like a serious seventeen-year-old, was still wearing the same shy clothes. She has never married. Or so I have heard.

I walk rapidly across the Park. The reassuring cloud of honeysuckle around my front door, as I approach it, suddenly makes me stroke the reassuring beard around my mouth. What do they conceal from the world, this honeysuckle and this beard? All I can see beneath the sweet-scented tangle above the living-room window is darkness within. Then I glimpse the shifting colours of the television and its faint reflection on two small inert alien faces. Cheryl's children. I long for them not to be there. I unlock the front door. For once, I find, Timmy is not asleep. He is sitting at the top of the stairs, sobbing. By the exhausted mechanical sound of it he has been sobbing for a long time. 'Now here's your Dad,' says Cheryl, standing in the living-room doorway. 'You tell *him* you're not going to bed. It's nothing to do with me. *I* don't make the rules in this house.' She goes back to collect her own two from in front of the television. They are both younger than Timmy. 'I'm sorry,' she says to me, as she bundles them out of the front door, 'but what can I do?'

I apologize to her. But then what can *I* do?

I turn off the television. The only sound in the house is the occasional last convulsive sob from the top of the stairs. I go up and sit a couple of stairs below my son.

'It's not fair,' he says.

What can I say in return? He's right – it's not.

'I hate Cheryl,' he says.

I remain silent. I hate Cheryl, too. That's not fair, either, of course. Nothing's fair.

I shift myself a stair higher, so that I can reach up and stroke my son's head. If whatever happened to Summerchild hadn't happened, I think, once again, then . . . then Timmy and I might have had a rather better quality of life.

10

By three-twenty, which was what the alarm clock by the bedside said the last time I looked at it, I have moved on from thinking about Timmy and Cheryl and her children, and Cheryl, and Timmy, and Cheryl's children, and Timmy, and Timmy, and Cheryl, and Timmy, and begun to think about Summerchild and Serafin, and Serafin, and Timmy, and Serafin, yes, and *Serafin*.

A very simple thought comes to me, like an angel entering the room. I could go and talk to her.

What? Go up to Oxford? – Yes! She's probably still living in the same house, still teaching, still struggling with the Marmite and the Spinoza.

What, some time next week? – Some time *this* week! In the morning!

Go to Paddington? Get on a train? – Other people do brave and sudden things like going to Paddington and getting on trains! I've done them myself!

I see myself on the train, in holiday mood, then walking past sunlit honeyed stone walls with doorways opening into quiet inner worlds of lawns and laughter. I'll go! But then I arrive outside the house. Its door is closed and unwelcoming. Have I phoned to say I'm coming? Or am I trying to take her by surprise? I don't know whether I've phoned or not . . . I don't know what I'm doing . . . She's not there, in any case. It's the middle of the long vacation. She's abroad – she's away for the entire year on sabbatical . . . No, here she is, opening the door. 'Yes?' she says. She looks motherly; the hall behind her is full of bicycles. No, the bicycles went years ago, she looks grandmotherly – she's divorced and the children have left home – this is a different house. I start to explain that I'm from the Cabinet Office. I'm writing a report on her former colleague, because suspicions have been voiced that she is the agent of some foreign power – though, I hasten to add, I personally regard this as nonsense, and am convinced he died simply because she somehow . . . I don't know . . . drove him mad . . .

I sit up in bed and switch the light on, shaken awake by pure embarrassment. Of course I'm not going to talk to her. I'm a Civil Servant, not a Police Inspector. My job is to go to Whitehall, not Oxford, and to read the appropriate documents, not interrogate witnesses.

I get up and listen at my son's door. I half hope he's awake, so that I can go in and sit with him, and stroke his head. But, of course, he only wakes when I'm asleep. I sometimes think that's what wakes him – an obscure sense of loss, an occult awareness that I am no longer conscious. I creep downstairs and roam pointlessly around. Now that the lights are on I don't suspect that she drove him to suicide. The idea is ridiculous. I don't suspect anything. I have no idea what happened. They may after all have been passing secrets to Soviet agents. Serafin may have been Russian, may have disappeared back to Russia. The idea that Summerchild was murdered by Naval Intelligence seems at least as plausible an explanation as anything else I can think of . . .

Natural Man. Yes. I do faintly remember some stir about the book. We might even have a copy of it. Lynn sometimes used to buy books like that before she . . . before. I run my eye along the shelves. Set texts I acquired at Manchester; set texts Lynn got at Keele; various important books bought since which were going to change the way we thought and lived, but somehow failed to. The books look dead; no one reads them any more. No sign of *Natural Man.* But there is an ancient paperback by E J Maitland. Didn't Serafin say he was her husband? It's entitled *Fair Do's: Studies in the Perception of Social Justice* – the kind of thing Lynn used to buy before I met her. Serafin's being Mrs Maitland, it seems to me, is the unlikeliest thing of all about her. Not that I know much about him, just that my philosophical friend Kevin Rice despised him. Too much plain common sense and rugged North Country integrity for Kevin's taste, as I recall. I take the book down. It was published in 1973, when Lynn was seventeen. There's a photograph of Maitland on the back. He doesn't look much like a philosopher to me. He's smiling out of a rugged face, with thick black eyebrows and curling hair. He's wearing a heavy raincoat in the photograph for some reason, though it doesn't seem to be raining, with the collar turned up, and he's got a pipe in his mouth, though there's no sign of any smoke coming out of it. There's something baldly *there* about him which inclines me, like Kevin, to distrust anything he says. He is a Professor, I see from the biography inside, and the E stands for Edward. I imagine his friends call him Ted.

I open the book at random. 'What these experiments show us is that human consciousness can be *re-set*. The scale on which it registers experience can be adjusted upwards or downwards. You might think of it like the clock in your hall being set forwards or backwards at the beginning and end of Summer Time, so that it registers nightfall as coming first later and then earlier . . .'

I can imagine what Kevin would have said about this kind of thing. I see Ted Maitland going to football matches in his grubby belted raincoat and having grubby affairs with his students. I seem to remember reading about him recently, living in California, married to someone who is noted for being controversial in some kind of way. Now that I've seen his photograph and read his prose style, I can't imagine how he and Serafin ever contrived to live together.

The more I think about it the bleaker the home life of Professor and Mrs Maitland begins to seem. Every door of the house I open seems to reveal the author of *Fair Do's* (and no

71

doubt something rather more respectable, to keep up professional appearances, on someone like Kant), tremendously *there*, as on the back cover of his book, his eyebrows and hair curling coarsely. Here he is in the bathroom, wearing his grimy raincoat with the turned-up collar. Here he is sitting up in the marital bed, his jaw ruggedly clenched on his unlit pipe.

This is what Dr Serafin is escaping from every time she pedals furiously to the station to catch the train to London (one of those bicycles in the hall is hers) with the portable typewriter lodged insecurely in the basket on the handlebars. The little room under the eaves must seem a refuge, Summerchild's diffidence and deference and fine copper hair a welcome relief.

Except that it's four in the morning and Dr Serafin's home life is largely inside my head. Or *entirely* inside my head. Is this possible? I'm beginning to get very confused about exactly where my head stops and the rest of the world starts. Which side of the beard is Ted Maitland's belted raincoat on?

I go back to bed. The curtains are light at the window. I stroke my beard, as if it were Timmy's brow, trying to soothe myself to sleep. One thing I think I know now, though – where she has been hiding all this time.

11

March 27th 1974.

Dear Prime Minister,
In spite of the most helpful representations and advice from
my staff, I have decided to continue submitting my reports to
you in the informal way I settled upon initially . . .

Friday morning. The last day of the week, and the last day
I shall be spending up here in my private tower, high above
the politics and the Park, where the phone never rings, far
from Bartlett and Kyle, cut off from Milmo and Gedge. There
is a carpet of sunshine on the floor and blue sky filling the
windows. The people walking across the Parade down there
are in a world of their own; no great glass eyes are turned
inquiringly up towards me. All the strained confusions of the
night are over, all the sleepless impatience to get on with the
job. Now that I'm back here at last, sitting on my two boxes
with the heap of riddled typescript in my hands, I feel soothed
and slowed. I'm looking out of the window, putting off the
moment when there will be nothing left to find out and all
this has to end. I've tracked Serafin down. She's where I
realized in the middle of the night she would be – where no
doubt she always was – safely tucked up in *Who's Who* and
the *Universities Year Book* under 'Maitland, Mrs E J'. And yes,
she has three sons. She's divorced, but she hasn't emigrated
or defected – she's still a Fellow of Somerville, and still living

at a solid address in North Oxford. Born in 1930, so she must be on the verge of retirement now. She hasn't written any more books, or held any more public appointments. Nor is there any mention of her time with the Strategy Unit.

I've got quite used to Serafin, I realize. I think Summerchild has, too. He's sitting here, looking out of the window like me, slightly amused, though probably not very surprised, that his advice has been rejected. He has a master (or a mistress) with a will of her own – always more engaging for a Civil Servant, whatever outsiders think. He reads on, to find what new horrors are in store:

> ... You will recall that the first task we set ourselves, in default of any clear instructions in the matter, was to decide what exactly we were doing, and that to this end we proposed to examine some of the various concepts involved. This will constitute what we might term the Prolegomena to the inquiry proper. We made a start today with the notion that seems to me most central to our inquiry – the one with which, as it happens, I personally have most difficulty. This is *the quality of life*.
>
> My original intention was that the entire Unit should participate in the debate ...

Just a moment. What's this about the entire Unit? Have I missed something? Apart from Summerchild and a Clerical Officer, the Unit at the last count still consisted of one single member, Serafin herself. Has she appointed more members in the interval, or is she proposing to talk to herself?

> ... However, Mr Summerchild has persuaded me that taking part in a discussion of this nature might lie outside Mrs Padmore's job description, and could involve us in difficulties with her union ...

Mrs Padmore? Serafin was proposing to involve the *Clerical Officer* in the discussion? This suggests a naïvety on Serafin's part amounting to a kind of idiocy. I suppose she suggested it in deference to the participatory politics of the time. Even so, it puts her judgement into question, to say the least. I can't help admiring the skill with which Summerchild got this mad toy out of her hands, by offering her the alternative piety of deference to trade union sentiment.

... So in the event our discussion group consisted of Mr Summerchild and myself ...

Well, if a hostage has to remain behind in enemy hands then it's clearly better that it should be Summerchild himself.

... and if this sounds as though I were conducting a tutorial, then I make no apology. The tutorial, after all, is in essence the classical way of doing philosophy. It is the Socratic method, where the philosopher asks simple questions which prompt the inquiring follower to think out the issues involved for himself ...

'Simple questions ... inquiring follower ... think out the issues involved for himself'? Madam, if my colleague were not bound by the traditions of the Civil Service – not to mention the obsolescent demands of gentlemanliness and his own natural diffidence – he would walk straight out of that door and never come back.

... Whether Socrates himself was ever helped towards a clearer understanding of matters by this process Plato does not tell us, but I must say I have always found that a tutorial strongly stimulated my own thinking. The most illuminating insights in philosophy are almost invariably the simplest, and a great deal of my most original thinking has been done in response to the innocence of my pupils – particularly of first-year students who are still philosophical virgins. Mr Summerchild (who tells me that he read classics at Cambridge) turned out to be eminently suitable in this respect. In fact his very first answer put the concept in an entirely new light for me. 'What do *you* understand by the phrase *quality of life?*' I asked him. He said he thought it was something to do with *washing-machines*, which for a start I found deeply puzzling. I felt rather as I should if, on my asking him what he would like for lunch, he had replied 'thriftiness', or 'thirty-seven degrees Centigrade'. After a few minutes' silent reflection, however, I saw that the difficulty arose because we had read the phrase in quite different ways. I had assumed that it meant the characteristic of being alive, livingness, whatever it is that makes life life. Mr Summerchild, however, was evidently feeling his way towards a quite different sense – the idea of some kind of grading system for our experience, of some variable level of satisfactoriness to which life might attain, and which, as he implied, might be enhanced by various practical means. As soon as I had seen this reading of the phrase it at once seemed more plausible. Indeed, I recalled the Government's commitment to 'work towards' the quality that we were studying, and could not understand exactly what I had envisaged by the notion of working towards the condition of being alive rather than dead. So this was the first fruit of our collaboration, the test of our method! I see it as the so to speak Preface to the Prolegomena!

I imagine she leaned eagerly over the desk towards me, as towards a pupil who has made a good point in his essay, smiling and nodding encouragingly. 'Yes!' she says. 'Good! Well done!' And I must not only sit here and endure all this – I must read her account of it at the end of the day, and think of something polite to say about it before I find ways of rewriting and neutralizing it.

What *do* I say, in point of fact? Isn't this my own handwriting running sideways down the narrow margin? I turn the typescript . . . Yes: 'I wonder if it might not be helpful to make clear to a lay reader what precisely the connection was between Socrates and Plato.'

What else? Nothing, apparently. Nothing more in the margins, nothing at the end. That's my only comment on all this nonsense.

I don't understand. What's happening? Am I becoming mesmerized? Does this woman, as she leans across her desk murmuring her little words of encouragement, exert some personal magnetism which is incomprehensible to those who haven't met her?

Or am I playing some deep game, as I was with the choice of accommodation? Am I tempting Serafin towards her own destruction? Have I decided to submit all this to the Prime Minister's office as it stands, to lay it all just as it is before Francis Tite and let fate take its course? If so, it doesn't seem to have worked – there's still sheaves of the stuff to come. I lift another heap of pages out of the file and something falls out on my knees . . . A photograph.

It's a snapshot of a woman with a broad, simple face, her greying hair drawn straight back from her temples. She is sitting at a desk, smiling out of wide-set eyes, leaning slightly forward and gazing straight into the camera with a kind of fervent intensity.

It's her. No doubt about it. I'd imagined her leaning forwards and smiling, but not looking like this, somehow. She is smiling plainly and openly, without a trace of irony. She is not smiling like a university lecturer who has just got off the train from Oxford, but like a peasant woman who has just arrived in a hard-class compartment from Saratov. She has some kind of black shawl over her shoulders. It should be over her head. Because, yes, she is Russian. Openly and blatantly Russian.

And her eyes are bright blue.

So that's what she looked like. She was – how old? – forty-four. And she does indeed have some kind of magnetism, even in a snapshot . . .

The photograph is not very sharp, but the shape of the window behind her is recognizable at once, and in the over-exposed whiteness beyond the glass I can just make out the roof of the Scottish Office and the aerials on top of the Admiralty. She is sitting exactly where I am sitting now. The photograph must have been taken from about twelve feet in front of her, where I surmise Summerchild's desk was.

It was presumably taken by Summerchild.

What *is* going on? In all my years in the Civil Service no

one has ever brought a camera into the office and started taking snapshots!

I assume he wasn't posing for snapshots himself . . . I give the absurd mass of typescript another shake. Several more items come tumbling or fluttering out over me . . . A dentist's appointment card. Two 5p stamps. A dried cornflower . . . How on earth did all this rubbish get into the file?

And yes, another photograph . . .

He is sitting at his desk, with the window I'm looking at now beside him. His face is rather out of focus. I have the impression that he was moving back, away from the camera, with instinctive diffidence, even as the photograph was taken. There he is, though, with his freckles and the ginger cloud of surprise around his head. He's at least five years younger than her and he has an ironic smile as elusive as hers is guileless. He looks not like a peasant from Saratov, but a Senior Principal who has just got off the train from Greenwich.

I wonder at what point in this insane course of tutorials did teacher and pupil begin taking snapshots of each other.

I turn back to where I was in the text.

. . . We shall meet next week for our first formal session. This I shall record on tape, to be transcribed by Mrs Padmore and forwarded to you unedited.

I turn to the next document on the tag and suddenly I am in a quite different and entirely familiar landscape of calm, double-spaced, wide-margined, cleanly typed Government A4. 'April 3rd 1974', says the heading. 'Transcript of first working session'. I feel even more uneasy to find the alien proceedings wearing such an everyday look.

Before I begin to read I push some boxes across to the place where Summerchild sat facing me and dust them to make him a desk and chair. I stand his face on the boxes that represent the chair, propped up against the wall behind. Then I put her face on her desk, supported by a heap of loose files. She gazes at him, from as close as she can lean forward. He looks guardedly back, from as far as he can lean away.

And I make a place for myself where I can watch them both out of the corner of my eye while I read.

12

SERAFIN: ... whether it's recording or not. I'd just better try ... No. Alexander did explain how to use it but ... I think I must have picked up Paul's one by mistake.

This is how the transcript begins. Not a very auspicious opening. I expect the Establishment Division refused to supply her with a tape-recorder (and for good reason, one might think), so she's brought one of her children's instead. I imagine the batteries are nearly flat. There's some kind of dried food stuck on the volume control. The microphone only works when you shake it. And no one's told Mrs Padmore not to type all this bit.

I'll just have another ... No. It looks as if it's recording, but every time I press Play ...

The Prime Minister's going to enjoy reading this. Something to keep him occupied through the odd thirty seconds of the week when he's not actually reading some other report.

... You see? It just plays that horrible music. I'm sorry. This must be one of Paul's tapes. I'll try again. Now, I press Play ... No. I'm sorry about this ...

SUMMERCHILD: Don't you have to press Rewind before you press Play?

SERAFIN: Rewind?

She hasn't pressed Rewind. Of course. And by now the Prime Minister has moved on to the next sterling crisis.

Oh. Yes. Good. Thank you . . . That's better. I'm sorry about that. Now . . . To recapitulate: 'the quality of life', as you understand it, is some property which is in one way or another promoted or enhanced by *washing-machines*. Now, I take 'washing-machines' in this context to be a synecdoche (no doubt humorously ventured) for domestic machinery in general.

SUMMERCHILD: I imagine it is. But, look, I'm not really the best person to ask about this, I'm afraid. It's not a phrase I've had occasion to use all that much.

SERAFIN: But you *have* used it? You've read it, for instance?

SUMMERCHILD: I suppose so. In minutes and reports, and so forth.

SERAFIN: You've never written it?

SUMMERCHILD: Oh, very possibly.

SERAFIN: Also in minutes and reports?

SUMMERCHILD: I imagine it was.

SERAFIN: Which you regard as being different from using it in private conversation?

SUMMERCHILD: I suspect I do.

SERAFIN: I find your repeated appeal to what you *suspect* you think and what you *imagine* you did deeply suggestive. We tend to assume, I think, in normal usage, that *I* have to suspect what you are thinking, and to imagine or conjecture what you mean by an expression, but that *you* have some direct and privileged access to your intentions which enables you to *know* what you mean. But you find it quite natural to resort to conjecture yourself to establish what you think and what you mean. However, that is by the way. I am taking it for granted that if you used the term, even in minutes and reports, you must have meant *something* by it. Yes?

81

SUMMERCHILD: Of course. I should imagine I meant . . .

SERAFIN: 'Imagine' again!

SUMMERCHILD: I'm sorry.

SERAFIN: No, no! This is fascinating!

SUMMERCHILD: I – how shall I put it, then? – I assume I meant . . .

SERAFIN: 'Assume'! Yes! Good!

SUMMERCHILD: I assume I meant more or less what everybody else means.

SERAFIN: You've no idea how deeply helpful all this is to me in a private capacity. I think I may now have seen how to proceed in a paper I'm writing at the moment on unconscious intention. But we're letting ourselves be distracted from the matter in hand. (If you're interested in following up the question of how we know what's going on in our own minds you might have a look at Duncan: *I Know What I Know – or Do I?* – Proceedings of the Aristotelian Society, Spring 1971, or just possibly my contribution to the symposium on recursion in the current *Analysis*, though this is a little technical.) Now, back to the actual contents list of your mind (imagined, assumed, or however else established) when you use the term 'quality of life'. Let's see if we can locate the boundaries of the concept, as you yourself use it, a little more firmly. Does the class of things which to your mind promote or enhance the quality of life stretch far enough from the kitchen door to include the family television set?

SUMMERCHILD: Oh, yes.

SERAFIN: You're very definite about that!

SUMMERCHILD: Am I? Yes, well, let me rephrase that . . .

SERAFIN: No! Don't rephrase anything! What we're after, I think, is what you are *naturally inclined* to say, without conceptual hindsight.

SUMMERCHILD: Yes, well, I don't really ever watch enough television to have an opinion. I simply assume . . .

SERAFIN: Another assumption! Excellent!

SUMMERCHILD: I mean, since we seem to have got on to household appliances in general . . .

SERAFIN: Yes, but we have jumped into a really rather different category of household appliance, haven't we? Washing-machines, and similar sorts of domestic machinery, are intended to save our time and labour. Now, no one could claim that a television set saves *time*. On the contrary – it uses up the time we've saved with the dishwasher and the vacuum cleaner. And I think one might go on to argue that far from saving labour it *creates* it – that its function is to give one the task of understanding it. So let's ask ourselves a naïve question. Why do people watch it?

SUMMERCHILD: Because, well . . .

SERAFIN: Yes?

SUMMERCHILD: Because they – I don't know . . .

SERAFIN: No, no! Say it!

SUMMERCHILD: This is very silly.

SERAFIN: If by 'silly' you mean 'simple-minded', then take heart, because simple-minded is what we are struggling to be. We are aspiring to the state of *village idiots*, to whom everything is a source of amazement. So, people watch television because . . .?

SUMMERCHILD: Well, because they enjoy watching it.

SERAFIN: Exactly. Thank you. They enjoy watching it. Let's leap from the television to the central heating. Do they have central heating because they enjoy it?

SUMMERCHILD: I think the simple-minded answer is yes again, isn't it?

SERAFIN: Is it? Do *you* enjoy it? Do you sit there thinking, 'My word, I'm enjoying this warmth! Goodness, but I find the evenness of the ambient temperature hugely entertaining!'

SUMMERCHILD: No.

SERAFIN: You don't notice it.

SUMMERCHILD: Well, I've noticed it quite a lot these past few months. I've noticed very distinctly every time it was turned off.

SERAFIN: You notice the central heating if it's turned off. Yes. You notice it if it's not there to be noticed. What should we think if someone tells us: 'I enjoy roast potatoes, but only at meals where I'm served boiled potatoes?'

SUMMERCHILD: Actually, what I do really enjoy is an open fire.

SERAFIN: Well side-stepped! So you don't have central heating at home?

SUMMERCHILD: Yes, we do.

SERAFIN: So we can prefer what we're not aware of enjoying to what we *are* aware of enjoying?

SUMMERCHILD: Possibly. We can certainly prefer not carrying endless scuttles of coal up from the cellar.

SERAFIN: And thereby have time and energy left to enjoy the open fire which is by our very preference not there to enjoy?

And so it goes on. For many pages they consider the idea of enjoyment. They consider it simple-mindedly, of course. The simple-mindedness of their consideration makes the object of it complex in comparison – so complex that it becomes difficult to understand how mere mortal man has ever managed to enjoy anything. If indeed he has. It begins to seem unlikely that there is any such thing as enjoyment. They consider it (if it exists) in relation to such things as sauna baths and chicken vindaloos. Held in the mad intensity of their village idiot's gaze not only enjoyment but saunas and vindaloos begin to seem implausible. Not even in my conversations with Kevin Rice have I come across anything quite so exasperating.

The morning ticks by. *My* morning ticks by. I've no idea where they've got to.

Now they're beginning to wonder if enjoyment is really what's at issue after all. They have cautiously emerged from the kitchen and bathroom by this time, and moved on to the garage.

SERAFIN: Do you find the word 'motor car' on your list?

SUMMERCHILD: What list?

SERAFIN: The list we have been consulting. The list that you apparently keep inside your head of things that enhance the quality of life. (More intriguing byways opening off the main road here! Let us ignore them.)

SUMMERCHILD: Oh, I think cars are usually included on these occasions.

SERAFIN: Good. Now, wouldn't it be possible to imagine someone who maintained *both* that motor cars were on our list of things that enhanced the quality of life *and* that travelling by motor car frequently took more time and demanded a greater outlay of labour than using various other means of transport? Even that it was less comfortable – less entertaining – less *enjoyable*? If we met someone who held this view he might justify it by saying something like: 'I prefer travelling by motor car from Oxford to Westminster, let's say, or from –' Where do you live?

SUMMERCHILD: Greenwich.

SERAFIN: 'From Greenwich to Westminster' – which I should think would involve somewhat similar considerations – '*even though* it takes longer, *even though* I can't read or watch television to keep myself entertained at the same time, *even though* it demands a greater expenditure of concentration and nervous energy – and, one might possibly add, physical labour in pushing and pulling the various levers and pedals involved . . .'

SUMMERCHILD: Also there's nowhere to park.

SERAFIN: Yes. Good. Parking difficulties – so *more* time – *more* nervous energy – *more* pulling back and forth at the steering-wheel and the gear-lever – none of which, he might tell us, he in any way enjoys. 'Even so,' he might insist, 'I *prefer* this means of transport because I find it consonant with a certain feeling I have about myself – because it expresses a certain style of being that I find congenial – because I find the kinaesthetic sensations it affords, even the physical efforts and nervous tension, somehow *involving*.' What are we to say to that? I think we are perhaps beginning to find the conventional notions of convenience and comfort, of enjoyment and enter-tainment, inadequate. We are beginning to find that to explain what we understand by the quality of life we have to introduce a further notion which we could call *texture*. Now, can we *generalize* this? Can we see convenience, enjoyment, etcetera, as *cases* of texture? I wonder whether we can speak of the *smoothness* of having little to do . . . the *bobbliness* of being entertained . . . the *thickness* of being warm . . . the *knittedness* of being kinaesthetically involved . . . I wonder . . . The sugges-tiveness of metaphor once again! I start to feel life like cloth under my fingers . . . Hairiness . . . Tweediness . . . Clingingness . . . Snagginess . . . Hm . . . .

SUMMERCHILD: Shall I turn it off?

SERAFIN: I'm sorry?

SUMMERCHILD: The tape-recorder. I thought perhaps I should turn it off. You hadn't spoken for some time.

SERAFIN: Hadn't I?

SUMMERCHILD: I do apologize. I've interrupted your train of thought.

SERAFIN: I was just thinking how often philosophy begins with the promise that if we can manage to get our thinking right about some basic concept we can then go on to restruc-ture our thinking about everything else – and how rarely this later part of the programme is ever reached . . . Why – how long was it since I spoke?

SUMMERCHILD: Oh, about fifteen or twenty minutes.

SERAFIN: I think I was also thinking about the tape-recorder. I think I was supposing it would be on your list and wondering why. It's not entertaining us or making us feel comfortable. It's not saving our time or labour.

SUMMERCHILD: I suppose it's saving Mrs Padmore's time and labour.

SERAFIN: You mean that if we didn't have the machine she would have to be in here taking a shorthand note? Good. *Good.* So *our* having the tape-recorder is affecting the quality of Mrs Padmore's life – which, however, has an indirect effect on the quality of *our* life, given the I think not unreasonable premise that an improvement in the quality of someone else's life offers us some kind of pleasure or satisfaction, or at any rate spares us discomfort or guilt; though whether this is what I had in mind when I borrowed the tape-recorder this morning I think unlikely. I believe a better practical explanation of my *intentions* might well be offered once again in terms of texture. After all, one does the same with clothes. If I'd been working at home today I should have put on my old skirt and my old pullover, so as to have something comfortably rough and worn around me. But as I was coming up to London to work in more formal circumstances I selected my new skirt, which is somewhat smoother and less worn, together with my new pullover – oh, no, how odd, this *is* my old pullover – but – ah, now I remember, yes, worn over a cotton shirt – which again is something smooth. I believe I picked up the tape-recorder in much the same spirit – because I felt that whatever we did here ought to have a rather *spontaneous* feel to it, and yet at the same time be noticeably *hard-wearing.* That it should be *light* but *long-lasting* ... *translucent* but, as one might say, *mothproof* ... Though just a moment ... ... What?

SUMMERCHILD: Sorry. I was turning the tape over. We'd got to the end.

SERAFIN: Oh yes. I was just thinking. I may have taken off in the wrong direction entirely. Let me think a moment ... ... What?

SUMMERCHILD: I was putting a new tape in.

SERAFIN: What was wrong with the old one?

SUMMERCHILD: It had run out.

SERAFIN: Again? They seem to be very short tapes.

SUMMERCHILD: Ninety minutes. Forty-five minutes a side.

SERAFIN: Yes, you see, I have been attempting to identify and generalize the various things that we perceive as affecting or as constituting the quality of life. But what they have in common is something both blindingly simple to name and blindingly difficult to think about. The common factor is that *we do so perceive them*! And *this* is what we should be examining – *what it is* to so perceive them. Look, the question of *what* we want is a sociological one, which we answer by asking people, or by observing their behaviour. The question of *why* we want it is a psychological one, which we answer by much the same means. The *philosophical* question – the deep question – the question that we, I think, are here constituted to examine – is *what it is* to want them. I think we shall find ourselves distinguishing between what it is to want what we haven't got and what it is to want what we *have* got. We may find the latter is the more elusive and the more central question, which opens out into what it is to like and to love, what it is to be content, and what it is to be happy. Yes, I believe we may find ourselves forced to approach the whole question of happiness, which philosophers have gone round and about for so long. The idea of happiness is surely the sun at the centre of our conceptual planetary system – and has proved just as hard to look at directly. It seems to me possible that here in this room we might between us just conceivably be able to make a first . . . *How* long did you say these tapes are?

SUMMERCHILD: Forty-five minutes a side.

SERAFIN: So what time is it now?

SUMMERCHILD: Five to two.

SERAFIN: Oh, no!

SUMMERCHILD: I didn't like to interrupt you, but if we want lunch in the canteen . . .

SERAFIN: No time for lunch, I'm afraid. I've got to be back in Oxford by four for a meeting of the Research Fellowships

Committee ... Also I've got to get something for the boys' dinner first ... Look, if you don't mind a bit of running you could just come as far as the Tube with me and we could continue this conversation on the way. We'll have to be quick, though ... What's holding you up?

SUMMERCHILD: Sorry – I'm just turning the tape-recorder off.

13

I'm running back to my office to make all the phone calls I should have made already this morning; Summerchild is running just in front of me, a pace and a half behind Serafin, trying to catch the various pearls now flying back unrecorded over her hurrying shoulder. He is also carrying an armful of her books and papers, and fielding an orange which rolls free from the overloaded briefcase she is cradling to herself. Another orange goes bounding away up the corridor ahead of them, under the feet of one of Summerchild's colleagues who is approaching from the opposite direction, coming back from lunch. He recovers it neatly, just as Serafin dives for it herself and sets more oranges cascading. I see Summerchild's colleague glancing at him curiously. I catch the colleague's eye as he passes me. His mouth twitches almost imperceptibly. I dare say that mine, under the cover of my beard, twitches faintly back.

Not that I don't have the most intense professional fellow-feeling for Summerchild. It's nearly two o'clock and he has had no lunch. As I follow them past Security and out into Whitehall Serafin is dropping library books and wild phrases about the metaphysics of desire. Security gazes after her. I nod at Security drily. . . Hold on, though. What am *I* doing out on the street? I was going to my office! I go back past Security and get a slightly curious look myself. *I'm* going upstairs to the canteen; it's Summerchild who's going up Whitehall. At least, I assume he is, to get the Bakerloo from

Trafalgar Square. He'll feel obliged to go all the way to Paddington with her – she'll never manage all that stuff on her own. He'll find himself going into some supermarket in Praed Street, buying fillets of plaice and frozen broccoli for her sons' dinner . . . She'll have lost her ticket . . . He'll end up running after her along the platform, bundling books and plaice and Government papers in through the window of the carriage at her as the train moves out . . . It's quarter to three by this time and still he's had no lunch . . .

I can't help laughing . . . But what's this? My laughter suddenly dries up. I can't open the door of the canteen . . . The canteen's shut already! Of course – it's quarter to three – *I'm* not going to get any lunch . . . Just a moment – what's going on? It's not quarter to three *here* – it's quarter to three at Paddington! Here in the Cabinet Office it's twenty to twelve and the canteen's not shut already – it still hasn't opened. Then why am I hungry? I'm *not* hungry! I won't be hungry for another hour and twenty minutes yet! All right – so why am I standing outside the door of the canteen . . .?

My office is where I'm supposed to be. As I go back downstairs I begin to feel that this woman is making fools of us all – of Summerchild, Tite and Harold Wilson, of Ken Hurren and myself. It is right that our procedures should be subject to challenge and change, but her idea of turning a Government Advisory Unit into some kind of Oxford tutorial is an absurd perversion of everything that has been so slowly and painstakingly developed over the years. It illustrates only too clearly the dangers of inviting outsiders to meddle in the machinery of Government. And the investigations she is proposing to undertake are eccentric even by the standards of visiting academics. No wonder the report was never published. No wonder the Government of the day tried to conceal that it had spent public money on bringing some dotty lady down from her high table to tell us *what it is to want what we want*. Underlined, of course, which must surely make it mean something. Perhaps we should launch a new investigation into *what it is to underline what we underline*. Or what it is to speak so emphatically that even the phlegmatic Mrs Padmore feels obliged to underline it.

So this is what the great glass eye thinks may have been leaked to our enemies – an inquiry into the nature of happiness. Yes, better they should see the plans for a nuclear submarine than this! 'The sun at the centre of our conceptual planetary system . . .' The Americans landed on the moon in 1969; five years later an agency of the British Government is launching an expedition to some metaphorical sun. A state secret, certainly. I feel, as I sit here in my own office, with my own files in front of me, a physical sense of shrinking inside my skin. I am embarrassed. Embarrassed for Summerchild, of course. Embarrassed, too, for Tite and Harold Wilson and me. Embarrassed for the great glass eye, if ever it should find out.

In fact I feel more than embarrassed. I feel angry. I am not much given to anger, but there is something indecent about these raw pink naïveties. The nation where this debate is being launched has just emerged, in the spring of 1974, from a confrontation between Government and unions so destabilizing that some people had been daily expecting to see tanks in Whitehall. Industry has only just been restored to normal after being reduced to a three-day working week. Offices are still heated only half the day. Streets and homes have been plunged into random darkness. And all this minor misery is occurring in an island set in a leaden sea of even greater misery, in a world which is presumably going to end, sooner rather than later, in some cataclysmic downpour of misery beyond imagination. Upon this charming scene enters a woman whose marriage is about to break up. She sits down in a quiet room, provided at public expense, and begins to lecture a man who is shortly to be found dying by the dustbins. 'Now,' she says, 'let's talk about *happiness*.' Underlined.

My hands dart indignantly about my desk as if they were offended mice, opening files, annotating minutes, picking up the receiver. My voice rushes out of its kennel at people like an irritated terrier. 'Jessel,' it snaps. 'Yes . . .! No . . .! Before

Cabinet on Thursday . . . At ministerial level . . . proceed with some urgency . . .' And all the while my mind is thinking how beside the point all this talk of happiness is. What constitutes the quality of *our* lives, Summerchild's and mine, is hands opening buff-coloured files, is slow-turning towers, pressure from colleagues, and walking the length of Whitehall. It's the sense of decisions moving closer, the steepness of the stairs, words, more words. It's thinking of Lynn and Timmy, and thinking of Lynn not being Lynn any more. It's the Saturdays going out to the hospital, the smell of floor-wax and urine in the corridors, the helplessness, the moments of despair . . .

Happiness! This is the Government service, not a holiday camp! *Happiness!* When even Summerchild isn't happy! The quiet man with the violin, who goes home to play trios with his quiet and loving wife and his quiet and loving daughter, in his quiet and well-loved house along that quiet and rural lane, with London lying quiet at his feet – and even sur-rounded by this best of lives he's plainly a depressive! I, Jessel, saw the heaviness in his legs as he walked up the lane. I, at seventeen, heard the heaviness in his lungs as he sighed, the heaviness in his voice as he fetched those few reluctant words up from the depths inside himself. Happiness! Who told them to start drivelling on about happiness? No one. They're blundering about like a ship in the fog, with no terms of reference to steer by. One day their terms of reference will be agreed and there'll be no mention of happiness anywhere in the document. They'll find themselves chartered to carry pig-iron and cheap tin trays, just like everybody else; and by that time they'll be down in the South Seas loading rainbows and moonbeams.

I know the kind of people who talk about happiness. They're the ones with strained white smiling faces and desperation in their hearts. They're so happy! – Expect tearful phone calls and suicide attempts. They've found the secret of happiness for all! – Stand by for the labour camps and the mass graves.

I'm over-reacting. But why doesn't she just shut up and get on with it, like everybody else? With work, with statistics about the distribution of washing-machines, and evidence from economists and sociologists. With life, since we're stuck with it. With not embarrassing the rest of us. *We've* got to get on with it, after all. *I'm* getting on with it. I get on with it over lunch – a sandwich and a green apple from the canteen, eaten at my desk. I get on with it most of the afternoon, and I've still got a stack of unopened buff envelopes in my hand as I head doggedly back up the little twisting staircase and sit down on my hard box seat to get on with it again up here, a task which now looks likely to keep me here after everyone else has gone home. Some of us don't have time to ask ourselves what we're doing in this world. We're too busy listening to the outpourings of others.

What I'm doing at this point, actually, is jumping up and forcing the windows open to get some air into the room. The high blue summer weather goes on and on and by mid-afternoon it's hot up here under the leads. There is the sound of a brass band playing somewhere, and a bumble-bee sweeps erratically past, miles above the pollen on the plane trees. In the lead-lined gutter behind the parapet, just down the slope of the roof beneath the window, is something white with writing on it. I reach out and recover it. It's a plastic marker, pointed at one end, of the sort that people stick in flower-pots to identify them. *Pelargonium hortorum* 'Elizabeth Angus' it says. Someone in this room once had a geranium on the little sill outside the window, scarlet against the blue of the summer sky. The plant and the soil it grew in have long since spilled from the toppled pot and been washed away in the winter rains. The plastic pot itself has gone bouncing away across the rooftops in the spring winds. Only the words remain, and the notion of that flaunting colour.

Pelargonium hortorum . . . I file the marker, on top of everything else, in my Summerchild file. Summerchild, yes. The name on the front looks subtly different, now that the *Pelargonium hortorum* document has been added to the record. He's not indignant, he's not embarrassed. He's *amused* by the turn events are taking, like me, even ironically helpful. I look at his contribution to their first working session. 'I imagine so . . . I suspect I do . . .' They're as smilingly elusive as his expression in the photograph on the boxes opposite me, as charmingly imprecise as the photograph itself. I go and sit beside him on his boxes and feel much the same as he does. There she is, in the other photograph, guileless and fervent, leaning forward across her desk, philosophizing away at me from the broad steppe of her Slavic soul. I lean back in my seat, smiling ironically over the hedge from the little back garden that serves as a soul for the English. Yes, I believe I'm beginning to enjoy myself. Some odd irresponsibility is stirring in me as I listen to Serafin's preposterous diatribe. I am released from the gravity of routine, light-headed in the thin air at the top of the building. Even before our report has been completed, the quality of my life has been improved.

Summerchild, I am beginning to think, has considerable inner resources. When we all left the office this morning he was hurrying off to Paddington a pace and a half behind his wide-eyed philosopher, fielding stray oranges and packets of plectra. Now I see him coming back in the middle of the afternoon, with, I hope, a railway sandwich or two inside him, apparently not in the least put out at being employed as a busboy. I believe he is already carrying the geranium. He puts it in the sun on the window-sill. Where are we by this time? April. Inside the glass, then – it will go outside later. But already I have the impression of warm spring sunshine. The miseries he mentioned with the heating were in the past. The terrible winter is over.

Now what does he do? Well, he collects up the tapes from the tape-recorder and takes them downstairs to Mrs Padmore.

'How many copies?' asks Mrs Padmore.

'Oh, just the one, I think, Mrs Padmore,' he replies drily, 'until we've got ourselves a shade more sorted out.'

Because this is a top copy of the transcript in the file, not a carbon. It was never forwarded. So far Summerchild has evidently managed to keep everything under control.

Then what? With Serafin back in Oxford and Mrs Padmore hard at work on the tapes he has a little time on his hands. He waters the geranium, then picks up the phone.

'Tite,' says the voice at the other end. 'Summerchild,' says Summerchild. 'Would it be a convenient moment . . .?' 'It would indeed,' says Tite. He can hear a new note in the grating depths of Summerchild's voice. There is slightly surprising news to hear about the Unit, the section of his empire upon which the fate of the whole department may well depend. From the sound of Summerchild's voice the news is either surprisingly good or surprisingly bad.

So Summerchild locks up his office and goes down the narrow staircase. In some much larger and loftier room on the first floor, with net curtains at the window and the mulberry tree at the back of the Scottish Office just beyond, Tite waves him to a seat. I picture a sharp little man, with sharply pointed shoes and sharply pointed ears. 'Well?' he says, sharply. 'Yes, well,' begins Summerchild, scratching his head in amused perplexity. 'I think we may have a bit of a problem on our hands . . .'

Or perhaps he doesn't. There is a great weight of paper still to come in the file. 'Well?' demands Tite, a little too sharply – and Summerchild becomes rather less forthcoming than he had intended. He looks at the window over Tite's shoulder and says something like: 'Oh . . . early days yet.'

'Not trying to fetch in too many people off the street, is she? That's all I'm worried about.'

'We haven't got that far yet. We're still pretty much sharpening our pencils.'

'Yes, well, keep me posted.'

'Of course.'

He doesn't want Tite intervening. I realize that now. He is evidently enjoying his little flight of philosophical fancy. Believes he can get the aircraft back on to the ground all by himself when the joy-ride is over. Has begun, I should say, to feel a little proprietorial about Serafin, in the way we do about our masters, and at the same time a little protective.

Just as Tite himself, it occurs to me, is going to be doing when he goes into the witness-box at Summerchild's inquest later that summer and tells the Coroner – I turn back in my file to the copy I took of the cutting – that Summerchild was working on conditions of employment in the Civil Service at the time of his death. Just as the Prime Minister, or whoever briefed him, will be doing a few months after that when he tells the House that the report that Summerchild was working on was the comparability study which has since been published. Was it Summerchild they were feeling protective about, though? Or was it themselves?

So when Summerchild steps out up Whitehall at the end of the day he is still hugging their secret madness to himself. Because I was wrong; he *did* have secrets; he *was* carrying a headful of them up Hyde Hill Lane every evening. And somebody *has* been covering up for him – smoothing his footprints out of the mud, rubbing his fingerprints off the door handles.

There he goes across the concourse at Charing Cross with the rest of the commuters. Nine minutes it's taken him this evening, no more – almost as fast as me. He can't wait to get home to share some sense of his pleasure with Anne and Millie. And naturally when he gets there he can say nothing. He smiles a few secret smiles and shakes his head when Anne and Millie look at him. His inability to explain makes him smile again. Millie laughs. Anne watches them both silently. If spring is like this, what will summer bring?

And next day back he comes – ten minutes from the ticket barrier to Security, even in the morning rush – eager to see what new lunacy is in store at the top of the stairs.

Yes, what next? I'm naturally pleased to see Summerchild feeling. . . I was going to say happy, I realize. Happi*er*, let's say, and no questions are begged. We can be happier without being happy. In fact, the further we are from whatever happiness is, the more scope we have to be happier. All the same, I can't help feeling a little anxious about this relish he is revealing for anarchy. I put my Summerchild file aside and turn back to the Quality of Life. The transfer of Mrs Padmore still threatens on the first page. I go to the back of the file and sort out the next complete document.

It's more of Mrs Padmore's typescript. Another Socratic dialogue. My eye skips down the page. 'Happiness' is the first word it lights on – and, uncontrollably, away it bounds at once, as affrighted as ever.

14

But then I go cautiously back to take another look. I realize
with hindsight that the dread word was preceded and calmed
by the word 'notion'. Yes, 'the notion of happiness'. This is
what she has been 'giving some thought to', she says – 'the
notion of happiness'. And at once all the blood runs out of it.
The wild piping creature that haunts the woods is hoisted up
by its heels on the butcher's hook and it's just dead goat-
meat ready for dissection. I am relieved. I had been fearing, I
realize, that she would ask Summerchild if he personally was
happy.

I realize something else, too – I am a little disappointed. I
had secretly been hoping to see my colleague tortured a little.

Various ways in which the term has been used by philosophers ... Yes, yes ... References to Mill and Nietzsche ...
Fine ... Summerchild mentions Kierkegaard. Good God. Much
enthusiasm from Serafin over this. 'Yes, yes! Good, good!'
etcetera. Much, I imagine, eager nodding. Hopes here of a
good second, at the very least ... Now a brief diversion into
the lives of the saints ... Summerchild rather well-informed
about St Teresa of Avila. He's doing the Civil Service considerable credit, I must say.

All right so far ... Hold on, though. I think Serafin is
starting to edge away from the notions counter.

SERAFIN: Don't you begin to feel you have heard the whole
debate before?

SUMMERCHILD: No, I don't think I do. I don't think I have heard anything remotely like it before.

SERAFIN: Isn't it very similar to the kind of discussion people used to have about ethics? What is goodness? What is *the good*? Is it analysable? Is it an absolute? Is it intuited directly, like greenness or blueness? Etcetera. Nowadays, of course, we understand that it was this way of talking about ethical abstractions that made them seem so mysterious. In everyday life we talk about things being good and bad, and we know perfectly well what we mean. So what philosophers have said is, Instead of talking about good in the abstract, let's look at the way people actually use words like 'good' in non-philosophical contexts.

SUMMERCHILD: As in the phrase 'good sewage effluent', for example?

SERAFIN: Yes! I thought you said you read classics?

SUMMERCHILD: I did, but a friend of mine in college . . .

SERAFIN: Good! Well picked up! If you want to read the discussion of 'good sewage effluent' for yourself you'll find it in Hare, *The Language of Ethics*. Yes, and there's a rather odd smell in this room . . .

SUMMERCHILD: I don't think I can . . .

SERAFIN: Slightly disgusting.

SUMMERCHILD: Oh, the geraniums, perhaps.

SERAFIN: The geraniums?

SUMMERCHILD: On the window-sill. I thought they'd brighten the place up.

Geraniums, yes. And not just one, evidently. Two, three – a whole display of them. And perhaps, as the spring draws on, there will be more floral tributes. I look round the room. Now it seems like a conservatory, full of potted camellias and azaleas. A *Ficus benjamina* in the corner. A room vine climbing up the old chimney-breast . . . Something else about the chimney-breast, I realize, has been worrying me for some time now. Two tiny marks, side by side, half an inch apart, about head height. I go across and look at them from close to. Yes, two neat holes, where a pair of steel pins were driven into the masonry to support a picture hook. There are two more on the wall by the door. A single one over Serafin's desk. Another single one over Summerchild's. They had plants on the window-sills and pictures on the walls. Not posters, fixed with sticky tape or drawing-pins. Framed pictures.

They had a hammer to drive the nails in. And all this provided by Summerchild, from the sound of it.

SERAFIN: Oh yes. Good . . .

Because she obviously hadn't even noticed the sudden splash of blood-red petals against the white April cumulus.

. . . Where were we? Yes, as in expressions such as 'good sewage effluent'. Exactly. Good! Good!

SUMMERCHILD: Or as in that expression, perhaps.

SERAFIN: What expression?

SUMMERCHILD: 'Good! Good!'

SERAFIN: Good! Yes!

Very good indeed. He is politely but quite openly starting to mock her. Perhaps this is why he is buying flowers and pictures. He is beginning to feel at home up here. He has taken Serafin's measure and knows that he is on top of the situation.

Not that Serafin seems to realize. On she sails like the Titanic:

Well remarked! So what I propose is that we put the notion of happiness back in its box and restrict ourselves to the word 'happy', which people do in fact use in everyday circumstances.

SUMMERCHILD: Yes, well, I have made a list of organizations which I believe would be interested in giving evidence . . .

SERAFIN: Good. Or rather . . . no, *good*. We might at some later stage wish to move on to institutional usages of the word. I imagine that a psychiatrist, for example, would apply the word to the behaviour of a patient according to rather technical criteria which would indeed provide an analogy with what a sanitary engineer means by good sewage effluent. But in the first place I believe we should direct our attentions to unschooled lay usages of the word.

SUMMERCHILD: You want what are sometimes called 'ordinary people'?

SERAFIN: Exactly.

SUMMERCHILD: I don't think that should present any problems. The department has contacts with a number of opinion-sampling and marketing organizations. I think we'd simply need to specify whether 'ordinary' means selected on a randomized basis or according to a specified distribution by age, sex, class, etcetera.

SERAFIN: Thank you. But I think for our purposes we might define 'an ordinary person' as 'anyone who is not a professional philosopher'. A Civil Servant, for example, would be a perfectly ordinary person in this context.

SUMMERCHILD: Very kind of you to say so. I've explained before, however, why I should be reluctant to involve Mrs Padmore . . .

SERAFIN: I wasn't thinking of Mrs Padmore.

SUMMERCHILD: So you were proposing . . .?

SERAFIN: To continue with our present procedure.

SUMMERCHILD: Ah.

SERAFIN: If you'd be happy with that arrangement . . . And already we've found ourselves with the word on our lips! 'I should be happy with this arrangement,' you say ... At least, I *assume* ...?

SUMMERCHILD: Yes, yes, yes.

SERAFIN: Perhaps I was a little ahead of myself?

SUMMERCHILD: No, no. I should be happy with this arrangement.

SERAFIN: Thank you. So, yes, you tell me you are happy with a certain proposal. Now let's jump straight in and catch this one on the wing. A simple question first: how do you *know* you are happy with this arrangement?

SUMMERCHILD: Well, I think I felt ...

SERAFIN: You *felt*. Yes. You were aware of a particular feeling. Some identifiable affective *event* occurred inside you. Can you describe this event at all?

SUMMERCHILD: Well ...

SERAFIN: Was it – let's start at the *heavy* end of the scale – was it a moment of ecstasy?

SUMMERCHILD: I think 'ecstasy' might perhaps be putting it too strongly.

SERAFIN: Let's move down the scale a little. A surge of joy?

SUMMERCHILD: Well ...

SERAFIN: Not a surge of joy. All right. Was it a shock of delight? A wave of pleasure? A glow of contentment?

SUMMERCHILD: I think perhaps ... I don't know ... I think I do in fact get a certain ... well, yes, *pleasure* out of our conversations ...

SERAFIN: You sound a little uncertain!

SUMMERCHILD: No, no ...

SERAFIN: You sound as if you are making a cautious discovery about your feelings for the first time. But you didn't have to stop and examine your feelings before you announced that you were happy with the arrangement! Am I right? You didn't have to focus some kind of internal microscope, as you seemed to do when I challenged you. You didn't have to hold slides of this unidentified emotional entity up against the illustrations in the textbook before you could declare your findings! 'Are you happy with the arrangement?' I asked. 'Yes,' you replied at once, 'I'm happy with the arrangement.'

SUMMERCHILD: No, well, I suppose I . . .

SERAFIN: '. . .was not conducting any internal examination at all,' you tell me. 'I was not identifying a feeling – not reporting upon the occurence of an event – I was simply signalling my acceptance of a proposed course of action. I was declaring my agreement. I was committing myself to a policy.' You might have *felt* nothing at all. Might even have felt displeasure at the prospect. Imagine that somehow I *knew* you regarded the proposed arrangement with distaste. All the same, you tell me you're happy with the arrangement. I think you would be just a little surprised if I shouted 'Liar!' There would be no contradiction, would there, between your *feeling* of distaste and your *declaration* of intent?

SUMMERCHILD: Yes, but when I say I'm happy *with* something . . .

SERAFIN: '. . . I'm using "happy" in one specific turn of phrase, which is some kind of extension of its basic meaning.' True enough, I reply. But if we could grasp some of these small particular uses we might be able to follow them back to the main river. Look after the pennies and the pounds will look after themselves. Shadow your *bagmen* and they'll lead you back to Mr Big. We've put a tail on 'happy with'. Let's try following 'happy about', and see if he's going to the same address. 'Are you happy,' I ask you, '*about* the way we are pursuing this investigation?'

SUMMERCHILD: Oh . . .

SERAFIN: And you pause. Are you examining the state of your emotions? I think not. You are examining the progress of the investigation. 'Yes, I'm happy about it,' you tell me.

SUMMERCHILD: Well, I'm not sure that I *am* all that happy about it . . .

SERAFIN: Or 'No, I'm not happy about it.' But in either case, aren't you still declaring something rather than reporting on anything? Aren't you once again in some sense signalling your acceptance of events – or your non-acceptance of them? Isn't it – look, *I* know – isn't it like your signing or not signing the minutes of the last meeting? In fact you tell me you're *not* happy with it. You *won't* sign the minutes. 'Why not?' I demand. You don't tell me it's because you've got a lump in your throat, or an ache in your heart, or a sensation of nausea in your stomach. You may have all these symptoms and more – and yet they still wouldn't constitute grounds for refusing to sign the minutes. 'Why won't you sign?' I ask – and you tell me where you think the record is wrong. 'Why are you unhappy about the way we are proceeding?' I demand. And you identify some point or characteristic of our discussion. Which is?

SUMMERCHILD: Isn't it all a little beside the point? The thing about being happy is that you're happy. I mean, when you're actually *happy* – I mean just *happy* – not *with* anything or *about* anything . . .

SERAFIN: How about happy *that*? Or happy *to*? You wouldn't like to trail those two rather innocent-looking characters back to headquarters?

SUMMERCHILD: No, I'm thinking about when you're simply . . . well, *happy* . . .

SERAFIN: Hold on. Let's make sure we're comparing like with like. What we're examining, if you recall, is particular usages of the word. So what you're saying is: 'Let's look at the case where someone says, quite simply, "I'm happy." Yes?

SUMMERCHILD: Exactly! If someone says that, then it's because he feels . . . well . . .

SERAFIN: Happy?

SUMMERCHILD: Yes!

SERAFIN: He might be lying.

SUMMERCHILD: Yes, yes. But . . .

104

SERAFIN: And you make a gesture which the tape-recorder won't pick up, but which suggests, I imagine, impatience with pedantic nitpicking. All right – you might be *mistaken*. Is that a trivial objection? Looking at you from the other side of the desk I might feel you have *misdiagnosed* yourself. I might feel – imagine now that I'm a rather severe confessor, or a psychoanalyst faced with what I believe they call denial, or the flight into health! – I might feel that you are concealing your deeper feelings from yourself. To which you of course reply that the concept of misdiagnosis implies the possibility of *correct* diagnosis, and that I am able to discount the evidence of your feelings only by reference to other feelings. I'd like to come back to the notion of self-misdiagnosis later, if I may, possibly at some future session. But let's leave aside the whole question of the *truth* of the statement, which I think is going to lead us, if we're not careful, to the hideout of some other gang altogether. What I think we might with advantage look at now is not the *grounds* for saying 'I'm happy', but the *occasion* for saying it. The reasons for giving utterance to the words rather than not giving utterance to them. *When* does one say, 'I'm happy'? *Why* does one feel it necessary to make it public? People say things to serve some purpose. What purpose might be served by announcing that you're happy? What use might the statement have? People don't suddenly say things out of the blue, without a context. In what circumstances might you say 'I'm happy'?

SUMMERCHILD: Well . . .

SERAFIN: In what circumstances *have* you found yourself saying it?

SUMMERCHILD: Me personally?

SERAFIN: You personally!

SUMMERCHILD: Well . . . (*Laughs.*)

'(*Laughs*)' is presumably a rare example of Mrs Padmore's editorializing. I wonder exactly what sounds on the tape the word represents. Quite noticeable ones, I should imagine – she hasn't found it necessary up to now to make any special record of the other small vatic events – gasps, hesitations, groans, sighs – that the conversation must have involved. '(*Laughs*)' I take it, therefore, is not a single mirthless bark but a whole sequence of barks. I imagine it perhaps starting as one, and then escalating, as Serafin waits, smiling eagerly at her pupil, and Summerchild hunts back through his life for the required circumstances, covering his retreat with bursts of fire as he goes. Thus: (*Laughs.*) Pause. (*Laughs, laughs.*) Pause. (*Laughs, laughs, laughs . . .*)

I look away. My eye falls on the geraniums by the window, which all the way through this conversation, presumably, have been continuing to scent the office air. With a perfume that she characterizes as slightly disgusting. And blushing scarlet, of course, as they do so.

I return to Summerchild, who has retreated as far as laughter will stretch and found nothing.

SERAFIN: You never have?

SUMMERCHILD: I can't recall . . .

SERAFIN: In what circumstances *might* you find yourself saying it?

SUMMERCHILD: Well . . . (*Laughs.*)

More (*laughs*)! Are these the same noises? Or have we moved from minor to major? Has my colleague simply got the giggles?

SERAFIN: I see! (*Laughs*).

Now *she's* off! I understand why the universities have been cutting back their philosophy departments.

. . . All right, let me suggest a possibility. You might say it as a boast – perhaps in the hope of rendering me envious or jealous.

SUMMERCHILD: I suppose I might. (*Laughs.*)

SERAFIN: But then you're not the kind of man who would wish to arouse painful feelings in other people, so let's find some more plausible circumstance. Well, you might do it to reassure me. Yes? Sensing some anxiety on my part about your reaction to the work I am asking you to do, you tell me, 'I'm perfectly happy here.'

SUMMERCHILD: 'I'm perfectly happy here ...' Yes, I can imagine saying that.

SERAFIN: Have indeed just said it.

SUMMERCHILD: Yes, though ...

SERAFIN: Though only, so to speak, experimentally. Not as the instrument of an actual assertion. I understand that.

SUMMERCHILD: Well ... 'I'm perfectly happy here.' I think I am perhaps ...

SERAFIN: To some extent saying it? To some extent trying it out, but to some extent actually ...?

SUMMERCHILD: 'I'm perfectly happy here.'

SERAFIN: ... saying it?

SUMMERCHILD: Yes. I'm perfectly happy here. Saying it, saying it.

SERAFIN: You've taken the inverted commas off?

SUMMERCHILD: I think I have, yes.

And he has, too. Or someone has. I glance back at Summerchild's last remark, and see that the inverted commas before and after 'I'm happy here' have been neatly expunged with Tipp-Ex. Mrs Padmore, having typed the interpretation of the remark, has gone back and altered its semantic status to fit the interpretation. She is obviously following this insane dialogue with remarkably close attention. No wonder; in her entire career as a Clerical Officer she has never typed out anything remotely like it.

SERAFIN: You are not happy about the way we are proceeding, you told us a moment ago . . .

SUMMERCHILD: Well, I'm not absolutely sure I'm happy about it . . .

SERAFIN: Not absolutely sure you're happy about it. Of course. I'm sorry. Not absolutely sure about that, yet absolutely sure – yes? – that you are perfectly happy here.

SUMMERCHILD: Yes, well . . .

SERAFIN: No, no, this is interesting! I don't feel any contradiction at all between these two statements. Because that 'perfectly', that 'here', are just as limiting in their way as 'with' and 'about'. It's entirely open to you to reject our way of working but to accept with equanimity the fact of our working. To which I reply, 'All right, let's think of the circumstances in which you might wish to say "I'm happy" in the most general sense, without limitation to any implied purpose or situation . . .' Well, suppose we were not sitting here engaged in a job of work. Suppose we were old friends who were meeting again after not seeing each other for many years. We were at university together. I stayed on to teach philosophy – you went off to London and disappeared into the Civil Service. Now here we are, sitting face to face across a table in some little restaurant with a bottle of wine between us . . . 'Are you happy?' I ask you . . .

SUMMERCHILD: Actually, I do feel a little as if I were coming face to face with my past in some kind of way. As if I were back at university. Tutorials . . . Discussion groups . . . Walking round the streets at night talking to people . . .

SERAFIN: Good! Yes!

SUMMERCHILD: A feeling of – I don't know – looking down and seeing the world stretching away over the horizon. Back into the past. Away into the future. Knowing that huge things are going to happen, but not knowing what they are . . . Sorry.

SERAFIN: Not at all! A feeling of wide horizons – open possibilities – this is the atmosphere we need to do work of this kind.

So, we're old friends meeting . . . Or – I know! Yes! Even better! We're *in love*! Yes? I sit here gazing into your eyes. You sit there gazing into mine. 'Oh, I'm so happy!' I cry. 'I'm completely happy! I'm utterly happy! I'm wildly happy!' Etcetera. Yes? Isn't this *exactly* the kind of thing people say when they're in love? 'Are *you* happy?' I ask you. Isn't that *exactly* the kind of question lovers ask each other all the time? 'Are you happy?' I ask. To which you reply . . . .

Dots. Twelve dots arranged in groups of three. Mrs Padmore's way, if she is being consistent, of representing a notable silence on the tape. A silence long enough, I imagine, for her to use the fast-forward button. What's going on? The dots have brought us to the bottom of a page – an appropriate point, since we have also, surely, reached the nadir of these proceedings, perhaps of all proceedings in the whole history of the modern Civil Service. I find myself pausing for a few dots myself before I turn over the page to find where all this is leading. I take it that the proceedings so far are conjecture – that the two of them are not in fact gazing into each other's eyes – that Serafin is not waiting for Summerchild to supply an answer to her question. I should imagine she is gazing at the floor, pursuing some thought which has escaped sideways from the main line of march, while he gazes almost anywhere but at her. Out of the window, probably, at the healing impersonality of the April sky. With each passing second he is becoming more painfully conscious of quite how far he has been dragged from the track of normal professional propriety. Perhaps even she has begun to have second thoughts about the ballooning barminess of these proceedings . . .

No, I know what she's thinking. I turn over the page. Yes.

Sorry. I was just thinking that we might leave hypothesis aside. I might simply try asking the question, and see how you respond. So: are you happy?

I knew it. I *knew* it!
I lay the transcript aside and lean out of the window. The

same day is still going on out here, a little older, a little wearier. The same summer . . . I am looking down on the world, but it does not stretch away over nebulous distant horizons. It stops short at the Palace in the west, and the Admiralty in the north. I can hear her putting the question in the room behind me. 'Are you happy?' she asks him, she asks me. 'Oh, for heaven's sake!' I hear myself replying. But in fact that's not what I reply at all. Politeness remains, even after all the other laws of human discourse have been abrogated. 'Oh, reasonably,' I say with a smile and turn back to my work. But she is waiting with those wide blue peasant eyes of hers, nodding expectantly. I believe I hear myself beginning to talk to fill the silence – beginning to explain to her about Lynn – about Timmy and Cheryl . . . Shameful thoughts.

A curious little line of figures comes round the side of the Admiralty, walking slowly and wearily through the late summer afternoon in Indian file. The woman at the head is carrying a clipboard. The man in the middle has a tripod across his shoulder. They are bearing the one-eyed god from some unseen station of its progress to the next. Before I can establish whether they are the same votaries as before they disappear into the Horse Guards.

A salutary reminder. My report has to be on Ken Hurren's desk before theirs is on the Prime Minister's screen. I think I can interpret Ken's request for it to be done by the end of the week as meaning in his hands on Monday morning. That involves finishing it tonight, though. I go back to the file and find Summerchild's reply.

'Oh,' he says, followed by three dots. 'Well,' he says, followed by six. Each dot goes into me like a needle. 'Yes,' he says finally.

'Yes.' The raw little syllable sits there in all its nakedness. Yes, full stop. Not words we use much in the Civil Service, yes and no, even in the most impersonal contexts. In the presence of a question like Serafin's it seems as indelicate as an oath. Then again, it's impossible to guess from the transcript how it was said – whether it was flung down, shrugged off, tossed out, or uttered in some other way that put a hairpiece upon its baldness. It might have sounded as flippant as the question was importunate.

He says it again. 'Yes . . .'

Now he's repeated it, of course, I take it less seriously. And those three dots after it . . .

A third yes. Another three dots. As good as no, surely.

'Or rather,' he continues. Three more dots, during which, I imagine, he is looking evasively out of the window. He is doing something, at any rate, which makes Serafin have second thoughts.

'I'm sorry,' she says. 'Perhaps that was an intrusive question.'

Yes!

'No,' he lies.

She says nothing.

'No, no . . .' he lies again, to give the first lie some company.

And he goes on gazing out of the window. What's he doing? A nasty suspicion comes to me that he is taking the question seriously. He is not politely evading it – he is actually thinking about it. Yes – 'I was just thinking . . .' he says after a while, then stops again, because he's still thinking.

I believe my colleague is going to confess. He has broken under interrogation. He has gone over.

'I was just trying to think,' he says, 'what I do actually . . . .'

He in his turn is reduced to twelve dots. His dots, in fact, appear to indicate a silence that goes on indefinitely. There is no more text to bring it to an end. After the twelfth dot, two thirds of the way down the page, the transcript of this long session tails away into blank paper.

I suppose what's happened is this: he has gone on staring out of the window, thinking, and she has gone on staring at him, waiting, with such absorption that neither of them noticed the tape had run out. The rest of the session, including Summerchild's confession, or his heroic refusal to confess, has broadcast itself about the little attic room, bounced off the walls, been absorbed in the carpet, faded to silence and passed out of history.

Or has it? I turn to the next document on the tag. It is a handwritten minute, from Summerchild to Serafin, dated two days later, entitled 'A Preliminary Submission'. The wording of the title sounds reassuring. I glance down the page. 'I . . . I . . . my . . . me . . .' It's some kind of personal statement. My foreboding returns.

I put the file down again. I am afflicted by that ambiguous unease which is produced by the prospect of starting some unwelcome task – a restless desire either to drink water or to pass it. I open the door to the little cloakroom in the corner, undecided about which form of relief to try, and hesitate between the brownish lavatory and the greenish tap. The sight of the greyish kettle beside the gas-ring, and of the yellowish mug which has been drying on the little draining-board for the last fifteen years, makes me think of tea. Yes, it's tea-time. I find a box of matches, then follow the piping up the wall from the dead gas-ring until I come to the stopcock that turns the supply on. Could there possibly be a last antique teabag in the cupboard over the sink? I turn the cuphook that holds the door closed . . .

There is indeed a teabag. In fact there are five, in an upturned cardboard lid. There is also an eggcup, a biscuit tin, a tin of Colman's mustard and a packet of Heinz cock-a-leekie soup. A few small green leaves are scattered about the bottom of the cupboard . . . How can there be green leaves, after fifteen years? I pick one up to examine it – then drop it in disgust. The green is mould. What the mould is growing on appears to be a cornflake.

A cornflake? Teabags, yes. Soup, just possibly. But *corn-flakes?*

On the upper shelf of the cupboard are four plain white plates, two plain white pudding-bowls, and another eggcup.

In the drawer beneath the gas-ring – a few grey pieces of cutlery, a corkscrew and a lot of corks. It looks as if they were making some slight effort of their own up here to maintain the quality of life.

I am retracing the footsteps of the lost expedition, tracking them through their abandoned log from one wrong compass bearing to the next. Now I have found their supplies. I am trailing them along the line of their tea-breaks and their modest working lunches of packet soup followed by something you eat with mustard. I am trying to get a sighting of them eating cornflakes and drinking twelve – fourteen – sixteen – nineteen bottles of wine.

I make myself a cup of milkless tea, vintage 1974, and take a cautious sip. It tastes brown and leaves a little dust crunching between the teeth. I find the flavour. . . appropriate, and take it back to my cardboard work-station. The Lea & Perrins box this time, where Serafin sat, so that I can keep an eye on Summerchild. 'I . . . I . . . my . . . me . . .' he pleads from the manuscript in front of me. And all the while, from the Saxa Salt box opposite, he watches me read, smiling his sideways smile.

Right. Let's see what he has to say for himself.

15

CONFIDENTIAL

THE QUALITY OF LIFE: A Preliminary Submission

Dr Serafin   S Summerchild
                                                April 10th 1974

With reference to our discussion on April 8th, and the question which was left unanswered at the end, namely as to whether I regarded myself as 'happy':

I have to confess that I had not anticipated the direction that your inquiries were going to take and I feel that my immediate responses were fragmented and unhelpful. You will, I fear, have found my monosyllabic utterances rather unrewarding material for *linguistic analysis* (which I assume to be the philosophical method you are following) – and my frequent silences even more intractable. I have, therefore, taken advantage of your absence on academic business to give the matter more thought and I feel it might be best if I set out the various considerations involved in written form.

I assume that what you are hoping for is not merely a simple yes or a no, but some discussion of the matter, and I shall therefore take the liberty of presenting the evidence in some detail and at some length. If I might interpose a personal remark here (not perhaps too inaptly, given the circumstances!) I have to say that nothing in my career so far has prepared me for this kind of work. A Civil Servant is, as you know, here to serve as best he can, in whatever way his masters devise, and

114

we do pride ourselves on our adaptability. I am in any case rather intrigued by the project! But I must ask you to be patient with my navigation in these uncharted waters.

It seems to me that, so far as my feelings about it are concerned, my life can be most conveniently divided into two halves:

1. Work.
2. Home.

The latter can probably be broken down again into:

(i) House.
(ii) Family.
(iii) The evening.
(iv) The weekend.
(v) Holidays.

At this point I take a sip of my disgusting tea. I can't help noting that, whatever Summerchild is going to say, he is at least going to say it in his own way. He has not given up the running battle between them over the question of form, which started out with his victory on accommodation. Now the fight has shifted to the mode of procedure. She has picked home ground and imposed the tutorial format on him. But he seems to have succeeded in executing a ragged but effective withdrawal, hesitating and equivocating his way back at the last session until night fell over the battlefield. Now he has had a chance to regroup and fall back on to the kind of terrain of which he is master – the written minute. What a different man he is on the page! He advances steadily and unhurriedly, with his battle-squadrons laid out in paragraphs i, ii, and iii, in sub-paragraphs (a), (b) and (c), in Introductions and Conclusions, his red hair gleaming like an oriflamme. If he is going down to defeat, as I suspect he is, he is doing it in style.

1. *Work*. (NB. I am excluding the present proceedings from consideration here, since they are entirely untypical of what I do.) I find it difficult to identify any overall feeling about my

work. I cannot recall actually thinking to myself 'I am enjoying this.' I can recall on occasion thinking 'I am not enjoying this.' But the occasions were, I think, fairly infrequent. This relative freedom from negative reaction is what I imagine most people mean when they say they are happy in their work.

On analysis, I believe I can distinguish three characteristic phases into which, speaking very generally, my work falls:

(i) beginning a piece of work,
(ii) being in the middle of it, and
(iii) finishing it.

(i) I foresee with trepidation and execute with unease. (iii) I look forward to, but then usually fail to take much pleasure in, because (a) having reached it, there is no possibility of looking forward to it, and (b) it brings with it the prospect of (i) again.

Where I feel most at home is (ii). (i) is behind me, and (iii) is still a pleasure to come. During (ii) I am usually sitting at my desk, quietly getting on with things. This quiet progress is both thrown into relief and varied by endless interruptions. I sigh and click my tongue at these, of course. The phone again! Someone else putting his head round my door! Another committee coming up, another summons to the Permanent Secretary's office! But I realize, as I sit here in the offices of the Strategy Unit, away from my usual desk and my usual routine, and charged with scrupulous self-examination, that I look forward to being interrupted, and that I also get a certain satisfaction from these sighs and clickings of the tongue.

Since most of my work necessarily consists in (ii) rather than in (i) or (iii), I think I must conclude that on the whole I am happy in my work.

And I think *I* must conclude that, in spite of the well-established format, something is going seriously wrong here. This may look like a minute, but it's *not* a minute, and it's getting less one with every line. The gyro-compass inside Summerchild has developed some mysterious fault and, unremarked by the crew, the plane is veering further and further off course.

Another thing: does Dr Serafin have full security clearance? If not it seems to me possible that Summerchild could be opening himself to proceedings under the Official Secrets Act. I'm not sure, now I come to think about it, whether the Act covers Civil Servants' emotional states and behavioural quirks. If it doesn't, then it should be rapidly amended.

I take an absent-minded sip from the mug beside me. Ugh! A moment of panic. This isn't coffee! This is no more coffee than Summerchild's minute is a minute! What's happening to the world? Oh, yes, I remember – it's tea . . . But it isn't tea, either! At this point its provenance comes belatedly back to me. I take the mug out to the cloakroom and tip the dusty brown nothingness away down the sink.

I go back to the minute. Perhaps we shall be on safer ground with:

2. *Home.* Home, I realize on analysis, is not a concept which has definite geographical or social limits. For me it begins to be noticeable at the railway station where I get off the train each evening, and becomes gradually stronger, like a magnetic field, as I walk up the hill. By the time I turn into the little lane where I live it has become so intense that I usually slow down. There is an analogy here, perhaps, with 1(i) – a desire to postpone (iii), the moment of arrival.

There is also just possibly an analogy between the interruptions I described in (ii) and the unadopted state of the lane. The various potholes and puddles seem to suggest that the satisfaction of being a road is still something to be looked forward to. There is still room for the imagination.

(i) *House.* By the time I reach it, at this time of year, the house itself is usually nothing but one or two lighted windows in the darkness, with perhaps my wife and daughter (see separate headings) visible inside. I sometimes stand there in the darkness for a moment, watching them, putting off the moment when I walk up the five tessellated steps to the front door. The third step is cracked and breaking away at the edge. Every evening, as I see this crack, I think the same thought. The thought is about how I must find someone to mend it before it gets any worse. I am slightly irritated to find myself

117

thinking the same thought at the same point every evening, but also rather comforted.

This, I believe now that I examine it, is because underneath this thought, like a warm underblanket, is a reassuring additional thought, viz:

'Every evening, as I see this crack, I think the same thought.'

And underneath that thought (I think!) is another one – another underblanket, insulating the underblanket above – and which, so far as I can make out through the layers on top of it, runs something like this:

'Every evening, as I see this crack, I think the same thought: "Every evening, as I see this crack, I think the same thought."'

Summerchild's third step, I am beginning to realize, is not the only thing which is cracked. For the first time I can imagine some dim trail of obsession, some weird recursive delusion, leading out of this little room, down the spiral stairs, and out to some wildly mischosen destination . . . Across the Horse Guards down there to the doors of the Admiralty . . .

Actually I believe I remember that crack. Now Summerchild has mentioned it, I believe I remember looking at it during the long silences in my conversations with Millie. To me that crack signifies not reassurance but youth and hopelessness.

And I know what he means about the long vistas of precedent, like endless suites of anterooms, that open backwards from these recurring moments. Every evening, as I lift my key towards the lock of my own front door, the same thoughts formulate themselves – the same sudden loss of courage, in my case, the same leaden fear about what I shall find. And, yes, the dull weight of that moment includes the dull weight of the same moment the evening before, which includes the dull weight of the evening before that, which . . .

Back to work. Or rather back to home. Now *his* key is going into the lock:

... with a practised rippling smoothness like a boat gliding over a quiet dark river. Then I am inside. There is warmth around me and small sounds from other rooms, of voices, footsteps, a chair scraping, the television. Above all there is a smell of great ordinariness and naturalness that I should recognize anywhere in the world like a familiar voice. Now I think about it I believe I can identify a mixture of floor-polish and dust ... cooking, certainly ... books, yes ... a touch of mildew ... and an old and comfortable smell which I suppose is from Millie's cello case in the corner.

I put down my bag and open doors until I find my:

(ii) *Family*. This consists of:

a. *My wife*. Her name is Anne. We have been married for eighteen years. When she hears me come into the room she doesn't look round or say 'Hello'. She simply tells me something, as if I had been there all the time. 'Dorland Henry's dead.' Or: 'The Porringers are coming to lunch on Sunday.' Or: 'Jane Ryle says she hasn't slept for three nights.' She is a historian, or more properly a micro-historian, and she is writing a history of our hillside – the road I walk up from the station and the various lanes and alleyways that open off it. She has been doing it for three years and expects to be working on it for at least another three.

At the moment, though, she has secretly put this aside and, unknown to me, is working on another project entirely – a micro-history of myself. This is intended as a present to me on my fortieth birthday in July. I have naturally been very careful not to discover anything about it, but I have a feeling that she has commissioned little tributes from friends and childhood recollections from my sisters. She has found a number of old photographs that will come as a great surprise to me. I believe she has even phoned an old school friend of mine whom she avowedly dislikes and asked him for the manuscript of a symphony we once composed together. This was in the days when we were both planning to be great composers.

I should imagine she is writing an essay herself. The other contributions are probably mostly of a somewhat facetious nature. But if I know her she is composing something more like an entry in a good encylopaedia, or perhaps a chapter in her own book. I expect to read a full and objective description

of what's on the site now, together with a documented recon-
struction of how it came to be like that. My eye fell on a page
she had left on the kitchen table the other day and I had
noted, before I could avert my eyes, a pretty scholarly history
of my conversion to double-knotting, after an incident when I
was unable to get out of the train at Greenwich one evening
and found myself being carried on to Maze Hill, because
someone was standing on the trailing lace of my shoe. There
was also what looked like a very perceptive account of how I
decide, when I get up in the morning, whether to wear my
new shoes or my old ones. I also found an envelope lying
around in the bathroom the other day with a list of numbers
on the back, and when I asked her about it, she took it silently
out of my hand. I realized, thinking about it afterwards, that
they were the numbers of the various different bus-routes I
used on my way to school, together with the relevant extracts
from their timetables.

So I open the door to wherever she is, and there she sits
with some leather-bound quarto volume of local archives open
in front of her, writing about the way I lace my shoes. I wait.
Without looking up from her work she tells me something she
has done or discovered or thought or decided during the day.
'I saw Mary Seal this afternoon.' Or: 'Sally Terris's eldest
daughter is getting married.' Or: 'I'm going to keep the bicycle
pump in the drawer with the secateurs.' I'm not entirely clear
what I do at this point. Do I reply? I don't think I do. Do I say,
'Oh'? Probably not; it doesn't seem a very interesting thing to
say. 'Hello'? No, it's too late in the conversation by this time to
start saying 'Hello'. Do I offer her some piece of information in
return? I sometimes turn the possibility of this over in my
mind, but only rarely does a suitable piece of information
present itself. I imagine I stand just inside the door for a few
moments, looking into the corner of the room in a companion-
able way.

I should describe myself as happily married.

After I have seen my wife I continue on my way to find:

b. *My daughter*. She is called Millie. She is seventeen. She is
doing A-levels in Latin, Greek and Classical History, and cello
Grade Six. If she is not practising I tap on her door. In
appearance she takes after me, in conversational style after

her mother. 'I'm going to Athens next summer with Louisa Stair,' she says. Or: 'I hate Mr Margery.' (Mr Margery is her cello teacher.) Or: 'The cat's got fleas.' What do I say to this? I believe I say nothing at all. I nod, perhaps, and look around the room. She is doing her homework. But since she is rather ostentatiously concealing it with her arm as she talks I imagine that it is in fact not homework at all, but a contribution to her mother's *Festschrift*. In spite of all this secrecy, I happen to know that it takes the form of a humorous catalogue of my supposed states of mind, arranged from one to ten like the Beaufort Scale. 'State 1', it begins. 'Complete stillness. Book falls out of hands. Eyes unable to rise above floor-level. Insufficient energy even to sigh.' When I saw it the other night, tucked inside the cello part of one of the piano trios we play, she had got as far as 'State 7 – Moderate Gale: Intervals of laughter. Words are spoken, including frequent stories of own childhood. Humming occurs, together with attempts to balance glasses of water on edge of playing cards and to perform unaccompanied violin partitas.'

I feel silently amused at this as I stand there in her doorway. I am silently pleased to be the object of such closely observed mockery and silently proud of her cleverness in carrying it out. I probably smile slightly before I go out of the room and come back downstairs to commence:

(iii) *The evening*.

The first part of the evening consists of:

a. *Dinner*: I find it difficult to give an account of dinner. We eat, of course, which I enjoy. Sometimes we talk. What happens when we talk? Millie says something and we listen. Sometimes Anne disagrees, whereupon Millie disagrees back and conversation rages. Occasionally Anne says something, at which Millie disagrees, and we're off again. Very occasionally I say something myself and Millie glances mockingly at me, then looks at Anne to see how she is reacting. We respond more with glances, it occurs to me, than we do with words. For quite long stretches of the meal these glances, with perhaps a few small frowns and smiles, are all we need to sustain communication. Yesterday evening, for instance, I realized that I was smiling to myself (I was thinking about writing this minute!) and it set off a substantial debate, conducted entirely

121

in silence. So far as I can reconstruct events, I was gazing at the water jug when the exchange started; I discovered I was smiling when I realized that Anne was watching me; whereupon I looked at her interrogatively; she looked at the water jug with a slight frown; Millie glanced at each of us in turn, then picked up her dessert spoon and studied that instead; I watched her smiling at the spoon; which made me start smiling again; which made Anne start looking at me again; which . . . kept us all occupied throughout the main course.

After dinner Millie and I wash up, which brings us to:

b. *The rest of the evening.* This I often spend working (see Section 1 above), or in the kind of silent conversation described in 2 (iii) a. Sometimes I get out my violin and we all three play some music together, which is a kind of combination of work and conversation – it has all the tense absorption of the one, and all the anxiety to reach the end, together with all the wordless companionability of the other. And sometimes the evening simply passes and I can't tell you how. What happens? Nothing happens. I read. Or I half-read. Or I fall asleep. Or I just sit there, not even asleep.

There is some truth in Millie's ridiculous Beaufort Scale, I have to admit. I do have eventless evenings when the book falls out of my hands. How often do they recur? I don't really know. When I am down in States 1 or 2 it seems to me that I am always there, with all the flags hanging limp and absolutely still, and not a breath of air moving. Now I am up to something like State 4 ('Raises dust and loose paper'), according to the only reference to the original scale that I can find in Registry, or perhaps 5 ('Small trees in leaf begin to sway') it seems to me that States 4 and 5 is where I mostly am.

I should like for the purposes of this inquiry to reconstruct an average evening, an ordinary evening, a typical evening. Then I could measure the speed of the wind inside me and know where on the scale I was in general located. But no average evening comes to mind. They are all slightly different and all the slight differences cancel each other out. The almost overlapping outlines become a blur. The only evenings I can recall are fixed in my mind precisely because they are different from all the others.

I remember the evening when the tank burst and live water

came tumbling and gleaming down the stairs.

I remember the evening when four of our oldest friends came to dinner and no one could think of anything to say, and they all fled in terror. I remember the burn of shame as we stacked the silent, abandoned plates. I remember Anne suddenly laughing, which she never does, and putting her hand on my arm.

I remember the evening when Millie mysteriously fell in her room and broke her wrist. I remember the shock of fear when I heard her scream and the sickening jolt of pain through my stomach when I saw the angle of her hand to her arm.

So all I actually remember is unhappiness? Not at all. These weren't unhappy things. Dismaying, awkward, painful, even sad. But that's not to say unhappy.

In any case, I clearly remember one evening that was unambiguously happy. It was last month – our final power-cut. This is why I can see and hear it so clearly – because there was no electric light and there were no electric sounds. We ate by the light of three candles and our eyes all shone like children's around the table. Every time one of us leaned forward for the salt the flames wavered and curtsied with ridiculous deference, like three nervous waitresses. And when we laughed at this they started back in absurd confusion. If we'd raised our hand to them, or even spoken sharply, they'd all have had instant heart attacks.

I think this was the day you asked me what the quality of life was. Yes, because suddenly the answer came to me, as I watched the candles. It was *lightness*. I mean in both senses of the word. It was brightness and it was weightlessness. It shone and danced in the darkness, and without it there would be nothing; but one hand raised against it and it could lightly cease.

Yes, yes – because that's how the evening started. I stopped in the lane for a moment, as I often do, before I climbed the steps to the front door, and looked in through the windows. The lights were off in the living-room, but the television was on and I was amused to see a little bluish-grey man talking seriously to the empty armchairs. Anne and Millie were both in the kitchen and they were having a serious talk as well. Or rather, they were having a serious silence. Millie was standing

123

at the table with her hands resting on the back of a chair, looking down at the tablecloth. Anne was at the stove, with her head turned towards Millie. She was watching her intently. I had the impression that they had reached a moment of reflection in some important exchange. Millie's hair was close to the light over the table; it looked like a burning bush. My hair; Anne's thoughtfulness. What could be more familiar? But suddenly they looked like two strangers.

And then they were gone.

Everything had gone. Anne, Millie and the kitchen. The little grey man and the living-room. The house. The lane. London. The world had ceased to exist. Silently, effortlessly, between one breath and the next. I was surrounded by blackness and silence. There was nothing in the world but me.

For a fraction of an instant I thought I had ceased to exist myself. But then in the next fraction of the same instant I realized that if I *thought* I had ceased to exist then I existed – that the very thinking of this thought was me.

It's ridiculous telling all this to a philosopher. I had merely discovered what your pupils discover in their first term when they read Descartes. It's taken me twenty years to catch up. Though what came into my mind when I realized wasn't *Cogito, ergo sum*. It was a picture – a picture of a pearl necklace that my mother used to have, which lived inside the little drawer on her dressing-table, in its own special case lined with black velvet. The pearls were artificial and when the string broke they got scattered and lost and forgotten about. But the black velvet case remained in my mother's dressing-table. I used to take it out sometimes, undo the little golden clasp, and run my fingers over the softness of the velvet inside. It seemed to me richer and stranger than the pearls themselves had ever been – and richer and stranger still now that they had gone.

So that for a moment was me – a black receptacle on a black night. Then the external universe began to return. The outermost limits came first – the sky, with a pale shine of overcast through the bare branches of the trees. Then my family; or at any rate the beam of a torch moving about in the kitchen. But what stayed with me all evening was that fraction of an instant when I thought I was dead. I hadn't been frightened, that was what surprised me. I hadn't even been

124

alarmed. It had seemed the most natural thing in the world. Lightness, that was the thing. The lightfootedness with which life comes and goes. The lightheartedness with which one might watch it happen.

Then after dinner we took the candles into the living-room with us. We were three glowing faces and three pairs of shining eyes in a houseful of mad black dancing ghosts. Nobody felt like working. We sat round the piano with the candles in front of our music stands and played one of the trios we know best. Behind Anne I could see another pianist, looming hugely over the wall and ceiling, waiting to turn the pages. Behind Millie a second cellist sawed and fingered in support. I could feel the presence of the dark violinist at my own back, too. And everything I couldn't say, everything I couldn't play, this dark violinist could articulate perfectly.

Halfway through the final allegro the world came into existence again, as quietly and effortlessly as it had gone. We all went on playing without taking our eyes off the music. But Millie gave a little cry of disappointment, and that's what I felt, too.

I have just rung a colleague in the Electricity Division of the Department of Energy. He tells me that the power-cut in south-east London that night began at 7.37 pm, and ended at 9.54 pm. So that was 2 hr 17 min of definite happiness.

Conclusions. I see, on re-reading this minute, that I promised further sections on the weekend and holidays. But this will involve an examination of the whole question of walking for pleasure, which is what we most usually do on these occasions. I realize, now that I think about it, that even our weekend walks in the countryside around London, with their character-istic mixture of dullness and reassurance, are going to take quite a lot of analysis. But the great hikes we undertake on our holidays, usually in the Highlands of Scotland, or some other bleak, wet, cold hill country that I got to know in the days when I used to go climbing by myself (and there's another subject we might discuss!), habitually entail a complex of discomfort, exhaustion, irritation, confusion, sheer misery and intense exhilaration so closely intertwined that I shall have to leave them to be considered on another occasion.

All in all, I think I have said quite enough for one minute.

Indeed, I have said considerably more than enough. I have gone much further than I intended when I set out on this report and am already beginning to regret the substantial breach in normal departmental procedures which this has involved. I think, in the circumstances, I shall not submit this manuscript to Mrs Padmore for typing.

Returning to a more traditional style of presentation, and returning also to the question at issue in the light of the evidence presented above, I should like to offer the following conclusions:

I believe a good case could be made out for saying EITHER:

(a) that, as a man who is happily married, with congenial work and fortunate domestic circumstances, *I am happy*.

OR:

(b) that, as a man whose responses are so dulled by routine that he can recall only 2 hr 17 min of unambiguous happiness in the past few years, *I am not happy*.

I think it unlikely that there is any further evidence which would put the question beyond doubt. What seems to be required now is something more in the nature of a decision.

This decision, if it were not to be entirely arbitrary, would presumably be based upon considerations of style or general policy. It would be, in fact, in the nature of a political decision and as such one which Civil Servants are accustomed to leave to their masters. I think, therefore, that I must ask you for a ruling.

16

I shift this extraordinary document across to the stack of papers I have read, then get up and walk about the room. I am rather shaken, I have to confess.

An audience. That's all he needed for everything to come pouring out. All those words he had hoarded for so long and released so grudgingly. An audience he couldn't see, like the priest beyond the grille, the analyst behind your head. Even Summerchild, in all his discretion.

She has put little red ticks at intervals down the margin, has this unseen audience, as if it were an undergraduate essay. 'Good!' she has written, next to Summerchild's claim to be happily married. 'Yes!' she agrees eagerly, beside his conclusion that the issue needs to be settled by a policy decision. He has offered madness in the form of a minute; she has accepted it in the form of an examination answer.

Outside the window, down in the reasonable world below, the light among the trees in the Park is becoming golden. The week's work is over. People are walking towards their leisure arrangements; taking each other's hands; sitting on the hard, dry grass; beginning the evening together. They are being happy. Being happy and not knowing it yet. Being alive and never quite realizing.

What Summerchild is doing, now he has someone to do it for, is living the last dozen years of his life, which have gone by without his quite taking them in. He's being retrospectively happy. He wasn't anything much at the time. He was *depressed* – I saw him coming slowly up the lane, I heard the reluctance of his words to face the world. And now he realizes that his slowness was a pause for savouring, that his silence was full of unfelt feeling. He makes another leap, now he's started, and sees three particular candle-flames, three particular shadows, all charged with particular feeling. But I know what he saw at the time – three mere candle-flames and three mere shadows. He ate his dinner and said nothing, played his violin and felt nothing, worked when the lights came on again and went to bed without another thought.

And now it all comes bursting out. Happiness. Because I don't take his manoeuvre at the end seriously – his request for guidance. This is afterwards, when he has got up from the couch, when he's making a date for the next appointment and putting on his overcoat in the hall, returning to his ordinary guarded self before he walks out on to the street. Anyway, we've all written minutes offering our masters a choice of options when we and they both know perfectly well there's only one.

Oh yes, he's happy, all right. Now. I suddenly find all those years of dragging footsteps and dragging monosyllables a tiresome indulgence, given the circumstances of his life. He's like a country gentleman who insultingly dissimulates his wealth beneath ragged pullovers and patched elbows, while the rest of us are struggling to conceal our penury beneath well-cut suits we can't afford.

Yes, he's happy, poor devil. He's also becoming slightly deranged. But I imagine this often happens – people are for all practical purposes sane as far as the analyst's door and become mad as they stretch themselves out and explain their sanity. And he's being less than frank. He's talks about States 4 and 5. He says nothing about States 7, 8, 9 and 10. Millie's evidently seen him with the slates coming off the roof and the storm cones flying. How does he feel then?

He's a simple manic-depressive, as Millie could evidently see, and he's talking himself up like a balloon from the safe plains of the depression into the thin, high air of the mania.

He's working himself up to walking into the Admiralty and telling them he's getting messages in his head from Russian submarines. Or that he's happy. Some embarrassed naval intelligence officer sends for Security, perhaps a doctor. His deranged visitor won't stop talking. There is a struggle . . .

No, but it's ridiculous. This is the public service. What imaginable public purpose can be served by all this nonsense? What is Serafin's report going to conclude, on the basis of the evidence submitted here? That everyone ought to live on unsurfaced streets? That we should all fail to maintain our front steps? That we should cut off the electricity and make everyone live in the dark?

I walk up and down the little room again. I am quite unreasonably disturbed by the document I've just read, I realize. I trace part of my feeling to an entirely ridiculous mixture of relief and pique that I don't figure in it myself. My occasional presence at Summerchild's front gate, keeping Millie from her pious labours on the birthday book and obstructing his view of the cracked step, evidently never reached a sufficient level of generality to impinge upon him. But my disturbance goes deeper than this. I can't help feeling a sense of loss and betrayal. Somewhere behind the massive classical forehead of the Cabinet Office a part of the brain has collapsed and failed. In the midst of this complex grey order the room I am sitting in is falling away into chaos and night.

And now I come to think of it the light in here is not what it was. I glance at my watch. Twenty to seven. . . I must get this finished tonight. But my God – Timmy! Cheryl . . .! No – Friday – weekend – Lynn's mother . . .! Phone! Check!

I run down the spiral staircase and along the empty corridor. On either side doors stand open to empty offices. Everyone has left for the weekend. No need to go back to my own phone – I can use one of these. As I dial I become aware of the emptiness of the building beneath me, like a great abandoned liner. Shut away in other odd corners of the vessel, no doubt, are a few more lone souls like myself with work to finish. We could all be happy, too, if we had audiences, if we had private tutors nodding and smiling and ticking our work. We could go all go comfortably demented together . . .

'Hello?' queries my mother-in-law's voice uncertainly, not knowing how to announce herself in someone else's house. I start to apologize for being held up at work. She apologizes as well, because she couldn't find any frozen peas for Timmy's tea and he wouldn't eat the broccoli. I apologize for the lack of peas and for my son's intransigence. She apologizes because there seems to be no hot water coming out of the hot tap. I apologize for whatever's gone wrong. She apologizes because she can't remember where I keep Timmy's clean pants. I apologize for Timmy's needing them . . .

Back upstairs I look out of the window. If I could see the one-eyed god down there now I'd lean out of the window and tell it everything. About Summerchild and his mania. About Timmy and his pants . . . I'd let them know what we were like in here behind our austere surnames and our net curtains. But even the great glass eye has closed for the weekend. I am alone in the world.

17

Mrs Padmore's impersonal Government typescript again – we are into another tutorial. Serafin is plainly taken aback by Summerchild's essay, in spite of her encouragements in the margin. She hadn't, she confesses, been expecting anything so personal or so comprehensive. She is 'astonished', she says, 'impressed', 'grateful', 'deeply interested'. Under this warm rain of *thank yous* and *goods* Summerchild retreats once again into the shelter of odd monsyllables. 'Well . . .' he says. 'Oh . . .' Twice he (*Laughs*) but says nothing.

I am sitting on his box now, in the hope that the hardness of Saxa Salt's cardboard will somehow make a change from the hardness of Lea & Perrins'. So Serafin is leaning eagerly towards me as she compliments me and I have to recognize that, however taken aback she was to read my minute, now we are face to face again the initiative is clearly back in her hands. She goes through the essay line by line, bright-eyed and encouraging about every point in turn. I skim and skip through Mrs Padmore's typescript, conscious of having a long way to go yet before I reach the backyard of the Admiralty and can go home to find what my mother-in-law has left in the oven for me. All the same, I can't help feeling a certain glow of pleasure on Summerchild's behalf. Everything I have written apparently goes to confirm her general thesis that statements about being happy have a strongly performative content . . . One so to speak *names* oneself as happy or unhappy, in the same way that one names a child . . . If one has difficulty in knowing what to say, even after reviewing everything that might count as evidence, as Summerchild says he does at the end of his report, this is precisely because the choice seems largely arbitrary without the context of a purpose, as the choice of a name might, without the example of fashion, or some saintly model, or grandparents to placate.

She has been thinking, she says, about the case they discussed before, of the two people in love who say 'I'm so happy' to each other. Here, she thinks, there is a clearly visible purpose, an intention to reassure. But it seems to be combined with another element – the urge to exclaim, to cry out, which they must examine in due course. They might conclude, she thinks, that this is yet another example of a performative – that it is an *enactment* of rejoicing. But with the difference, presumably, that it is at any rate in part involuntary – that it springs from some kind of internal imperative of its own, which one either feels or does not feel. Summerchild, evidently, when he came to write his conclusions, did not feel it.

What interests her most is his account of the power-cut. 'Because,' she says, 'there you commit yourself, without any difficulty, without any request for a ruling from me, without any special context of purpose, to the view that you enjoyed "2 hr 17 min of unambiguous happiness"'. Can he identify any purpose he felt he was serving with this statement?

I laugh at this. Of course I can identify a purpose, I tell her, sitting here where Summerchild sat. I was boasting. Have you really failed to understand that? I wanted you to think I was a rather more complex and interesting person than you imagined. I wanted to demonstrate it to *myself* – I wanted to demonstrate that I was more interesting than I'*d* imagined. And yes, I was rejoicing. Don't you ever rejoice?

But all Summerchild manages to get out under the gaze of those bright blue Russian eyes is No, he doesn't believe he had any particular purpose . . . Some kind of *need* to cry out, then? Not so far as he can recall . . . The best general explanation he can manage is that he said what he said 'because it was true'.

I imagine a slight puzzlement clouding the candid gaze at this point. Serafin knows, as a philosopher – even *I* know, as a Civil Servant – that the truth of something can't be a *reason* for saying it. I can imagine Kevin Rice's sarcasm, if I'd tried this on him in that first year of his on the philosophy course. Why did Summerchild stop at the power-cut? he would have asked. If truth was a sufficient reason for saying something, why didn't he also tell her the size of his grandmother's shoes, or the distance from Rugby to Reykjavik, or a statistic or two from his old studies of comparability?

Serafin doesn't press him on this, though. She has gone off in a slightly different direction.

'I have to say,' she tells him, 'that I find your account of those two and a quarter hours very moving. But I don't know why. The account you give of them is rather neutral. You list a series of external events and your thoughts about them – but all these events and thoughts might equally well have constituted an account of two and a quarter unhappy hours.

'My first reaction is that these thoughts and events must have been accompanied by some kind of very distinctive inward *feeling*. I suggest this with reluctance because, as I'm sure you can guess from the general drift of my questions, my hope is to keep everything out in the open air, where we can all see it, not locked up in private mental safes. But if there was such a feeling you don't mention it.'

'Well . . .' says Summerchild.

'You may say this is because it's very difficult to put such a feeling into words.'

'I did mention . . .'

'A feeling of lightness, yes. Good. Thank you. But lightness is not in itself happiness. There is no inherent connection, surely, between lightness and happiness. You might use the same word to describe the kind of feelings one has with a high temperature. You might use it to suggest some sense of rootlessness, or insignificance, or ineffectualness.

'It seems to me . . . I don't know how to say this . . . that the

133

happiness is not something extra. The happiness, for you, is somehow an aspect of the flames and the shadows you're seeing and the thoughts you're thinking. This is why you mention them. This is why I sense the happiness from your mentioning them. Happiness is the mode of your perception.'

'Yes,' says Summerchild. Whether he says this dubiously or emphatically, whether sincerely or falsely, feelingly or soothingly, Mrs Padmore does not record. What she does note at this point is twelve dots.

I watch Serafin carefully as these dots tick by. She is looking out of the window – thinking, of course, pursuing her trade. She is also perceiving the redness of the geraniums on the window-sill and the racing whiteness of the ragged April clouds beyond, though in what emotional mode I cannot guess.

'I was thinking about your front step,' she says finally. 'The one with the crack in it. I find your account of that deeply suggestive. I think we have to look at your perception of the flames in the context of your perception of the step. The sense of uniqueness in the flame experience derives from its contrast with the sense of repetitiveness in the step experience. And *that* is rooted in the cyclical nature of your life, with its regular movement between work and home. The location of your work is determined by its collaborative nature and the historical associations which have grown up around it; the location of your home by a combination of social and economic factors . . .

'I'm beginning to see that my very different perception of the world is conditioned not so much by inherent differences of outlook and character as by a different complex of socio-economic factors. If I can isolate no single episode of identifiable happiness in my recent past then this may simply be because of the different nature of my economic activity. I don't make regular journeys to and from a place of work each day. My places of work are scattered – college, various lecture-rooms, libraries. Often workplace and home are the same.

'My work is not cyclical in the sense that yours is . . . I see this surprises you.'

'No, no . . .'

'And it's true that universities keep regular terms. Lectures and tutorials are given according to predetermined timetables. I can only say that I don't *experience* my work as cyclical. Each day brings a bewildering complex of hazards which I have never quite foreseen. Now I'm running out of the house to go to college. Now I'm running back to take Paul to the doctor. Now I remember I have a lecture at eleven. Now I remember I've no food for lunch. Now I remember my lecture-notes are in college . . .

'I never think "This is what I thought at this time yesterday" or "This is what I shall be thinking at this time tomorrow". Yesterday and tomorrow scarcely exist. Today occupies the whole horizon. The next few hours – the next few minutes – running to wherever I am running to at this very moment. Lecture-room – shops – college. College – home – shops – home – back home for whatever I've forgotten . . . x variables, arranged in 2^x permutations.

'I run into my study for half an hour's work. Good. But in my mind I'm running all over the house still. I'm writing about Leibniz in the study – Paul's upstairs, I can hear him practising his electric guitar – no sound of Nicky, which is worrying – Leibniz, Leibniz – Alexander, shouting at Paul to keep the noise down – phone ringing – is that the police saying Nicky's in trouble again? – Leibniz, yes – the sound of the front door quietly opening, which is my husband coming in without disturbing me – must make a hotpot for dinner – will my husband be in for dinner? – and where *is* Nicky? – and somebody's coming for a tutorial, but when? – what am I saying about Leibniz? – the front door softly opening again as my husband goes out without disturbing me . . .'

More dots. Summerchild says nothing. I don't know where he is looking while this distressing outburst is going on. I'm keeping my eyes firmly fixed on Mrs Padmore's typescript. So, I imagine, is Mrs Padmore.

'I find this very painful,' says Serafin suddenly. 'But you have been rather surprisingly candid with me and I have the sense of being under some kind of obligation to repay your confidences in kind.'

Still Summerchild says nothing. Professional embarrassment has apparently overcome even ordinary politeness.

'Another element which reinforces the cyclical nature of your day,' she says, 'seems to be the fairly regular presence of your wife and daughter at home in the evening. My family function more as yet another set of random variables. I find it quite difficult to know how many of them are likely to be in the house at any given moment. Alexander sometimes says whether he's going to be in or not. So does Paul, but his statements don't have any measurable predictive value. Nicky's not usually there to be asked and when he is there he's not usually awake.

'Then there is the question of love. I imagine I feel no less love for my sons than you do for your daughter, if such a profoundly unverifiable comparison can be supposed to have any very definite meaning, but the form which that love takes is almost exclusively anxiety and anguish. Even in the case of Alexander, who does his best to protect me from the others. My worry in his case is about what this loyalty costs him in lost independence. And even with Alexander my feelings don't find expression according to any very fixed timetable.

'My husband frequently passes through the house at some point during the day, but not with any distinguishable regularity, and without any predictability at all, since we have an understanding he is not to be asked questions relating to his future whereabouts.

'Or for that matter questions relating to his past whereabouts. Or to his feelings about me or our children. Or indeed about anyone else, or anything else. Or questions which seem to imply some interest in his general aims or hopes or aspirations. There may be some classes of question to which he responds more warmly, but I have not been able to identify them with any certainty.

'You described the sudden disappearance of your family at the onset of a power-cut. What I recall with similar vividness is the converse – the sudden appearance of my husband when a power-cut ended.

'It was in the hall. I was feeling my way past the bicycles in the darkness, when the darkness disappeared, if one might put it like that, and there instead was my husband, almost as close to me as the darkness had been. I was very taken aback, not so much at finding him in the house, as by his largeness when observed from so close to, by the surprisingly broad section of the visual field that he occupied. I imagine we must have passed quite close to each other on previous occasions. I can only suppose we normally avert our eyes at such moments.

'He, I think, was not unduly surprised to see me. I suppose he had heard me struggling past the bicycles. I imagine he thought that if he said nothing and held his breath I might just possibly struggle past him as well without realizing he was there.

'He was not, in any case, looking at me. He was looking at what he was doing, which was buckling the belt on his raincoat, in preparation, presumably, for going out. So we stood there in a slightly awkward silence. I could not ask him where he was going, or where he had been, or imply a comment upon the frequency of his presence in the house by any expression of surprise at his being there. I felt that the events of my day would be a reasonably neutral subject of conversation, so I told him that the Prime Minister had rung – because, yes, that's when it was. It was the power-cut that started when the Prime Minister was on the phone.

'I remember that he considered my statement quite carefully. He was gazing over my shoulder at the front door by this time. Then he said he would be out that evening. I said I should have to go up to town the next day. I explained that I was going to see the Prime Minister, because he had offered me a job. My husband said he would be out the next day himself.

'And yes, what I felt was the converse of what you felt. You felt a sense of lightness. What I felt was a sense of heaviness, of almost overwhelming heaviness.

'You described yourself as happily married. I should not so describe myself.'

I was right about the home life of the Maitlands, then. But I'm beginning to become a little disconcerted by Summerchild's behaviour. Even this extraordinary confession by Serafin is apparently received in silence. It's not the first time that a Civil Servant has received a personal confidence. We have even, sometimes, had them from our masters. They have on occasion had to inform us of domestic tragedies, have felt free to ask our advice about their marriages and their relations with their children. Not usually in working sessions, it has to be admitted, for transcription by the Secretary and circulation to all interested departments. These things do come bursting out at the most unsuitable moments, though. Standing side by side in the urinals after the meeting. As one is is hurrying away to catch a train. At a moment when one's mouth is too full to reply. I imagine we have coped no less well than any other class of human beings. We have peed manfully on and offered our condolences, just like everybody else. We have given up hope of getting home in time to see our own children and offered fatherly advice about theirs. We have emptied our mouths and opened our hearts.

In this case, anyway, it was Summerchild who bared his soul first. And got the most gratifying response. He must surely have foreseen that he would be offered a glimpse of Serafin's soul in return. He must have been ready with a response of his own.

Not a word.

Or not a word that has been recorded. Yes, perhaps he is registering sympathetic interest in some way that can't be picked up by a microphone. He is looking at her, say. Not out of the window, for once. Not at the floor. Not at the back of his hands. At *her*. Intently. So intently that there is no need for words.

This changes the picture entirely. He is not embarrassed. He is sitting here with his red hair on fire in the April sunshine, and his blue eyes fixed on her blue eyes, and he is *rapt*.

I quickly glance at the rest of the page. I am beginning to feel a profound unease, which her next departure does nothing to relieve.

'The only perceptual experiences I can easily bring to mind which are in any way like yours during the power-cut,' she tells him, 'have occurred in dreams.'

Dreams. Of course. They are going to start telling each other their dreams.

'Sometimes,' she says, 'everything in one's dream seems imbued with a sense of *easiness*. Have you had this experience?'

A direct question. No recorded answer. I assume he nodded.

'I mean a sense that everything is self-evidently for the best. That everything is beneficent and smiling. A sense of . . . yes, of *lightness*. Thank you for introducing this notion into the debate.'

I smile. *He* smiles. I assume he smiles.

'I had a dream of this sort the night before last,' she says. 'I see even as I say it that it may have been in some way a response to reading your account of the power-cut . . . I was at home with my mother and sisters. My mother had a special – I'm not sure how to put this – a sweetness, a softness. I knew she was dead, you see, but I knew it didn't matter. Death was simply like mist on an autumn morning. It looks impenetrable, but one can move through it quite effortlessly. And suddenly one is in front of a building one knows – suddenly the postman or one of the neighbours comes out of the whiteness – and they're strange and familiar all at the same time. Strangely softened and strangely ordinary. It's rather absurd that they've been there all the time, with only this strange white misunderstanding between them and oneself. One could have reached out and touched them. It's as if they were playing hide-and-seek.

139

'Anyway, there she was, after all. We were living in the attics of some great house in the country. The house was full of staircases and I ran up them quite effortlessly, flight after flight, because I knew my mother was at the top and she was pleased with me.

'I had a baby brother and I was being very nice to him. I let him play with all my most precious books and I took him on my knee and put my arms round him. He kept kissing me the way Alexander used to when he was that age – putting his arms around my neck and pressing his lips against mine and laughing. But it wasn't Alexander in my dream. It was my baby brother. I never had a baby brother. He had emerged from the mist as softly and naturally as my mother . . .

'And then it all changed. The sun went in and it started to rain. There was no more lightness in things. I could hear the raindrops on the roof. They were large, bulky raindrops, the shape of shoes and wallets, and they were being put down carefully and quietly all over the tiles of the roof. Some of them fell off the roof and rolled away under the furniture in the garden . . .

'That must have been the money. The small change in my husband's trouser pockets. Because when I woke up he was crawling around the bedroom floor in the dark. I could just see the gleam of his shirt-tails. He had no trousers on. He was picking up coins and doing it very quietly, so as not to wake me.'

Twelve more dots. And Summerchild? No comment. So on she goes.

'I don't think I can be as precise as you about how long my experience had lasted. I assume, from the studies that psychologists have made of dreaming by measuring eye-movement, that it was only a few minutes. It can't have started before 12.35, when I shut my book and put the light out, and it must all have been over by about one . . . At least, I imagine it was no later than one. Why do I imagine that? I think because of my husband's tone of voice, when he heard me moving about. There was a slightly reproachful edge to it.

Also – yes – the choice of words. I think he said, "You're still awake, then." When it's noticeably after one the tone is more solicitous. And the wording changes. He tends to say, "Don't wake up."

'I should make clear that these are only approximate times. It's difficult to check them against the alarm clock, because that involves switching on the dial-light, and that has obvious analogies with asking my husband the time, which I assume to be excluded under our understanding about questions relating to his past and future whereabouts ... ...'

Yes, twelve more dots. And then, at last, Summerchild speaks.

'I'm sorry,' he says.

For seven long pages he has been listening to the recital of her wretchedness. For seven long pages he has been restraining himself from crying out, offering advice, running to her side. Then for twelve long dots he has been cogitating his reply. Now it all comes bursting out. 'I'm sorry,' he says. I think one must assume, in all fairness, that what he lacks in loquacity he makes up in sheer intensity. And her rejoinder is even shorter:

'Oh ... ...'

I imagine this 'Oh' is accompanied by some kind of shrug, a wave of the hand. She has shrugged off his sympathy as unnecessary – has brushed aside her feelings as of no consequence – has dismissed her entire experience of life.

And on they sit through those next twelve dots. The April sun comes and goes at the window. Rain falls and ceases. A few floors below, in the front part of the building where the Cabinet Office works, the staff of the Joint Intelligence Secretariat struggles to promote the secret subversion of the world without and to control the counter-subversion of the world within, unaware of the even more covert undermining going on beneath their own eaves. In Oxford Paul opens a fresh packet of plectra, Nicky sleeps, Ted Maitland creeps in and out of the house, for once unheard by his absent wife. In Greenwich Anne pastes another aspect of Summerchild into

141

her book, Millie stands outside their house on her way home from school, looking out over London and the distant towers of Whitehall, with me beside her, looking at the weeds growing out of the crack on the third step.

Then Summerchild stirs (I imagine), sighs (perhaps), and says very simply, without qualification or preamble:

'I should say that happiness is being where one is and not wanting to be anywhere else.'

'Yes,' says Serafin. 'I believe it is. Thank you.'

This brings them to the bottom of the page. I wait for a moment before I turn over, my heart somehow both sinking and rising at the prospect of where this exchange is plainly leading.

'No!' I want to tell them. 'No more! No further! Stop there!'

'Yes!' I want to urge them. 'Go on! Don't stop now!'

I turn the page.

Nothing.

No more pages. That was the end of the transcript.

18

So, good God, they'd hearkened to my advice and stopped there! Not uttered another word. Realized that somehow, rather suddenly and unexpectedly, they'd hit upon the answer to the question which had been asked. Understood in a flash, without any need to say so, that they'd solved the problem and completed the first phase of the Unit's work. Very sensibly decided, without wasting another word or another minute, to wind up the session and go home. Concluded their investigations for good, even. Had seen nothing left to do but write the report and wait for the New Year Honours List.

Or else they'd hearkened to my advice and *not* stopped there. Had seen where the conversation was leading and discreetly switched off the tape-recorder. Or, rather more plausibly, since the text ended at the bottom of a page, forgotten all about the tape-recorder, then removed the remaining pages from the transcript later, when they saw what was in them.

Well, let's have a look at the next document on the tag. Will it be the final report, or simply the minute of the next session, with their professional aplomb recovered and everything back to normal – or at any rate back to what passes for normal in this small mad corner of Government history? Or have things got beyond that point . . .? I pull the next document round from the back of the stack.

It's not a minute. It's a memorandum, a single sheet with two brief paragraphs of text on it which I seem to have read before. Yes – I saw it when I first opened the file.

FROM: Clerical Supervisor, Personnel

TO: Secretary, Strategy Unit, and Director, Economic Secretariat

DATE: April 18th 1974

With effect from today's date Mrs L Padmore will be transferring from the Strategy Unit to the Economic Secretariat.

A replacement Clerical Officer for the Strategy Unit will be appointed in due course.

I turn back to the previous minute. It is dated April 17th, the day before. Yes. I think I see what happened.

What I think I see is Mrs Padmore coming in to work in the room downstairs on the eighteenth. She puts her handbag down beside her swivel chair, then hangs up her raincoat and folding umbrella and rubs her hands. It's mid-April, so she unbuttons her dark green cardigan and loosens the silk scarf her sister gave her for Christmas, but it's still not very warm in the office and she decides not to take them off altogether. She sits down at her desk and finds a bundle of cassettes held together with a rubber band which have been left in her in-tray overnight. She rubs her hands again, and sighs, and puts on her headset. The pages begin to emerge from her typewriter. Summerchild looks round the door for a moment, on his way in to work in the room upstairs. He nods and smiles. She nods and smiles back. Apart from that her face is expressionless. Is she thinking about the life she is transcribing, with the three graceless sons and the faithless philosopher in the loveless house in North Oxford, or is she thinking about her own life, childless but content, with the loyal Local Government Officer in West Norwood? Every now and then she stops typing, and waits, and leans forward to press the fast-forward button. Then she types a row of full stops.

As she comes to the end of page . . . yes, page seven . . . she begins to frown. She seems a little anxious about something. She winds the finished page out of the machine and reads it through. Then she adds it to the stack on the desk and winds the next sheet of paper into the machine. 'Page 8', she types in the top righthand corner and presses the foot-switch.

But after she has typed the first few words she stops. She gazes silently into space, listening consciously for the first time to the little world inside her ears. She frowns again. I believe she even flushes. Is it embarrassment, or is it anger at being caused embarrassment? What's going on in there? My imagination is running riot.

Abruptly she pulls the headset off and stops the tape-recorder. She buttons up her dark green cardigan and tucks in the silk scarf her sister gave her for Christmas. Then she picks up her handbag, collects her coat and umbrella from the stand, and goes off to see the Clerical Supervisor . . .

So Mrs Padmore's gone and the transcript has stopped at the bottom of page seven. But then what happened? In due course, presumably, as promised by the Supervisor, the new Clerical Officer was appointed. She arrived, put her bag down beside the swivel chair, etcetera etcetera, unbuttoned the dark blue cardigan her mother had knitted for her birthday, etcetera etcetera, put on the headset, ran the tape back to find her place, then took off the headset again to introduce herself to Summerchild when he arrived for work. Smiles, nods, a short discussion of the weather and the upkeep of the potted plants, brief mutual demonstrations of agreeableness. Then the new Clerical Officer put her headset back on, listened to what came next on the tape – and promptly walked out in her turn. In due course another Clerical Officer was appointed, and so on . . . And out they all walked, one after another, without ever managing to complete page eight . . .

No, of course not. Summerchild had quietly withdrawn the offending tape by this time and the new Clerical Officer had set to work on transcribing the next session instead. I reach automatically round the back of the stack to find it . . . But there's nothing there. The memorandum is the final document on the tag.

I put the file together with all the other material I have accumulated in the course of my investigation and look in the Squeez-Ee box for the continuation file. No sign of it. Was there a slip at the end of the first file saying where it was continued . . .? No.

One by one I open all the cardboard boxes in the room, and scatter the files across the floor. It's eight o'clock and down at floor level the low red evening light shining straight across the room from the windows above my head is making it curiously difficult to see. I crawl round on my hands and knees, peering at the title on every single file. Time and tiredness have reduced me to the posture of some nocturnal animal snuffling through the garbage in the twilight. Grunting slightly, I crawl round again, rechecking the titles and snouting clumsily through the contents they describe. I am a very stupid animal, condemned to go backwards and forwards over the same ground, without system or certainty.

Still nothing. And suddenly hunger and weariness descend upon me. It's half past eight and I haven't eaten since I lunched off that single sandwich at my desk. I have been sustained by being on the point of finding the answers to all my questions. Now I can't even stay on all fours. I collapse on the floor and sit in the middle of the chaos I've created, sulking like Timmy. All my efforts and I've got nowhere. Mid-April, with another two months to go before Summerchild's death, and I've come to the end of the written record. I hurl empty boxes and files about the unforthcoming room.

I can't think any more. What have these tiresome idiots done? Have they wound themselves up at the end of their notorious session on the seventeenth? Without even writing a report? Or has someone been through these files already and destroyed them? Tite, perhaps? The Security Division? Maybe the great glass eye has somehow got here before me . . . Or Summerchild himself . . .

I lie down on the floor, pillow my head on a heap of buckled minutes and close my eyes. I have a curious feeling of being watched. I open my eyes and, yes, they're both watching me. She is smiling and leaning forward, eager to encourage me in the pursuit of knowledge. He is leaning back, his head half turned away, profoundly sceptical. He does not believe I am going to achieve that knowledge.

Well, I'll have one more go and then I'll give up. Perhaps I missed a folder somewhere . . . One lot of papers tucked inside another lot . . . It's madness, of course. I know there's nothing here. I'm exhausted. I don't know what I'm doing . . .

Stop. Wait. Take a break. Make myself another cup of that delicious tea-dust.

I switch the lights on. Under the bare bulbs the ruins of the room look like the aftermath of some shameful party. I retreat into the little cloakroom in the corner and light the gas under the kettle. Opening the cupboard to find another teabag I'm almost tempted to try the eatables. A bowl of cock-a-leekie soup, perhaps, or a spoonful of mustard – even a few of the mouldy cornflakes. I give the biscuit tin a forlorn shake – and it rattles most hearteningly. When I open it . . . out they come tumbling. Chocolate wafers. And they're not mouldy – they're not even soft. They're crisp and dark . . .

And made of plastic. With two neat holes and a little window in each one. And with labels on them, written in Summerchild's neat hand: 23/5/74 . . . 4/6/74 . . . 29/5/74 . . .

Tapes. Dozens of them.

I pick them up and put them down, looking at the dates. I have the final missing two months in my hands. I also have an odd sensation in my stomach. A shock of elation, perhaps. Or just a pang of frustrated hunger, of disappointment that they're not after all chocolate wafers.

Then I realize that I have no access here to a tape-recorder. I'm going to have to take the tapes home to play. I'm going to be spending the entire weekend on them. *Listening* to them. Listening to two awkward middle-aged clowns falling distastefully in love with each other.

Yes, I feel quite sour about it, now the element of uncertainty has been removed. I have found what I was looking for, and getting what one wants is a notoriously fallible source of happiness. As these two moulting lovebirds are doubtless about to discover.

I am tempted to put the tapes back in the biscuit tin and ask for a transfer, like Mrs Padmore.

19

'I once started whistling at a meeting with the Minister of Agriculture.'

Summerchild's voice! Suddenly, out of nowhere! Or rather, out of the loudspeakers in my own living-room. Obscurely ashamed and flustered, I rush to turn the volume down before Timmy or my mother-in-law walk in. I put my head close to the loudspeaker; I have no other way of playing the tapes.

'It was a phrase from the B flat trio. We were talking about the effects of metrification on poultry feed suppliers. It suddenly seemed to me that Schubert had said everything there was to be said on the subject and said it far better than I ever could.'

The voice comes back to me at once from those few forgotten remarks in the lane in 1974. It still sounds as if it has been fetched up from some source deep in the London gravel-beds. But the flow seems somewhat faster than I remember it, and – yes, this is what's changed – the water is no longer still and dark; it has a suggestion of effervescence in it.

'It was only the one phrase. No mention was made of it in the minute of the meeting.'

I can imagine what's happened. Serafin has started asking him about the higher states on Millie's scale. By the time she has remembered that this might constitute evidence in their inquiry, and turned on the tape-recorder, his recollections of

149

past gusts and gales have set the anemometer spinning again.

Here she is herself with recollections of her own. 'When I look back over my own experiences at the upper end of the register what I chiefly recall are moments of complete absorption in some conceptual problem. But the pleasure there was precisely my *unawareness* of my feelings – indeed, the loss of all sense of self.'

Her voice is warm, full and considered, but curiously brisk. It seems almost as unsurprising as his, as if all those pages of flying typescript had been somehow audible.

Timmy comes in. 'Daddy, Daddy,' he says, pulling at my sleeve. Now Summerchild has remembered an incident when Millie was younger and they saw a river-boat about to pull away from Greenwich Pier. Without the slightest idea where it was going he picked her up and jumped aboard at the last moment, because he was overcome by a sudden conviction that they should be going there, too. 'Daddy, Daddy,' says Timmy. 'What is it?' I ask, my head still close to the loud-speaker. 'Daddy, Daddy,' he says absently. I realize, from his abstraction, that he is listening to Summerchild as well. Slowly Summerchild discovers that he is aboard an office outing from the local Electricity Board and that it's going to be three hours before they can get off again. Timmy starts to cry. He's frightened, I realize; something about the voice has made him think of his mother. I switch off the tape and take him upstairs to play our weekly game of clearing up his room together.

By the time I can slip back into the living-room I am becoming as desperate as an illicit lover myself. The first of the tapes in the biscuit tin is dated mid-May; I still don't know what provoked the departure of the clerical staff. All the rest of the story, however, must be contained within this one tin box – if only I can manage to hear it. I switch on again. Summerchild's gales seem to have blown themselves out. I fast-forward hungrily and try another section. Still no words. But some kind of sounds in the background . . . small strangely remote and disconnected thumps and sliding noises. I bend close to the speakers, unable to imagine what's going on in that little room.

'Oh . . .' says an unrecorded voice.

I straighten up guiltily. My mother-in-law is hovering uncertainly in the doorway.

'I'm sorry,' she says, 'you're listening to your records.'

'No, no,' I say, 'it's just work.'

'Only it's the hot water again,' she says. 'I don't want to disturb you if you're listening to your records.'

'I've actually got a bit of work to do,' I say. She hesitates in the doorway. We are both listening to recorded footsteps going away across a room, then a door opening.

'They do keep you at it, don't they?' says my mother-in-law, still hesitating, reluctant to give up all hope of hot water.

'Do you mind if we take your skirt down?' says Summerchild suddenly.

I switch the machine off. 'I'm sorry,' I say.

'I'm sorry,' says my mother-in-law, leaving the room at once.

I should go after her and explain. Make clear, as soon as I have listened long enough to discover it myself, that Serafin's skirt has got wet in the rain, has been hung up over the sink to dry, and is in Summerchild's way as he prepares the lunch. Make her understand the simple directness of Serafin's action, the mere practicality of Summerchild's suggestion, the innocent forgetfulness which has left their little electronic eavesdropper still alert to hear all this.

I don't, though. I can't explain this without explaining how they have reached this intimate naturalness in the first place, this unthinking ease with each other. Because the very innocence of every syllable proclaims their complicity. How on earth, I wonder, now that I hear them through someone else's ears, have these two improbable candidates managed to fall in love with each other? What, as people ask in exasperation on these occasions, do they *see* in each other?

Perhaps, I think, as I listen to Serafin telling Summerchild about her father and his death, the question is not what people see in each other, but what they come to see in themselves. After all the years of silence, suddenly you're face to face with someone who has to be told about your life, and, as you tell it, as your listener listens, as he smiles and nods and exclaims upon the similarities and differences in his own life, you begin to hear the story yourself, you begin to glimpse your own shape and nature.

Saturday afternoon is visiting-time, of course. I resort to Serafin's solution and borrow my son's tape-recorder. I put it in the boot of the car with the tin of tapes. I have some confused idea that I will slip out of the ward at some point, leaving Joyce and Timmy with Lynn, and pursue my researches undisturbed for half an hour in the car park. It occurs to me when we get there that the car might be stolen while we are away, and all hope of my investigations with it, so I take the biscuit tin in with me. This means that I have to hold it all the time I'm talking to Lynn, because I realize that if I put it down on the dayroom table she will think I have brought it for her. As I tell her brightly about what Timmy has said and done during the week, and about the amusing problems with the hot water, and the heartwarming progress of summer through the garden, so far as I have noticed it, I find the tin moving bulkily about in the air between us, rattling with each move. Her eyes follow it with that dull fixity she sometimes devotes to inanimate objects in the room while some animate subject is trying to communicate with her. And when my budget of domestic news is exhausted and the tin has sunk back on to the arm of my chair, I find I'm gazing at it as well. I suppose Lynn is thinking about the biscuits inside and their forbidden sweetness (the staff are now making great efforts to control her weight problem, even if they can't control anything else). I suppose I'm thinking about the same. As I sit there, in the depressing cheerfulness of the dayroom, with nothing left to say to Lynn, and nothing much of Lynn left to say it to, I am suddenly overwhelmed, as Timmy is, by the sheer unfairness of things. *I* might have been forgiven, I think, if I'd found someone else – someone I could talk to from time to time about some subject apart from Timmy and the boiler and the aubrietia by the front gate. Someone who would give signs of hearing what I said. Someone who might look at me as I spoke, perhaps nod from time to time, even smile – even on occasion venture some reply. I should not have occasioned too much disapprobation in the department, I think, if I had furnished each coming day, each coming week, with some tender friend whom I could look forward to seeing without this sick dread, this leaden hopelessness. If I had set up a temporary home in some small unconsidered corner of my life.

But I hadn't done it – hadn't even imagined doing it. It was Summerchild who'd hidden those sweet biscuits in the tin. The man whose life was complete already. The man with the innocent red hair and the tactfully manifested mania to vary his tactfully manifested depression. I'd known from the first what was going to happen. From the moment I'd set their two faces opposite each other and seen the way she gazed and smiled, the way he smiled and half turned. I could have written most of my report then. I'd refused to admit it to myself, that's all. I hadn't wanted to believe that someone in the same, yes, *priesthood* as myself had behaved with such dull dishonour. Walking slowly up the lane in the evening, with his violin case in his hand – and all the time he was shutting his inmost self away in an old tin at the back of a cupboard in some forgotten garret. In *this* tin, that I am balancing on the flaking bentwood arm of the dayroom chair, that Lynn's gaze and mine are resting on with such absent intentness.

I stand up and say I'll send her mother and Timmy in for a bit. Her eyes follow the tin as it moves tantalizingly away towards the door, with all the sweetness of the world still shut away inside it. 'What?' I say, smiling disingenuously, 'This? This is just an old tin. Just work.' She turns her face away and looks at the wall. We have achieved some communication, after all. I have held the sweetness of the world in front of her, then taken it away again, and she has understood.

As soon as Joyce and Timmy have gone in I hurry back towards the car with my tin of sickly poison. But I'm stopped in the corridor by an old woman in her nightgown. She puts her hand on my arm and gazes blindly into my eyes, shaking and stinking and saying nothing. I back away and she follows me, clinging on to my arm, mute and blind and I think lost. I have to edge her towards a ward and find some member of the staff to take responsibility for her. So that by the time I'm back in the car park I'm hurrying and fumbling and I put the tape into the machine with the wrong side playing. A most extraordinary sound comes out. A voice – but not a man's voice, not a woman's voice. A high unearthly voice. Speaking, but not speaking words. Not talking about happiness or its childhood or the state of its front steps. Keening. Howling. Jumping thirds and octaves.

Music. Of course. Horsehair on catgut, speaking with piercing and slightly wavering poignancy about everything and nothing. A solo violin, to be precise, being played well but not quite well enough, struggling with something just a little too difficult. There is a lot of scrapy double-stopping which is not quite on either note. One of the Bach partitas, I think.

So this is the kind of contribution Summerchild is making to the debate by – I look at the label – May 13th. This is the department's view of the quality of life. The playing gets worse and teeters to a stop. There is a hollow knock as the instrument is put down on a hard surface, followed by what sounds like a sigh.

What view will Serafin take of this submission? Will she accept it? Reject it? Redraft it, for piano and woodwind?

The sigh is followed by various tiny indistinct sounds. I turn up the volume on Timmy's machine and hold it close to my ear. Inaudibly, beyond the windscreen, in the car parked in front of mine, a woman with a hopeful hairstyle and a disappointed face is explaining something infinitely long and painful to a man sitting with bowed head. Invisibly, beyond the plastic cover of the loudspeaker next to my ear, Summerchild is putting the violin back in its case . . . closing the lid . . . sitting down . . . while Serafin says nothing.

The back door of the car is flung open and Timmy clambers in, shouting rudely at his grandmother and indignantly snatching back his tape-recorder, which I have put down on the seat beside me with obscurely guilty haste. My mother-in-law gets in beside him, apologizing to me for his behaviour. I rebuke Timmy. Timmy shouts rudely back at me. My mother-in-law apologizes to both of us. There is another sound, too, as if someone in the car is sawing wood. Sawing once – in/out – then resting. In/out. Rest . . . 'What?' says Timmy, suddenly uneasy, as the other sounds in the car die away. We all listen. In/out. Rest . . . There is something horribly disturbing about it and I suddenly realize what we are listening to. It is the sound of breath being convulsively drawn and then at once convulsively released; the sound of a woman sobbing. I take the tape-recorder out of Timmy's uneasy hands and remove the tape. 'Someone at work,' I say.

By the time evening comes and Timmy is out of the way at last, I find myself moving restlessly through the house with the biscuit tin in my hands, full of twitching irritations and buzzing anxieties. How am I going to be able to write my report by Monday morning if I can't listen to the tapes? I am looking madly for somewhere to play them in peace. I keep opening cupboards and pulling down the suitcases on top of wardrobes, difficult though it is to imagine that I shall find a place for myself in a cupboard or a suitcase – until at last, under the bed in the spare room, I find a battered black leather box with a round bulge at one end, and I realize that this is what I was looking for all the time. I open it up and there, in its fusty-smelling blue velvet bed, is the dulled but still eloquent brass gleam. My trombone. I haven't played it since I left the local schools orchestra.

I assemble the pieces, and bend my lips into their old established pout at the mouthpiece. A little shakily at first, the great grunting brass voice speaks out, mine but not mine, me but not me, awakening the dead, and strange awkward brass vibrations in my lips and fingers and brain. I stop and put the mute on, but before I have played a full scale the door has opened a crack and Timmy has squeezed through in his pyjamas, gazing unsmilingly at this strangely transfigured father. I play 'Silent Night' to him, inappropriately enough, gazing at him no less solemnly over my unsmiling embouchure, then 'Almighty, Invisible, God Only Wise', and 'O Worship the King'. Nothing but hymn-tunes comes to mind, for some reason. I play flat, I miss notes altogether, but the dark tide of sound rises around us both with increasing strangeness, until I suddenly realize that Timmy is crying. He is afraid of it, and afraid of me.

I'm in a slightly strange state myself, and after I have calmed Timmy and coaxed him back to bed I don't know where to put myself. I fetch metal polish and start to clean the trombone. At once the acreage of dull brass seems to stretch out in front of me for ever and I abandon the cleaning and start to put the instrument away. But even the fiddle of taking it to pieces is suddenly more than I can bear. I leave it in bits on the bed in the spare room and go back to the living-room with the box of tapes. But of course my mother-in-law is in there already, jumping up guiltily from in front of the guiltily whispering television. I apologize – I don't know what for. *She* apologizes – neither of us knows what for. I run out of the house.

What's going on? How can I be walking about the streets in the warm summer twilight like this, full of strange electric unease, as if I were seventeen again, poised on the edge of some great abyss? I should have taken the car and Timmy's tape-recorder, and found myself a quiet car park to work in . . . I turn left . . . right . . . right again . . . Every garden I pass is overflowing with the sweet reek of summer. Where are my legs walking me to? The streets fall away behind me. I am emerging on to the great common that crowns the South London hills here. In the dry warmth of the evening the vast tableland of mown grass, criss-crossed by sparkling streams of distant car-lights, seems like a kind of urban high veld. Up in the great gentleness of the sky a bright star is approaching from the south, two more from the north. One after another they change direction overhead, murmuring easily to themselves now, and head down towards their Bethlehem in the golden west. I follow them, then keep close to the park wall at the edge of the plain where it turns back to the north, and walk beneath trees as gravely still as only living things can be. Now the ground is dropping sharply away in front of me, as I start down the scarp on the London side of the tableland. The well-known landscape of lights and towers opens at my feet . . .

And this plainly is where I'm going – Hyde Hill Lane, halfway down the hillside. I slowly walk the length of it, glancing at the Summerchilds' house as I pass. The curtains seem to be drawn; there is nothing but blackness beyond the glass. At the far end of the lane, where it joins the road climbing the hill from the station, I come to a halt. I look up the road – I look down the road. I have suddenly no idea where to go next. The internal auto-pilot that has got me here with so little conscious thought seems to have closed down.

So I turn round and walk back up the lane. I slow down as I pass the house this time, since there's no one in, and take a good look at the steps up to the front door. The third step *is* cracked, it's true – the whole surface of the step on this side of the crack has now broken up – and there are further cracks in the first, fourth and fifth steps.

At the upper end of the lane I stop again. I suppose I'm going back home, am I? But before I can decide I find that I have turned round and started to walk back down the lane. A strange thing to do. And when I get to the lower end I turn round yet again and come back up.

I find all this rather ridiculous. But there is worse to come. Five times I walk up the lane. Five times I walk down it. I have the feeling that control has somehow passed out of my hands. Five times I stop at the upper end of the lane and know that I am free to continue towards the open heath and home. Know that I could do it – *can* do it. Should do it – *will* do it. But don't. Turn round instead and walk back down the lane, laughing at this strange helplessness, shocked at it, alarmed at it, humiliated by it.

I know perfectly well by this time, of course, what I am up to. I am happening to be here when Millie comes along. I am happening to be walking along the lane just as she leaves the house, or comes back to it. I can be certain about my motivation here because I am an expert on the subject – I have happened up and down this lane ten thousand times before. But that was when I was seventeen! How have I got back here in adulthood, sauntering with this same insane casualness, stumbling over these same unevennesses in this same darkness, with this same knot in my stomach? I'm a grown man now! I could ring the bell! 'Hello!' I could say easily. 'I suddenly remembered that this was where . . . Suddenly thought I hadn't seen you for . . . Suddenly realized it was you I saw the other night . . . Suddenly wondered . . . Suddenly felt . . .'

I don't ring the bell, though. For the very good reason that there is obviously no one at home. They've gone away for the weekend. They're on holiday. It's a waste of time ringing the bell – it's simply more reasonable behaviour to happen to be passing. So, one last saunter up the lane . . . One last saunter down the lane . . . Up . . . Down . . . There seems to be no good reason why I should stop after the fifth time, if I didn't after the fourth. None for stopping after the twenty-fifth time, or the seventy-fifth. The more saunters I invest in the project, in fact, the more reason there is for investing just one more to recoup my investment.

And indeed, on my fifth trip down the lane I hear footsteps behind my back, and when I turn, there she miraculously, unbelievably, naturally, obviously, disappointingly is. I had expected her to be coming up the lane, back from the walk with the dog that I last saw her departing on – back from the station, like me or her father. But she is coming down it from the heath, the way I have come, the way she always used to come on her way home from school. There's no dog with her; she's coming from some part of her life I can't even guess at. Her face is shadowed by the single street lamp that is lighting the fuzz of hair around her head. I wait for her to catch me up. I don't pretend surprise – I don't need to. 'Hello,' I say, perfectly naturally. 'Hello,' she replies, no more surprised than I am. It's the easiest thing in the world.

We walk down the lane side by side. Conversation comes to me out of the deep reserves that age has provided – questions about what she is doing these days, and how her mother is, and whether she still sees various people whose names appear effortlessly inside my head again after all these years. She is working as an archivist for the local council, she says; her mother now suffers rather badly from arthritis; and no, she hasn't seen any of the people I've mentioned.

We get to her house. She stops. I stop. She looks up at the darkened windows of the house.

'I'm afraid my mother's away,' she says. I feel the promise of the empty house lurch through my heart, then understand that what she is telling me is that I am not to be invited in. So then I think: But she had *thought* of inviting me in! Which is a mile further than my own thinking had advanced! Then I think: None of these thoughts has any relation to anything in the objective world at all. And then I think: At any rate we are still standing here.

'I think I saw you as I passed the other night,' I say.

'Yes,' she says, after a very slight pause, 'I saw you.'

We are standing as motionless in the still summer night as the leaves on the trees. It is fifteen years since we stood here last.

'I'm sorry about your wife,' she says. I say nothing. I am thinking: So she has been hearing about me and not forgetting what she has heard. I have been in her thoughts.

'Yes,' I say. 'It's sad.'

And still we stand. Millie is looking at the ground. I am looking at the broken steps. This is the house I have been reading about; this is the lane. They have an intense, palpable reality that my own house and my own street have never achieved. So, it seems to me, does Millie. I have been reading about her, too, of course. About the secret smiles, that I have never seen. About the secret contribution she was making to her mother's book. (Yes, and what happened to that? Did her father read it before he died?) About the mad dark cellist at her back, that she herself never saw.

'Do you still play?' I ask.

She lifts her eyes and looks at me, frowning, unable for a moment to understand the question. 'Oh,' she says. 'No. I gave it up.'

A long time ago, evidently. Yes, of course. At the same time as she gave up the orchestra, at the same time as she gave everything up – when her father died. I have led us straight into the very subject that I now at once realize we must avoid. Her feelings about it plainly went to the roots of her life, and may do still. I remember my disappointment at the rehearsal she failed to come to. I remember walking up the lane afterwards and climbing these steps, to find out why. Her mother opened the door, but made no move to invite me in. She said something about Millie being unwell, about her giving up orchestra for a while. And I knew from the way she said this, from the fixed and unforthcoming look on her face, that there was something deeply wrong here, something that couldn't and wouldn't be talked about.

I called once or twice after that, but it was always her mother who answered the door. Millie was unwell, she was out, she was busy. She had turned her face away; it was all part of the great inscrutable awkwardness of death. So this is the first time since then that I've spoken to her. Too late to offer conventional expressions of sympathy now. Anyway, what could I say about it without disingenuousness? I can't tell her that I am engaged on retracing her father's steps through those last months of his life, that I have discovered the madness that had entered his blood.

Nor can I tell her that I have caught his madness, that the spores of it have remained alive in the files, like the spores of anthrax in the earth – that this, ridiculously, is why I am here talking to her again in the vertiginous stillness of the summer's night.

We continue to stand there in our silence. In a moment she will nod and smile, and say it was nice to see me again, and turn towards her door; and I shall nod and smile, and mention the possibility that we might run into each other again somewhere. Then I shall go on down the lane and our meeting will be over. But for the moment she is content to stand and look out over the lights of London above the houses on the other side of the lane. She doesn't want to end the moment, I realize, any more than I do. And we *shall* run into each other again. Oh, yes. I shall be strolling up this lane and strolling down it. Nothing good will come of all this, however. I can see that perfectly clearly. I shall always have one hand behind my back, holding the tin full of knowledge that I am hiding from her.

Now all the final nods and smiles have been exchanged. She is climbing the steps to her front door, I am continuing down the lane. I have a curious feeling of . . . elation? No, not elation. Peace, I think. *Stability*. A feeling of being set upon some course, and of being kept to it by a navigational system which some other hand than mine has programmed.

I am also starting to wonder about that day when I called to ask why Millie hadn't been at rehearsal. In my memory I can see the reporters waiting in the lane. But in my memory they are seen from a distance, not all round me as I go up the steps. And waiting is all they are doing. They are waiting for the door to open and someone to appear. Why are they standing so idle, when I am walking up the steps in front of them and ringing the bell – when the person they want to interview, the widow herself, is opening the door to talk to me?

There were no reporters the day I called. The day I saw the

161

reporters here was another day altogether. I saw the reporters and did not call. I have run two different occasions together in my memory. How strange.

So I saw the reporters here and went away again. Then I called the following week, after the next rehearsal . . . But, as I make my way back on to the heath and head for home I realize that this doesn't make any sense at all. If I knew Millie's father had just died I shouldn't have had to guess from her mother's manner that there was something wrong – I shouldn't have had to come round and ask.

So I suppose it must have been earlier, before her father died. I stop and stand still for a moment in the dark emptiness of the open heath. Her father was found dead on the Monday morning. I must have seen the reporters in the lane after the rehearsal on the Tuesday. And I must have called to ask where she was after some rehearsal during the previous week.

Yes, she gave up the orchestra, gave up the cello, gave up me – gave up everything, as I now realize – the week before her father died.

20

Each candidate has a white label on his forehead. This is the point. The labels could be white or black, but in fact they are all white. This the whole *point* of the thing.

I know this perfectly well every time I have my eyes open. Which I do now, at – what time? – 2.34 am. I can remember the whole puzzle perfectly well! There are three candidates for the job. The rule is that you have to put up your hand if you can see at least one white label on the other two candidates' foreheads, then put your hand down as soon as you have deduced the colour of the label on your own. Now, the first candidate says to himself, 'Suppose the label on my forehead was black. Then each of the other candidates would say to himself, "Suppose the label on *my* forehead was black . . ."'

But my eyes must have closed again, because what I am supposing is that the label on my forehead is red. Now, if the label on my forehead is red, then Summerchild says to himself, 'Suppose the hair on my head was red . . .' No, if my hair is red, and Summerchild's hair is red, then Serafin looks at us and says to herself, 'Suppose my hair is red, then Millie would look at us and say to herself, "Suppose my hair is red . . ."'

Because all three of us are red-haired. This is the point. I can see it perfectly clearly now I am awake. Summerchild, Serafin, Millie – all three of us! This is the wit of the thing . . .

Someone is stroking my red beard, trying to find out who's behind it . . . It's Timmy, leaning against the edge of the bed, woken by a bad dream. I get up and take him back to his

163

room, then sit stroking his red hair until one or the other of us has gone back to sleep . . .

I get back into my own bed. The point is that you *raise your hand* if you can see someone else with red hair. Serafin raises her hand. Summerchild raises his violin. I raise my trombone. I begin to play with great pleasure. The secret, I discover, is in the long, regular strokes of the slide. I laugh as I play – it's so easy and so delightful. The sunlight flashes on the bell of the instrument. It swells in the lovely warmth, and pulses, and melts, and all the sweetness in the world comes bursting out . . .

I am wide awake as I get out of bed this time, and the appallingly cosy warm wetness around my shrinking genitals turns soberly chill as the night air strikes it. I look very levelly at myself in the bathroom mirror as I wait for the water to run warm, and the same old face I went to bed with looks levelly back at me. My beard is trim and grey again, not wild and red. I think we are both shocked and surprised, my face and I. This hasn't happened to us for a number of years. What's going on? The great muddle of the world, the great muddle of the past, is reaching out for us, reaching into us, and we don't like it.

My face has stopped looking at me, though, I realize. I think it's thinking about something else. About how insidious, how overpowering, how irresistible that forgotten sweetness for one moment was.

Back in bed, I find that calm has returned, as unannounced and unexplained as the confusion earlier. I lie quite still for the rest of the night, wide awake, with my thoughts crossing my mind in quiet good order. I think about the rehearsals of the local schools orchestra. I try to recall that first rehearsal Millie was not at. But all I can remember is knocking on her door afterwards. I move back to the rehearsal before, the last one she came to. If I had known then that it was going to be the last time I should see her for fifteen years I should have fixed it in my mind, but I didn't. So I go back to the beginning of the year's rehearsals. From my seat high up among the boys in the brass at the back, I look down on the girls in the strings, all wriggling and giggling under our gaze; see for the first time the quiet ginger fuzz bent over a cello; contrive the first look at her face; first follow her wordlessly home; speak the first word ('Are you going this way?') . . .

Then I wake up and the bedroom is full of effortless Sunday sunshine. In my head, as easy and self-explanatory as the sunshine itself, I have the answer – the answer to all my problems, professional and personal.

Life, I have come to see, is nothing more nor less than an another way of writing *file*.

21

I'm counting the sobs, I realize. Five . . . six . . . I don't know why. Trying to preserve a sense of detachment, perhaps. Trying to prevent myself being too embarrassed. Seven . . .

I've gone back to the beginning of the same tape and listened again to Summerchild's violin solo, which begins without introduction or explanation. It sounds even stranger up here where it was actually played, in the little garret at the top of the Cabinet Office. Then the disconcerting silence after he has finished. No comment from its audience. No modest self-depreciation from the performer. Just the faint knock of bow against soundboard and the squeak of a loosened peg, as he puts his violin away. And all around me the oddity of Sunday. The emptiness of the building under my feet; the emptiness behind the net curtains I can see out of the window in all the other departments; the emptiness of the train coming up; the emptiness at my neck where my buttoned collar and tie normally sit. My tin of plastic biscuits and my son's red plastic tape-recorder perch at irregular angles on top of the files and boxes I scattered in my exhaustion on Friday night. Serafin leans forward on top of her box, watching with rapt, silent interest as Summerchild, smiling his oblique private smile, puts the mystery he has revealed back into its velvet-lined case.

And then she sobs. In/out, rest . . . (ten). Sits watching him, according to the still immutable photograph on her side of the room, with wide-open blue eyes – and sobs. In/out,

166

rest . . . (eleven). While he turns aside, as the evidence on his side of the room continues to insist, silent and very slightly out of focus. Certain faint sounds on the tape, however, suggest that he has put that diffidence away with his violin – that he is now across the room and at her side. He is crouching, as one must to comfort someone whose head is lowered in distress. He is kneeling, perhaps holding her hands in his, looking up at her in silent comprehension and sympathy.

On the thirteenth sob the sound changes. The in-stroke is followed not by a single out-stroke, but by a whole series of out-strokes – in/out, out, out, out, out . . . I have a picture of a steam train which has been standing in some quiet station, issuing little preparatory sighs as the pressure to depart built up inside it, and which is now moving out of the station and away to the ends of the earth. She is no longer sobbing but crying.

Perhaps I should have started timing her, now there is nothing more to count. On and on she goes, out across the steppe, hard-class back to Saratov, as if she had escaped from the smallness of these small islands for the first time in years. Not a word does she utter in explanation or apology; not a word does he utter in inquiry or consolation. She just sits at her desk – sits here, where my left foot is, resting on the edge of her box – and howls. While he kneels in front of her, as I suppose, holding her hands in his – kneels here, where my right foot is – and watches her.

She cries for a long time. A certain professional and even private curiosity has sustained me through the beginnings of this intimacy. But now the full distastefulness of the position in which I have been put begins to make itself felt. I'm trapped, like an eavesdropper behind a curtain. It's too late to come out and explain. A week too late. Or perhaps fifteen years too late. But I'm not even behind a curtain. I'm in the room with them, my unnoticed head bent as close to their heads as their heads are to each other, my surreptitious hands sandwiched into their handclasp. I resigned myself, when I took the Civil Service examination, to a way of life which would sooner or later require me to set aside various qualms and scruples, to exercise various undisclosed powers over my fellow-men – but I never envisaged anything like this. I have reached the least congenial moment of my professional life so far. And there is another month of the tapes still to come.

I press the fast-forward button. But this reduces her long-matured distress to a ridiculous high wittering of babyish protest, which seems merely to add mockery to intrusion. I switch back to normal speed. The least graceless thing I can do now is to sit her wretchedness out at its full natural length.

If it *is* wretchedness. Because as the awful sound goes on my moral claustrophobia begins to subside a little. A certain impatience sets in with the monotony of the proceedings, with the failure of the participants to make their feelings more articulate. Those of us with reports to write, I can't help feeling, would be grateful for a few footnotes to the text. It may be plain to Summerchild what's she's crying about, but, now that the first shock has passed, I realize that it's not to me. I imagine that it's for the unhappiness of her life up to now. But it might be for the happiness she has now discovered. Then again, it might be for the future unhappiness that she can foresee entailed by this present happiness. It would be helpful to me to know, since I have to make some professional estimate of its effect upon Summerchild. It might be for all three things at once. This is to suppose that she knows herself – and if she doesn't then it would be useful to know *that*.

At last the crying subsides into sobs again, as if, far out in the steppe, the train has reached some kind of destination. Then there is a deep sigh, as the remaining steam inside the locomotive is finally released, and at last a voice speaks. His, I suppose, from the pitch, but so small and strange that I can't associate it with that weary figure in the lane, that oblique smile still watching us all from the desk opposite. So soft and deep, and spoken to someone so close, to someone so other than myself, that I can't make out what it's saying. I run the tape back and play it again. 'Oh dear', it seems to be saying, twice over. Or rather 'Oh . . . dear', with an odd glottal stop in the middle, as if the speaker couldn't think how to get even that far with an articulate thought. I play it a third time. No, it's not 'Oh dear'. It's 'Oh my dear', with the 'my' articulated almost silently, as if he hesitated to claim this degree of possession.

Another sigh – I think hers. Then her voice, also small and strange, perhaps fearful: 'What are we going to do?'

For some moments there is nothing to be heard but that faintly audible unease which is the recorded sound of silence. Their breathing, perhaps. Their thinking. The last echoes of the question in the empty room. I bend my head towards the tape-recorder. The answer to this question is going to be of interest to all three of us. When it comes it is simple and decisive. The sound of silence is suddenly replaced by silence itself. They have for some reason at last remembered the listening machine, and switched it off.

I fast-forward through to the end of the tape. I ought to feel relief to have been so unexpectedly got out from behind my curtain. But I don't, of course – I feel absurdly cheated at not finding out what happens next. And I feel revulsion for their behaviour. I blame her, not him. She has very little to lose, after all; he has everything. He told her how happy he was with his family. He warned her. But she deliberately ignored it – merely sat there in reckless silence while he played his violin to her . . .

No, I blame him. Of course. He is, after all, a *Civil Servant* – he is professionally committed to bringing some measure of order to the great sea of confusion, strife and misery that constitutes the world outside these walls. She came in from outside, was part of that confusion. Nothing was to be expected of her but muddle and devastation. It was up to him to control her.

The tape clicks to a stop. My indignation is a little self-righteous, I realize. After all, I have had to cope with a certain amount of the world's confusion and strife myself – and in my case they are rather closer to home. They are the fabric of my life, just as they are of hers. But I've kept it well clear of this building! I haven't brought it in on my boots, like muck off the street. I haven't even brought it into town – I've left it at home, six stops down the railway line, where it belongs.

Misery, yes. Some people might think that there is a tiny element of this in *my* life. If some distinguished academic observer had started to examine *my* experience of the world she might have burst into tears – and at *my* life, not hers. But *I've* never seen it like that. *I've* never sat down in the office and wept, and had my hand held, and started confused entanglements with people in entirely different positions and grades.

I take the tape out of the machine and rootle through the tin for the next one. All right, never mind self-righteousness. Never mind my own life. What makes me laugh is the wonderful *unreasonableness* of their behaviour. These two set out on their preposterous search for happiness – and, against all the odds, they find it. At least, I assume that this is what informs all those silent mutual gazings, that mad violin solo. Here are two scientific investigators who want to study the properties of light. So they lift their faces to heaven and shout for someone to shine a ray of sunshine down on them. And lo, a rift appears in the clouds covering the sky, and out of the gloom a single ray, straight and perfect, falls precisely upon their heads. So what do they do? Do they reflect it and refract it, and reconfirm the laws of optics? Do they measure the calorific effect it produces in the skin of their cheeks, and calibrate the brightness of each other's hair? No, they gaze at each other for ten minutes, then they burst into tears. They ask themselves *what they're going to do*. What do you mean, what are you going to do? – You're going to dance and revel in the light, until you get sunstroke or the light goes out, and then you're going to sit down and tell the rest of us what it was like.

Only they're not, of course. They're going to get into the shade again as fast as they can and look for something to cover their heads with.

The next tape seems to be one labelled May 15th.

'Dear Prime Minister,' begins Serafin's voice briskly at once. 'I promised you, when this Unit was set up, regular informal reports on our progress, and you must feel I have been remiss in supplying them.'

Yes, they've got themselves safely out of the sunlight and back into the grey administrative shade. Her voice is firm and reassuring again and she evidently has more reportable things to report. She is even becoming house-trained – she seems to have been persuaded to give up writing to the Prime Minister on her messy little portable and to start dictating reports to be typed out in the proper way by Mrs Padmore. Or rather by Mrs Padmore's successor.

Except of course that Mrs Padmore seems to have had no successor. Serafin is dictating into the void.

She has paused after her brisk start. Now on she goes, still in the belief, presumably, that she is addressing the Prime Minister, gazing straight at him out of her wide blue eyes.

'But so much has happened in the past few weeks in the development of our inquiry that I have found it impossible before now to stop and take stock.'

She pauses again. A horrible suspicion comes to me. She *is* going to report the reportable? She's not going to try and . . .?

'New paragraph. The fact is that circumstances have granted us a rare opportunity to study some of the fundamental issues involved in our inquiry at first hand. I will give as full and truthful an account as I can of these circumstances, but I feel I must ask for this report to be treated in the strictest confidence.'

She is. She's going to tell the Prime Minister everything. I switch the machine off and take a deep breath. This is going to be even worse than hearing it happen. I go to the window and look down into the empty Sunday garden at the back of Number Ten. I imagine Harold Wilson emerging and standing there for a moment, taking a breath of air, as I am at the window, before he goes back inside to resume reading the extraordinary document that his Permanent Secretary has just gravely put into his hands. Or not put into his hands. Because it was never typed out – it doesn't exist – it never got outside this office. In fact it never got outside the cloakroom in the corner of this office – the cupboard inside the cloakroom – the biscuit tin inside the cupboard – the cassette inside the biscuit tin . . . Yet, as I look, I think I see the Prime Minister raise his weary pouched eyes towards the attics of the Government Commission . . . I start back from the window and switch on the machine again. There is a pause. Then out it all comes.

'New paragraph. The circumstances I refer to are these. I have become aware of certain feelings in myself with regard to Mr S Summerchild, the Secretary of this Unit . . . No, no . . . Mr S Summerchild and I have become aware of certain mutual feelings . . . have formed an attachment . . . have become somewhat emotionally involved . . . No, go back to the beginning of this paragraph . . . Let me put it quite plainly: Mr S Summerchild and I have fallen in love.

'New paragraph. I should perhaps explain that Mr Summerchild and I are both married – he, as I understand it, rather happily, I not. We are both fully aware of the possible consequences of our feelings, not only for ourselves but also for our families, and we are both fully conscious of the moral responsibility we bear. We realize, too, that our feelings may be unacceptable to those around us, and that it is going to be too difficult to accommodate these feelings within the framework of our professional relationship.

'New paragraph. Indeed, we have both been through intense anguish on these scores during the past week or two. And yet, bubbling up, around and through and over all our wretchedness, shamefully and irrepressibly, is the strange but entirely natural, omnipresent yet profoundly elusive, bright yet totally transparent presence which is the subject of our inquiry. In fact we have to ask ourselves, I think – and shall ask ourselves at a calmer moment – whether the intensity of our happiness is not in some way dependent upon the intensity of our anguish – whether in fact happiness and unhappiness are not logically interdependent.

'New paragraph. What we have to recognize first of all is that the situation is a source of firsthand evidence which is far too important to ignore, however painful the consequences. What we have to do next is to devise some definite framework for our investigation. I propose to begin by calling the two witnesses involved – Mr Summerchild and myself – to give separate testimony, and then, if it seems appropriate, to confront us, so that we can comment on each other's evidence. I propose to begin by calling myself, since Mr Summerchild is for once rather conveniently out of the office. Also, honesty compels me to add, because I can't wait to say what I have to say.

'New paragraph. Still, I must begin by trying to place all this whirling confusion in an objective historical context. I must report that I have been in love before. I have also been happy before. On occasion the two states have coincided. But I can recall nothing like the state in which I now find myself. I wake up each morning and a shining tide of anticipation of the day ahead runs through me even before I have recalled the cause of it. It's termtime and I can get down to London only two or three times a week. (And of course it has occurred to me that it is the restrictions on our meeting, like the violent alternations with anguish, which make the intensity of our feelings possible; and this, too, will be fully investigated in a later session.) I go through the day in Oxford like a candle. By this I mean that I am *alight* – alight with purpose – the purpose being to live until I see Mr Summerchild again. I also mean *consumed* like a candle – wasting away with the impossibility of waiting until that time should come. People speak to me – my sons speak to me – and I can't hear what they are saying – I can't find words in the world to speak to them. Then I hear everything – I am aware of every syllable and every glance, and I smile at people I have never seen

173

before – I touch my sons' arms, I touch their cheeks, I tell them things I have never told anyone. I sit through committee meetings and hear nothing, then propose huge schemes for raising and spending funds. I sit through tutorials, listening to the dull irrelevancies I have spent my life teaching, then locate and liberate the profoundest philosophical insights in them. I look at my poor husband and the tears start to my eyes for sheer pity.'

She has said all this quite evenly and calmly, but with superhuman fluency, without once stopping to think or to announce a change of paragraph. Now she seems to have reached the end of the cadenza. I can't imagine where she is going next. Nor, perhaps, can she.

'Outside my window in Oxford . . .' Nature, yes. Spring. Weather. And 'New paragraph', surely. Or has she has forgotten she is dictating a letter for the Clerical Officer to transcribe?

'Outside my window in Oxford the spring is becoming summer. Never, I think, has the process of becoming been so clearly and vividly articulated. A world of green is being constructed in front of my eyes, a calculus of birdsong and warm rain. I open the window wide and become quite straightforwardly the sum of my sensations. The smell of the air is intensely familiar – I am the self I was at this time of year in every year since I was born. And yet it seems to me that this is the first time I have ever smelt this ancient and lovely smell. I am a self I have never been before.'

She pauses again, perhaps merely to breathe. New paragraph, I take the opportunity to prompt her. But she's not listening. I was right – she's forgotten she's dictating. She's *talking* to the Prime Minister, not writing to him – she's leaning out of the window and telling him direct. Telling anyone who'll listen, telling everyone. Telling no one, since she must know that no one's ever going to type this. Telling herself, perhaps. Telling me, as it turns out. I listen, rapt.

'Then, unbelievably, I am on the train to London again. What do I feel now? Nothing! No anticipation, no light, no purpose. I have no sensations; I am no one. It is no longer possible to feel anything, or think anything, or be anyone, since he won't be there, since the train is going to crash, since there is some mistake and I am not in fact even on the train. I sit there frozen, blocked, knotted, unconscious, non-existent. I am as strikingly inert as some kind of explosive weapon which is not at the moment exploding.

'Now I'm inside the building where he is – I'm climbing the stairs. I suddenly lose heart and stop. He *will* be there, this is the trouble now, and I know that something is going to go wrong. I shall say the wrong word, I shall think the wrong thought, and everything will turn to desolation all around us. It's happened before; it will happen again. Whatever this terrible thing is I'm feeling I know one thing for certain – it isn't happiness! I've totally misidentified it! It's misery beyond enduring! I realize, now that I have reached this point in my report, that I am fundamentally mistaken in the direction that this investigation has taken. As soon as I have reached the end I shall go back and redraft it from the beginning.

'New paragraph, anyway . . . Where were we . . .? Yes, on the stairs. So now my hand is on the handle of the door. And what I feel now is . . . Let me think. I believe it's total indifference. I don't care whether I see him or not. In fact I have more than half a mind to turn round and go away. I could rather conveniently use the time to buy books and something for dinner, then get the train back to Oxford.

'But I observe that the door, with my hand on the handle, is opening. I'm not quite sure how this comes about . . .'

Her voice trails away. There is a click in the background, and a juddering of door out of door frame – the same click and the same judder as I have heard each morning this week as I arrived to start my day's work. The door has opened, and now Summerchild is standing silently in the doorway. I suppose he is looking at her. I suppose she is looking at him. No doubt they are smiling at each other. I get the impression that he hadn't expected to find her already there.

Sooner or later, I imagine, one of them will speak.

In the end it's Summerchild who obliges. 'Honey,' he says.

The voice is as low and reluctant as ever. The detached, free-floating, implausible endearment comes out of nowhere, like a bee on a summer's afternoon, and leaves nothing but silence behind it. He simply states it as a fact, slowly and carefully, as if he were briefing her on some small but arcane point of departmental procedure.

There is the clunk of something heavy being put down close to the microphone, followed by the rustling of paper and a soft thud.

'Celery,' he says, in the same way as before. *Celery?* I play it again to check. Yes, 'celery'. The originality of this endearment changes my perception of both of them. He becomes wilder and stranger, she taller and crisper . . .

'I thought we could dip it in the honey,' he murmurs. Oh, I see. He is taking groceries out of a carrier bag, not endearments out of his heart. His pronouncements sound factual because that's what they are – the facts of lunch. But now I know that, the courses of this little lunch for two up here in their private garret begin to sound like endearments after all. 'Olives . . . cornflakes . . . chocolate biscuits . . .' The words are shameless and it takes her a moment or two to collect herself sufficiently to reply. Then she murmurs in her turn: 'I caught the early train.' I find the intimacy of these words physically disturbing. They are beyond looks and sighs now – they are sensually and carnally absorbed in each other. You can hear it in every word and every silence. Celery dipped in honey; his little gastronomic caprice has the most graphic unconscious precision.

Another silence now, in fact. They are looking at each other, perhaps. Or they are looking at the groceries on the desk between them, as if the groceries were each other, and they are smiling to themselves at the beauty of them. For another moment neither of them speaks or moves. Then there is the scur of the jar of honey being pulled across the desk and picked up, the schlur of the head of celery . . . Footsteps. Hinges again, but different ones. I go over and check; I want to be sure I am following these moves correctly. Yes – the cloakroom door. From the tape-recorder in the office behind me I can hear him in the cloakroom in front of me, dumping the groceries down on the draining-board – here – then turning on the tap to wash the celery. While the sink is filling we open the cupboard. He puts the cornflakes away; I look at the handful of mouldy green flakes that remain.

I'm startled by the sound of her voice calling from the office: 'Close the door. I'm dictating something.'

I turn off the tap. 'What?' I say . . . *He* turns off the tap. 'What?' he says. I put my head back into the office.

'Go away!' she says. 'Close the door! I'll tell you when you can come out!'

He goes back into the cloakroom and closes the door. I stay where I am.

'New paragraph,' she says quietly. 'I want to say this now, while it's still fresh in my mind: when he arrived just then – when the door opened, and I knew it would be him, and it *was* him – *that* was happiness.

'When he opened the door, not knowing I was going to be here, and I *was* here, and he saw me, and he stopped, and he looked, and he smiled – *that* was happiness.

'When I saw *his* happiness . . . when I saw that he saw *my* happiness . . .

'Now still, while he stands just behind that door, washing the celery for lunch . . .

'I came to the conclusion in an earlier report, I think, that happiness was a state that existed only in recollection and anticipation – only in the past and in the future. I was wrong. It can also exist in the present. It exists now, as I say these words.

'I am at this moment happy. I know this with absolute certainty. I know this *incorrigibly*, whatever happens in the future, whatever retrospective revisions the future imposes upon my understanding of the world. I know it in the same way that philosophers once hoped to show we knew the experience from which we supposedly inferred the world around us.

'Here is what happiness is like: a sense of perfect fit. It's like holding up honey and saying "Honey". It's like holding up celery and saying "Celery". These things are exactly true. The honey and the "honey" are entirely congruent. "Celery" is made for celery, and celery is celery because "celery" is its name.

'I think we might find, as we investigate this further, that the notion of fit, or congruence, is not merely a subjective feeling. I believe we might be able to identify it as an objective aspect of the universe. We might discover, I think, that the schoolmen were right, and that in some important sense the world works as precisely and simply as a syllogism.'

The cloakroom door opens.

'All right?' says Summerchild. 'Perhaps we should do a little work before lunch.'

'I feel we've done enough for one morning already,' says Serafin.

And the machine is switched off.

22

I fast-forward through the empty tape. I'm glad she's happy. Naturally. She's deserved a little happiness, with the life she's had. Quite apart from her personal merits, I'm glad that someone somewhere – anyone anywhere – is happy. Not was, or will be, as we all once were and may be yet, but *is*. Is, at the moment of knowing it. Is, in the eternal present preserved out of the past on this piece of magnetic tape. I'm more than just glad; I'm quite shaken by her testimony. I shouldn't like to dictate a report to this effect, but I don't mind admitting it to myself: her happiness strikes a tiny answering spark of happiness in me.

And yet a few weeks after this Summerchild was dead, and apparently not a word did she have to say about it. No interviews in the papers, no evidence to the inquest. She, and all her feelings about him, were just about to vanish without even leaving a discarded body beside the dustbins.

What about *his* feelings? This is the important question for the purposes of my inquiry. I'm never going to get any direct access to *them*, because he's not going to start dictating reports on the subject to the Prime Minister. I suppose he's happy. All the outward signs suggest he is – his behaviour with the groceries, his long silences in her presence. She certainly believes he's happy and she is subjecting him to the closest possible observation. Am I happy about *his* happiness? I'm not sure. I suppose I ought to be, if I'm consistent – and *have* to be, logically, if I'm happy she's happy, because she

179

wouldn't be if he weren't. But then I think of Millie, covertly watching her father's moods, and I think, well, he *shouldn't* be happy. Anyway, here he is, coming slowly up the lane to where Millie and I are standing at the gate. He sighs . . . And he isn't happy, he isn't. But perhaps I'm remembering him as he was the first time I saw him, in the darkness of the winter evening. Did I see him as the spring wore on? Perhaps, by that merry month of May, he was changing, and all I saw was the character I had already set in my mind.

And then, suddenly, in the middle of nowhere, he is gabbling wildly at me in a high insane voice. 'Confidential F Tite – S Summerchild,' he squeals urgently. I take my finger off the fast-forward button and the voice drops to its characteristic low growl. But there is still something odd about it, even at normal speed, something slightly desperate. 'I feel I must request an immediate transfer to another posting . . .'

He's withdrawing. He's off, like Mrs Padmore. And at once I feel a pang of simple childish disappointment. He's not going to play – he's spoiling the game! I even have a twinge of moral disapproval for his cowardice in running away. Then I recover my more reasonable self; he's behaving rightly and I honour him for it.

He's having a struggle to find the right words, though.

'I should perhaps stress that my request has no connection with the nature of the work, which I have found intensely stimulating . . . which I have found personally interesting . . . which I believe to be of value. I am anxious, however, to avoid a difficult situation which I feel may arise within the Unit . . . which I feel may have arisen . . . which has arisen and which I fear can only become more acute . . . as a result of the personalities involved. There is no good purpose to be served, I think, by going into too much detail . . . by going into any detail . . . except to say that none of this is to be taken as implying any reflection upon . . . upon anyone. Certainly not upon the director of the Unit. Dr E Serafin has brought to a difficult task the most outstanding personal qualities . . . the most outstanding and inspiring personal qualities . . . the most astonishing and moving and . . . the most deeply . . . the most profoundly . . . very considerable qualities. I have to say that I personally find the prospect of leaving the Unit rather sad . . . more than sad . . . rather painful . . . very painful . . . more painful than I can bear to . . .'

His voice seems to have given out. He makes a few inarticulate attempts to continue, then takes in a convulsive mouthful of air and switches off the machine. He was just about to send his Permanent Secretary a sob.

I switch off my machine, too. I laugh a single laugh and then wish I hadn't. Poor Summerchild. He's in as deeply as her; I hadn't quite realized before. I feel curiously dismayed – as if I have somehow become responsible for his feelings. I'm also aware of a certain resentment that I should be constrained to wince at his pain without being dignified by the state that has caused it. Because he's in love and I'm not. He is in that mythical state, that much-sought land, that exclusive club where all men are kin. And I am not. Yes, I believe I'm jealous.

I turn on my machine. He turns on his and makes another attempt at the letter. This time he is seeking an even more urgent release from his problems. 'I feel I must ask to take immediate leave, followed by a transfer to another . . .' Again his voice goes and the machine is turned off. He makes a third attempt. 'I feel . . .' he starts and gets no further.

He feels. This is his great mistake.

Further along the tape the machine is turned on again and no words are said at all. There is nothing but the expectant sound of silence, going on and on and on. He is sitting there on his own, looking at the red light on the tape-recorder. This time he can't even get as far as the words 'I feel'. All he can manage is the feeling itself.

Eventually, with nothing recorded but a sigh, the machine is switched off and the tape runs blank to the end. So presumably he never completed his letter. He is still in his job at the beginning of the next tape (May 21st) and by this time he seems to have forgotten all his anguished scruples completely. He is talking to her this time and he is up again – up higher than ever. There is a kind of wild jauntiness in his voice, a wilful irresponsibility. I suddenly think of Millie's Beaufort Scale and have a vision of storm cones, and dustbin lids rolling along the street in the rising wind. And what he is saying, it strikes me as I listen, casts a considerable retrospective doubt on the seriousness of his attempt at resignation.

'There – it's on, it's recording,' he begins suddenly, out of nowhere. 'Everything's being taken down on this remarkable machine. Nothing's going to be lost. Don't worry.'

'But there's no one to type it out – they still haven't sent us a new Clerical Officer.' Her voice sounds almost cautious now by comparison. Leader, it seems to me, has become led, and led leader.

'As a matter of fact they have.' He laughs. I hardly recognize him. He is like a drunken man. 'They've sent us five.'

'Five? I'm not entirely sure I understand. There appears to be no one downstairs.'

'Five candidates for the job. Five different candidates sent along by Personnel. Not all together. At different times. First one, then another, and so on. Five possible Clerical Officers.'

'What happened to them?'

'I interviewed them.'

'When was this?'

'At various times. As and when. I rejected them. They were unsuitable.'

'All of them?'

'All of them.'

'What was wrong with them?'

'One of them had a cold. We obviously don't want a Clerical Officer with a cold, blowing germs over us all, bringing the whole Unit down.'

'Stephen . . .' she says anxiously. She sounds frightened. All the happiness has gone.

'One of them was carrying a book about economic theory, which I thought was a rather bad augury.'

'Stephen, we must start to work again! We're not getting anything done!'

'I'll type everything out myself. Why not? I can type. I can type quite fast and quite accurately.'

'It's not just the typing . . .'

'No – I can do a number of things that you don't know about. You've got various surprises in store for you.'

'Stephen, please! Stop! I don't like all this!'

'But we don't want anyone else around, do we?'

'We're not getting anything done, though! This has never happened to me before. I've never sat day after day, week after week, doing nothing. I wake at night sometimes in the most terrible panic.'

A great crack is opening up between them. In a moment the whole mistaken adventure is going to be as good as over. But then Summerchild's voice changes.

'We don't though, do we?' he says softly.

Her voice changes, too. 'What are we going to do?' she says sadly, as she said before.

There is a silence. 'I don't know,' says Summerchild finally, and the rising gale in his voice has suddenly dropped. The flags are hanging inertly against the flagstaffs again, the trees are not stirring. They sit like this for a long time. I suspect they're not even looking at each other. Then the machine is turned off.

Yes, what are they going to do? I suppose they are pursuing their inquiry without realizing it, even as they sit there in despair. Their mad quest for the nature of happiness was after all a side-trip, a wild dash for El Dorado, when what they had set out to do was to explore the entire continent of the Quality of Life. And if the quality of life has something to do with the awareness of being alive, as some of their earlier discussions seemed to be suggesting, then they are still hard at work; they are, I imagine, notably aware of their existence.

But the practical question remains: how are they going to pursue their examination of this condition? The answer emerges in hints and snatches from the next few tapes, as May gives way to June: they are going to keep house together up here.

It's the most natural thing in the world. They are going to make their nest beneath the eaves, like a pair of swallows, or a couple of June newly-weds.

Or, more precisely, *he* is going to keep house, since she is away in Oxford most of the time – the examinations have started and she is an examiner, on top of everything else. On one of the tapes there is a roaring noise in the background and a voice singing over it; it's him, vacuuming the room. Where the machine has come from and where the regular cleaners have gone – this is not explained. On another tape he is drawing her attention to the windows, which he has cleaned, and to the new tablecloth on the desk, which he has bought. They are eating lunch on it at the time – asparagus, so far as I can gather from her appreciative remarks, followed by cold chicken and salad, washed down with white wine. He has done all the shopping for the meal. He has cooked the asparagus. What in, I wonder. He has been buying various items of kitchen equipment – but not an asparagus saucepan, surely? He has chilled the wine. How? They haven't got a refrigerator! I become slightly obsessed with this question. I run the tape several times, with the sound turned up. I believe I can hear the clunk of a bucket at one point, as the handle falls back against the rim, and the dripping of water. I suppose he has bought ice. I suppose it must be the bucket he got from somewhere to wash the windows.

'This one?' – 'That one.' So the discussion starts at one of their sessions. 'Here?' – 'Lower ... lower still ... a bit to the right ... an inch higher ...' And there is the whine of an electric drill. They are fixing shelves and hanging cupboards. They are making the lines of holes in the walls on either side of the chimney-breast. He has brought in a Black & Decker – smuggled it out of the house, I assume, in his briefcase. I listen carefully to the voices in all these little domestic episodes. They sound practical and involved. The weather inside Summerchild seems to have become settled and steady; in the cheerful round of domestic labour the anguish has evidently been forgotten. It all sounds so natural! I shouldn't be surprised to hear that they were redecorating the Clerical Officer's room downstairs as a nursery.

Once or twice the phone rings. 'Summerchild ... Yes ... No ... Joint consultative machinery ... Put a paper up to Cabinet ...' As if it were a Government office and not a love-nest at all! And they resume their work. Or they resume their attempts to work. Serafin comes bustling in off the train from Oxford, throws her bursting bag of books down on the desk, admires the latest acquisitions, worries about the plants outside the window, then announces a topic for discussion. Happiness and the naturalistic fallacy, for example, or the concept of fun. Does happiness necessarily involve forgetting oneself, or does the highest happiness require that one remains in some way self-aware? Is the world of the happy man, as Wittgenstein declared, different from the world of the unhappy man? She suggests bringing in zoologists and examining whether the concept of happiness has any application in understanding animal behaviour. There are various notions connected with wanting and liking that she feels (and he seems to agree) need clarification. They have to investigate what it is to do what one wants to do and to be where one wants to be. There are problems with the idea of fit. They must give some thought to why it is that one likes being with whoever it is that one likes being with.

Now that I am actually hearing them, though, their tutorials are not quite the same as they appeared in transcript. They are somehow less definite than the typed text made them seem. The voices are further away from the microphone than I had imagined and their words don't have the same precision. There are long pauses, and disconnected noises, which seem more incisive than the words and which seize a rather greater hold on my imagination. It's difficult to follow the exact time sequence. Sometimes a new topic starts at right angles out of another, or out of a silence, as if the machine has been switched off and another day has dawned. It's plain that a major contribution to the coherence of the earlier proceedings was being made by Mrs Padmore.

One morning in early June they find themselves in difficulties over the notion of joy. What is it? A gradation of happiness? A direct and unanalysable emotion, as irreducible as the experience of whiteness or saltiness, which may (or may not) be a component of the much more general state of happiness? Which may be *mistaken* for happiness? Which may strike even in the midst of unhappiness, as freely as a stab of pain? Summerchild chases the notion around his mind, trying to find a remembered instance of joy to capture and examine.

'I imagine,' says Serafin slowly, 'that it's what you sometimes feel when you look at Millie.'

'Yes,' says Summerchild, after a long pause to think and with great decisiveness. 'I think it is.'

'I surmise,' says Serafin, 'that it's connected with a sensation of tenderness, of delighting in her, of going outside yourself, of losing all sense of yourself in your sense of her.'

She surmises? Hasn't she ever felt that same tenderness and delight with her own children? Not even when they were lying in her arms, gazing up at her, as absorbed in her as she now is in Summerchild? Or is she feeling it for the first time in recollection, as she gazes so intently at Summerchild and pictures her own feeling through the image of the feeling she can see in *him*?

'I suppose,' says Summerchild at last, 'that it's the feeling that comes from being with someone you love.' And maybe he is seeing it for the first time in recollection, too, as he gazes into those shining, eager eyes across the desk and sees the image of his feeling that she has formed inside herself.

A long silence. Then Serafin:

'Is it what you feel when you look at Anne?'

Another long silence. Summerchild has turned his head to look at the summer sky outside the window. And when at last he does reply he speaks very quietly and I can't quite catch his words. His feelings when he looks at Anne, I think he is saying, are 'more settled'. The question, like so many of these questions, is not pursued. Summerchild is suddenly holding forth, with a kind of insane procedural urgency, about whether a Government inquiry, even one into the most general questions of happiness, can really concern itself with the provision of joy. And then, as at most of these sessions, they find themselves distracted by some domestic detail – in this case, of where they are going to keep the wooden salad bowl he has just bought.

They seem to be separated now by the width of only a single desk and often the dialogue simply dies away to silence as they become absorbed in gazing at each other, or looking at the little pile of hands between them, some of them so smooth and round, some of them so thin and bony. I slide my boxes together in imitation. Their photographs are now only two feet apart.

Sometimes Summerchild laughs, for no reason which can be identified from the tape.

On one afternoon, from their passing remarks evidently very hot and still, the quietness of their contemplation is interrupted by a distant hum of someone else's conversation. They look out of the window and down below, in the garden of Number Ten, politicians in sweltering dark suits and African visitors in complex coloured robes are sipping drinks and finding sources of measured amusement.

Eventually the tape-recorder always seems to be switched off, without, or so it seems to me, much philosophy having got philosophized. There is in any case still no one downstairs to transcribe the proceedings. Personnel have apparently given up sending candidates and Serafin has given up worrying about it. Evidently no one in the outside world has noticed that the reports have ceased to emerge – plainly no one was reading them in the first place. The world has forgotten the Unit ever existed.

What does happen after the machine is switched off, though? Do they just go on holding hands in silence? Do they continue to talk about shampooing the carpet? Or do they . . . well – *embrace?* Do they kiss and caress each other? Does she kick her shoes off, loosen his tie? Does he unbutton her shirt? Slide her skirt back from her knees . . .?

Do they lie down? If so, where? Here, on the floor? On the stretch of carpet beneath these tumbled boxes and files? Their heads beside my feet – their feet only inches from the door? Why don't they keep the machine on and give us a recording of it all, if this is the heart of their happiness? I can imagine the little cries, the silences, the sudden practical concerns with a trapped arm or a cramped leg. I try to enter that closed intensity of mutual absorption and self-awareness. But I can't. All I can imagine is external events . . . someone knocking on the door, say. Yes, and at once the little sighs and frictions cease. The door handle is turned – the door is pushed against its lock . . . There are sounds of horizontal bodies suddenly becoming vertical in a restricted space, of zips and shoes and stumbles against furniture. The door is tried again. This time Summerchild manages to speak. 'Just coming!' Then a whisper – 'Get dressed in the kitchen! Keep the door shut!' The sound of the door to the stairs being unlocked. 'Francis! Sorry – I was just putting on a clean shirt for dinner . . .'

The scene is so vivid to me that I can feel the hot flush of shame. I can feel it – but I can't quite believe it. The picture I believe is one of them just sitting here doing nothing, like two children, the way Millie and I just stood there at the gate . . . I am brought back from all these thoughts, though, by the realization that there is something going wrong with the tape-recorder. For some time now it has been getting quieter and the sounds it emits less and less defined . . . I feel suddenly foolish. Of course – it's not plugged into anything, it must be running on batteries. It had never occurred to me. I should have brought some spares . . . And through the fog I suddenly realize that Summerchild is saying something about a *bed*. Is this just my imagination? I turn the volume up as far as it will go and put my ear next to the loudspeaker, but I can only make out occasional words . . . 'The bed . . . lie on it . . . our bed . . .' The words give place to some kind of confused rustling, as of tumbled sheets, and then it seems to me that the fast-fading

haze of sound settles into some sort of regular pulse –
shhh . . . shhh . . . shhh . . .

I turn the machine off at once. Imagining it is one thing;
actually hearing it is another. I am deeply shocked, I discover.
Shocked at them, certainly. Shocked also at myself, though,
for hearing them – for hearing *her*, still smiling at me from
the top of her box – for hearing *him*, Millie's father, who
walked up the lane on those winter and spring evenings, and
who looked at the grass growing out of his front step. Shocked
at my son's innocent red tape-recorder for uttering these
sounds, with what seems to be its dying breath.

And at once, needless to say, I turn the machine on again
and listen as the last faint thudding traces fade. It sounds like
panting breath, as if each downstroke of his body – somewhere
just about here, presumably, where the tape-recorder is now
reclining on top of the boxes – were forcing a sigh out of her.
The sighs merge into the indistinguishable chaos of the tape's
hiss and the rank rumpled bedclothes and the rifled files at
my feet and my own tumbled thoughts.

But a *bed*? This goes way beyond my imaginings. They
actually turned this office into a *bedroom*? How did they . . . I
don't know . . . how did they get the door open with a bed in
here? How did they get a bed up here in the first place? A
double bed? They carried a double bed through Security –
through the whole height and depth of the Cabinet Office –
up a spiral staircase? Or did they hoist it through the window,
out of the back garden of Number Ten?

I suppose I must find out, for my researches, exactly how
those sighs ended up. Even on a Sunday there'll be batteries
at one of the tourist shops in Trafalgar Square.

It's summer still out on the streets. I'd forgotten about
summer, in spite of the heat up there under the eaves. It's
this summer, too, I realize rather slowly, and not that one.
You can tell, if only because this one's better and much more
ordinary. Whitehall is full of heat and brightness and ordinary
people. So this is what ordinary people are like. They walk

189

round the important streets of capital cities with their children on Sunday afternoon, buying things to eat and not knowing quite what to do. They have brown hair, or none; they don't teach philosophy; they look as if they are leading one life apiece and not two. I make another interesting discovery from the clock over the Horse Guards – it's three o'clock in the afternoon, which may go some way to accounting for the strangeness of the world around me, since I seem to have forgotten about lunch.

I emerge from the souvenir shop at the end of Whitehall with enough batteries to power me through all possible permutations of sexual and intellectual intercourse, and add two hot dogs from a stand in Trafalgar Square and two cans of lager from the pub on the corner of Northumberland Avenue. As I come back through Security I hold up the souvenir shop's plastic bag, which is decorated with an implausible Union Jack motif and emitting a suspicious clinking of cans. But Security merely nods. I wonder if he would have raised an inquiring eyebrow if it had been a brass bedstead.

I lay out the hot dogs and open the first can of lager as the tape runs back, then hesitate. Which am I going to do first – eat lunch or listen to the tape? I don't think I can do both at once, given the distasteful nature of the tape. I suppose duty takes precedence. So the hot dogs lie respectfully cooling while I discover how Summerchild got the bed into the office. The answer turns out to be that he brought it in his briefcase. It's not *our bed* he's telling Serafin about – it's an *airbed*. She has evidently forgotten about the notes she was dictating in her excitement at this latest addition to their household furnishings and left the tape-recorder running as they pull off the rustling polythene packaging, then unpack the foot-pump he has bought as well. Hush ... hush ... hush ... goes the foot-pump rhythmically as he pumps up the airbed. I realize I have plenty of time to eat my hot dogs before there is a chance of anything remotely distasteful beginning to happen.

I stop chewing to listen in surprise, though, when the

pumping finishes, because they have picked the bed up from the only piece of floor it can conceivably be on and they are attempting to manoeuvre it somewhere else. Where can they possibly be putting it? There *is* nowhere else! A readily identifiable squeak – the cloakroom door is being opened. The cloakroom? There's no room to put it down in the cloakroom! Their voices become muffled and distant. 'Now, if you can just . . .' 'Hold on . . .' 'This way a bit . . .' What in heaven's name . . .? The hinges squeak again as I open the cloakroom door myself and gaze uncomprehendingly at the floor-area of the room. The only way they can possibly do it, so far as I can see, is to wedge the lavatory door open and have one end of the bed hard up against the bowl. I find the desperation of this arrangement even more disturbing than what I thought I had heard before.

There are little grunts, and knockings, and slidings, then something smashes. 'Just the milk jug,' says Serafin. 'Sorry – caught my foot on the washing-up rack,' grunts Summerchild, preoccupied. What? Either the washing-up rack is standing on the floor for some reason, or . . . Saucepans clatter . . . Or Summerchild is standing on the draining-board. They are being reduced to the most appalling contortions in here. Something hard is thumped three or four times by something soft, possibly a recalcitrant surface by a frustrated fist. 'Have to get some Vaseline for it,' mutters Summerchild. 'Be careful,' says Serafin. There is a sudden whooshing sound. 'Ah,' exclaims Summerchild with satisfaction. More slidings, more knockings and scrapings. 'All right?' asks Serafin. 'All right,' says Summerchild. His voice is very faint, after all his exertions. 'I've got it . . . Can you . . .? That's right . . . Foot on the . . . yes . . . Mind the . . .!' More saucepans jostle. She is climbing on to the draining-board as well! Wild, uneasy imaginings come to me. Some people, I have heard, can only derive satisfaction from intercourse performed standing up, against walls and in doorways. Others like to be tied up and shut in cupboards. But standing on draining-boards? Holding an airbed?

191

I feel a ridiculous sense of injustice, like a blind man who's been brought a jigsaw puzzle to do ... But now my hearing's gone as well! All sounds from the tape-recorder have ceased. Complete silence. What in heaven's name ...? My lubricious imagination has come to the end of its range. I can only think that they have ... spread the airbed out on the ceiling and gone to sleep.

I gaze upwards, wonderingly. And see at once what's happened. Of course. It should have been obvious just from thinking about it; there wouldn't be any light inside this little windowless room if there weren't a skylight in the ceiling.

I get up on the draining-board and push at the frame around the frosted glass above my head. It's stuck. My foot dislodges the mug I drank my dusty tea from and it clatters down into the sink like the milk jug before it. I'm tempted to give up; from up here there seems to be a great deal of empty space beneath me and I can clearly see myself clattering down off the draining-board in my turn. I try thumping the window-frame with my fist and from the sounds this makes I surmise I have found the right technique. With a sudden no less recognizable whoosh it gives and I push the skylight open. Now, get a foot on to ... what? The stopcock on the cold water pipe – yes. Push, trying not to think about the huge emptiness yawning ever vaster beneath me ... And my head emerges into a dazzle of baking sunshine and blue sky. I set my hands on the edge of the trap and heave myself up into a new and brilliant world.

23

I am in a kind of hot valley between the pitches of two roofs, closed off from the world by the moraine of the garret room behind me. Chimney-stacks rise out of the slate slopes like the exposed stumps of underlying geological strata. The sun beats down into this waterless gulch and its heat is reflected off the hard surfaces all round. No breath of air stirs. Here, in the heart of the teeming city, at the very centre of Government, is the hidden valley of explorers' dreams, the long-sought place of absolute seclusion under the open sky. Summerchild and Serafin could have taken their shirts off here, as I'm taking mine off now. They would have had to, on a day as hot as this, as I have had to. They could have wandered as naked as Bushmen.

In the flat gully that runs the length of this mountain state, like a dried-up river, there would just have been room for their airbed. What would the world have looked like to them, as they lay stretched out side by side? I take off my shoes and socks to make a pillow. But the leads are so hot under my feet that I go dancing wildly away down the gully to find a cool patch for them in the shade of a chimney-stack. I lay out my shirt and shoes in the sun, then take my trousers off and put them on top of my shirt to thicken the insulation under my back. I cautiously stretch myself out. The hot sun strikes down on my chest. The hot leads strike up into my back. I screw up my eyes and gaze into the great blue emptiness. There is nothing to be seen but a floater drifting slowly across the surface of my eye. There is nothing to be heard but an indefinable ghost of sound, which might be the last faint reminder of the world beyond the mountains, or merely the whisper of the blood inside my own head.

This was their Canaveral. This was the secret launch-site for the Government's rocket to the sun.

I have left my son's tape-recorder talking to itself down below, I realize; but then it's saying nothing – they've left her son's down there as well, listening unspoken to.

I take off my pants. My bush sparkles in the sun. I am a Bushman! The blood runs in my veins. I have a feeling of reckless simplicity. I welcome the possibility of the Special Branch appearing over the skyline on security patrol. I'd be delighted if Ken Hurren's all-knowing head suddenly rose from the skylight and his well-controlled mouth opened in surprise for just a second before some suitably unsurprised remark emerged from it.

June. Yes, by the middle of the month the exams she was marking were over and her vacation was beginning. She was probably able to get down to London every day. This roof, I realize, has probably scarcely changed in the last fifteen years. This is what they saw. This sky, this sun. These planes murmuring overhead on their way down into Heathrow. One's going over now. 'Passengers on the righthand side of the aircraft,' the captain is telling them, 'have got a good view of the Houses of Parliament and Whitehall.' Passengers on the righthand side of the aircraft look down and see naked tribesmen engaged in their ancient mating rituals, sunlit and unashamed, on the roof of some solemn state building. They feel a wild rush of anticipation. They have at last found the perfect holiday place, where pagan abandon is combined with Protestant plumbing.

Five miles up, a taut white rope is being hauled across the sky in the opposite direction by another aircraft too small to be discerned. We follow it, Serafin and I (or is it Millie and I, naked in the sunshine up here?), speculating learnedly but silently on the cargo of anticipation it carries.

We brush away the flies drinking at the rivers of sweat on our stomachs. We watch the martins dip and swerve above the chimney-stacks. Then the clouds pile and clear, the blue fades slowly into black, and the stars come out. We pull the blankets over us and look out into the immense calm lifelessness of the universe, back through all the huge quiet happinesslessness of the unpeopled centuries . . .

I open my eyes – I was beginning to doze. I've just realized what the special private appeal of this place is for Summerchild. It's like the unmade-up lane in his other life – an odd corner of space, unplanned and unaccounted for, hidden away among the regular framework of streets and offices. He emerges each morning from nowhere, into the overcrowded trains and through the public streets, then vanishes into nowhere again. And all this freely granted by heaven! At the taxpayer's expense!

But it's too hot to lie here. My beard is full of sweat. Parts of me that have never seen the sun before will shortly begin to burn and blacken and drop off. Summerchild, with his red-headed complexion, would have had his brains boiled by now. I put my shoes on my bare feet and walk about my kingdom, keeping my back to the sun. I climb a few feet up the slope, and press myself against the rough brickwork of a chimney-stack, as if it were another body, as if it were Serafin, as if it were Millie. Something moves under my hand – a foot of thin rope, hanging from a hook. It has gone grey and brittle – it powders as I rub it between my fingers. A piece of grey wood scratches at the brickwork – a clothespeg, its spring rusted fast, clenched on the rope like a dead man's hand.

So they didn't just lie up here and squint at the sky. He fixed up a clothesline, like the one in his own back garden, and they did their washing. What did they wash? Their tablecloth, their drying-up cloths. Towels, perhaps, to dry themselves after their shower. They'd have needed a shower at the end of a hot day up here – I need one now. It's not just the sweat – my hands are black and so is my sticky flesh

195

---

wherever I've touched it. A few hours of this and you'd be a Bushman from head to foot. But how could they have taken a shower? Well, they had a bucket – the one they chilled the wine in. They could have carted water up here by the bucketful and splashed it over each other like children . . .

My imagination is running ahead of me, dancing barefoot in the heat. I think they must have had water, though. Among the detritus that has collected on the grille over the drain, at the far end of the gully, are some shards of earthenware pottery and a split grey cane. I believe they were growing tomatoes up here. It was a complete civilization, with its own agriculture. I picture to myself a system, now vanished, for gathering rainwater from the slopes – dams across the runnels in the angles between one roof and the next, reservoirs in the high coombes behind the chimney-stacks.

My eye is caught by a series of marks scratched on the slates. They run slantwise across the bottom three courses of the south-facing slope, like calibrations on a ruler, but at intervals decreasing from right to left. In my present elevated mood, when all things in heaven and earth are manifest to me, I have only to glance up at the crocket on top of the garret roof to divine their significance. They mark the footsteps of the sun as it ascended day by day towards its apogee that summer, and the shadow cast by the crocket at noon as each day grew shorter. The scratches vanish into a blur, overlaid one on top of another where the days were levelling into the solstice, on June 21st. This was a people, I realize, who made primitive astronomical observations and had a calendar to mark the days as their world approached its end.

Still wearing nothing but my pale tan summer shoes, I edge my way cautiously up the slope above this miniature Stonehenge. Slates shift slightly under my feet. I don't like this at all – I've no head for heights . . . At last I seize the hot flashing on top of the pitch and peer carefully over it. Summerchild is balanced beside me, his hands next to mine. Together we are looking at the whole of London, drenched in the hot clear late afternoon light like a baklava in honey. We can almost see the strollers on Hampstead Heath to the north-west, and on Shooters Hill to the south-east. Immediately in front of us the other Government roofs in the Whitehall range stretch away, fold upon fold – the Scottish Office massif, with the Horse Guards chain behind it, and on the horizon the fantastic cloudscape of communications equipment on the roof of the Admiralty.

There's something else on the roof of the Admiralty, too – a little knot of people, half-hidden behind the parapet, intent upon some piece of apparatus. It's the glass eyes!

For a moment I have the wild sweet thought that I will climb up on to the pitch and balance there stark naked, waving at them across the mountain range that divides us, jeering at them, because I now know almost everything and they know nothing. But even more immediately than I managed to think this ridiculous thought I had already ducked prudently and shamefully out of sight.

I slither clumsily back down into the gully and pick up my clothes. I'm very shaken. So the glass eyes are up to rooftop level already, even if it's the wrong roof. Of course, a moment's reflection tells me that they weren't glass eyes at all – no one's going to let television journalists loose on top of Ministry of Defence property. All the same, my hour of elation has passed. Summerchild and Serafin and Millie have fled, and I'm on my own up here, absurdly naked and absurdly dirty. The sun, I feel, has definitely begun to recede from the solstice.

I throw my clothes down through the skylight and lower myself sickeningly after them. The essential foothold on the stopcock is invisible from above and I have to scrabble alarmingly for it with my foot, as I hang suspended from my elbows in the trap. One of the worst things about climbing up things, if you're nervous of heights, is the certainty that climbing down them again is going to be even harder.

Never mind. Back to work!

24

But I think the game's up.

I'm walking up the steep streets in Greenwich towards my house when I discover this. It's about six-fifteen, on Sunday, June 25th, in the world I am walking through; and nearly lunchtime, to judge from internal evidence, on Thursday, June 21st, the day of the summer solstice itself, in the world inside my left ear. They are getting very close to me now. But then of course they have to. They must just get their hands on Monday, June 24th before I reach Monday, June 26th. They'll be only a day behind me when Summerchild goes down.

I'm on my way home to put Timmy to bed. I suddenly thought about him having his bath. I was in the little cloakroom at the time, after I'd come down from the roof, trying to clean myself up at the sink before I went back to work. I was struck by the absurdity of it: here was I, washing with no soap, and there was he, bathing with no father. So I dried myself on my handkerchief, then I picked up the tape-recorder and the tin of tapes, and closed the door on this mad little universe at the top of the spiral staircase. I'll finish listening to the tapes tonight one way or another and get up at dawn to write the report. What I'm doing, now I'm out of the train, and climbing the hill towards my house on my own, is balancing the tape-recorder on my shoulder like a teenager and listening with my ear pressed up against the loudspeaker.

Summerchild is dictating something that he has announced as a position paper. He is also, by the sound of it, making lunch. The position paper, so far as I can understand what he is saying, is about the nature of time. His voice is uncharacteristically urgent and persuasive. He sounds the way one feels when one's running a temperature and not quite oneself. I believe he has caught philosophy. Like many patients who catch a disease they have never been exposed to before, he has caught it in a dangerously acute form. What he seems to be saying is that any understanding of happiness, or of the quality of life, must depend upon our knowing what it's like to experience something and to experience it now. So we need to think about what we mean by 'now'. The more often he repeats the word, the more difficult I find it to remember what if anything we do mean by 'now'. Or rather, what we mean by '*now*', since he gives it some strange insistent emphasis that makes the whole idea of the present time seem as remote and alien as one of those notions one gets into one's head in a delirium. Well, perhaps this is what philosophy is supposed to do.

What in fact we get *now*, that's to say at this point on the tape, is a pause for hurrying footsteps, and various muffled thumps and scrapes, which I think, from my growing experience of analysing the sounds inside that room, suggest some sudden crisis in the kitchen. Then more footsteps and the philosophy resumes. 'Now is *now*,' he urges quietly, 'but *now* it's no longer now. So *that* now isn't *this* now, and the now I called *this* now is no longer this now – it's *that* now – it's *another* that now.' I don't know much more about philosophy than Summerchild does, but I suspect that these gropings are like Summerchild's performances on the violin (or mine on the trombone) – enjoyable to oneself, but not the kind of thing one would like a professional to overhear. Which may be why he is talking so rapidly and quietly; I have a feeling that there is indeed a professional philosopher somewhere not far away – already coming up the stairs, perhaps, about to appear for lunch.

Another excursion to the kitchen. Then: 'People think, Well, *now* it's now – and *now* it's now – and now it's now and now it's now and now it's now – which means it's *always* now. They get the idea that the present is just one long continuous thing. But what I suddenly understood this morning is that each *now* is separate from every other *now* – that everything we see and hear and think and feel in *this* now is separate from everything we feel and experience in *that* now . . .'

I think at this point I begin to have some glimmering of what all this is about. I believe he has had some revelation, as he lay on the airbed up there in the broiling sun, which seems to explain to him how he can be simultaneously the same man who lives quietly tucked away in the secret depths of Hyde Hill Lane and the one who lives wildly concealed in the secret depths of the Cabinet Office roof. The answer is going to be, I think, that he is *not* the same man. He is infinitely many men, each of whom dwells independently in each moment of time, without reference to or responsibility for any of the others.

So it is ironical that he is just developing the theoretical infrastructure for this approach and obliterating various key sections of it with the clatter of what I take to be the crockery and cutlery he is laying for lunch on the desk very close to the tape-recorder – ' . . . This means that time is really a series of . . .' – crash! – '. . . like the particles that make up matter, and that . . .' – bang, bang! – '. . . are no more visible to us than the gaps between the electrons . . .' – when the blow falls. The fatal knock on the door, which I had envisaged as coming in the middle of intercourse.

It's a brisk double report that suggests courtesy but authority. Not, I think, Serafin arriving for lunch. Summerchild evidently doesn't think so, either. There is a moment's silence, broken only by a fork falling on the floor, while he stands wondering what to do. The door is pushed at, but it doesn't give – the very sound that I imagined – and then it's quietly but insistently shaken in its frame. Summerchild puts down the rest of the cutlery and crosses to unlock it and drag it open.

'Francis!' says Summerchild, with polite surprise.

Just as I predicted.

'Not a bad moment?' says Francis Tite.

'No, no,' says Summerchild.

'I happened to be in this part of the building,' says Tite.

He has come in and Summerchild is shutting the door behind him. He has an amused, easy voice that suggests a rather different sort of Civil Service from the one in which Ken Hurren has made his mark. As soon as I hear it a face comes to me. Polished red cheeks, tight little mouth, silver hair worn very slightly too long. A short man, full of blood and spleen, with a flower in his buttonhole. I think he was still around the department when I first joined, serving in various distinguished emeritus roles.

'Thought I'd see how you're settling in up here,' he says. 'You've done it up rather nicely. Bit remote, but that has its charms.'

He sounds as if he's visiting Summerchild's country cottage. But he's worried about something, as Summerchild will of course have realized – he wouldn't have come calling otherwise.

'Which may account for why we haven't seen or heard quite so much of you recently,' he says.

'Yes,' says Summerchild. He makes it sound like a rather lengthy statement. His voice has reverted to its usual cautious growl.

The conversation hangs fire. I imagine Tite is gazing at the knives and forks on the table.

'I was just making some lunch,' says Summerchild. 'Save going to the canteen . . . Sit down.'

A slight pause. Tite is looking at the chair he is being offered.

'Some kind of deckchair?' he inquires.

'I think it's what they call a director's chair,' says Summerchild reluctantly. Of course. All the furniture in their household is the sort that can be folded up and carried, not too conspicuously, through Security. There is no sound of Tite sitting down.

'I was a little concerned about you,' he says. 'You seem to be having rather a bad time with Personnel.'

He means that Personnel seem to be having rather a bad time with Summerchild. So this is the source of his disquiet. This is what's got him up the spiral staircase.

'Oh . . .' says Summerchild vaguely. I imagine he is shrugging.

'Seven candidates for the post, I gather, and all found wanting. Morale in Personnel is somewhat shaken.'

'I didn't feel any of them were really quite right for us.'

'No. Seven, though. Well . . . So you're quite without staff? You and Dr Serafin are coping entirely on your own?'

'For the moment.'

'She's not in today?'

Summerchild thinks about this for a fraction of a second.

'I'll go and look,' he says.

He goes into the cloakroom and closes the door behind him. Good God – she's on the roof! But what does Tite think at the sight of Summerchild disappearing into a cloakroom five foot long by four foot wide to look for his Director? He's probably guessed that there is a lavatory in there. Perhaps he thinks that Summerchild has gone to tap delicately on the lavatory door and murmur that the Permanent Secretary has come to call. It's not really possible to deduce, from the long silence that ensues in the office, what Tite makes of it. A few faint sounds suggest that he is walking round the room, perhaps examining the pictures on the walls. Including, I suppose, the photograph of Serafin looking at Summerchild and the one of Summerchild looking at Serafin. I can't imagine what he concludes. All I can imagine is the lower half of Summerchild, balanced on the stopcock behind the cloakroom door with his upper half disappearing through the roof. The upper half itself, up there in the sunlight, and what it's saying, are also beyond my imagination.

The cloakroom door opens.

'She's just coming,' says Summerchild gravely.

'Ah,' says Tite.

Another long silence, broken only by the tiny sound of a spoon being laid carefully down on a hard surface. Tite has picked it up from the lunch arrangements on the desk, perhaps to check idly on the hallmark.

'I got them at the Army & Navy,' says Summerchild. 'They were reduced.'

'Very nice,' says Tite.

Up on the roof, I suppose, Serafin has lost one of her shoes and put her skirt on back to front.

'I've obviously picked the wrong moment,' says Tite.

'No, no,' says Summerchild. 'She's just . . .'

Just what? I imagine that some rather unspecific gesture completes his explanation. There are muffled noises from the cloakroom. Just hanging by her elbows in the skylight, Summerchild's gesture is meant to indicate. Just searching blindly with her foot for the stopcock. Just . . . yes, just stepping on a lighted gas-ring and hurriedly stepping off it again. Things clatter about out there in muffled surprise.

'Do you think,' says Tite, 'that you ought perhaps to . . .?'

'No, no,' says Summerchild.

The cloakroom door opens.

'I do beg your pardon,' says Serafin.

'This is Francis Tite,' says Summerchild. 'I don't think you have actually . . .'

'I don't think we have,' says Serafin. 'How do you do?'

She is all smiles and wide-open eyes, without a trace of discomfiture. 'I was working out there,' she explains. 'I had one or two things to think about.'

'Very sensible,' says Tite. He's a man who's dined at many high tables, of course. He knows the ways of the world. I don't imagine it comes as any great surprise to him to find that a leading philosopher locks herself up in the lavatory to think.

'We all need somewhere to get away to,' he says. 'I'm tempted to do the same myself.'

'Do we have any kitchen paper?' says Serafin, in a different tone. She is speaking to Summerchild. 'I stepped in the butter.'

'I bought some this morning,' says Summerchild. 'It's still in the carrier.'

The cloakroom door opens. Summerchild, evidently, has gone for the kitchen paper; Serafin, shoe presumably in hand, is left alone with Tite.

'You'll have some lunch, of course?' she says.

I'm just turning into my own road when she utters these words. I stand still for a moment on the corner. She wants him to *stay*? She wants to delay his longed-for departure by an hour, while they make polite conversation about the choice of pictures on the walls and the provenance of the china? Or do the words just emerge of their own accord? Do all human beings connected as couples find themselves producing hospitality as helplessly as Alka-Seltzer and water produce bubbles?

Tite declines, naturally. 'How kind,' he says. 'Alas, though . . .'

The social process, however, has developed a momentum of its own. Serafin appeals to Summerchild as he emerges from the cloakroom. 'We've got enough, haven't we, Stephen?'

'Plenty,' Summerchild is obliged to insist. But what compels him to add that it's homemade clam chowder? What drives her to explain that it's homemade by Stephen and then, while Summerchild answers a telephone call, to offer a gratuitous gloss on their domestic arrangements by confiding that it's Stephen who does all the cooking? It seems to me that the social logic of the situation has taken over not only their behaviour but their feelings. They have now conceived the genuine desire that Tite should stay for lunch. When the receiver is passed to Serafin – it's her good son, Alexander, calling from Oxford – Summerchild takes over the urging. He detains Tite, who already seems to be halfway out of the door, with improvised solutions to all the problems that lunch will involve.

'We've only got two soup spoons,' he says. 'But I can use a coffee mug.'

'Another time, why not?' says Tite, edging ever nearer the Athenaeum.

'Then I can wash up one of the spoons for the next course,' says Summerchild. 'I can eat with a spoon and the bread knife.'

And then there is a sudden silence.

'What?' says Summerchild gently.

'Not bad news?' says Tite.

They must be looking at Serafin. In the silence that follows you can hear the small click of the receiver being replaced.

'Apparently my husband has left me,' says Serafin carefully.

I am standing on my doorstep by this time, in the golden evening light, with the tape-recorder pressed against my ear and the front-door key frozen in space halfway to the lock. An entirely predictable development, with hindsight. It would naturally be at a moment like this, just when you'd reached the dénouement of some quite other story in your life, that your husband would walk out. But before I can hear what happens next, and find out whether Tite is obliged by the conventions of sympathy to stay to lunch after all, or how Summerchild reacts to this fundamental change in their situation, the front door opens in front of me. Timmy is standing on the doorstep, looking simultaneously important and guilty. I can see at once that he is the bearer of bad news.

'Granny kept trying to phone you,' he says, 'but you weren't there. She got the doctor. The doctor's gone now. She doesn't know what to do. She's in the kitchen.'

I put my hand on Timmy's shoulder and go through the hall, sick at heart. Timmy follows me. In the kitchen my mother-in-law is putting things back in cupboards and drawers. I look round. Every storage space in the room has been neatly and systematically emptied. Every surface is covered with half-used packets of breakfast cereal, and rusting tins of peaches, and plastic bottles of detergent, with scourers and shoe-polish and tablecloths and slug-killer and dried-up paintpots . . .

'She must have walked all the way,' says my mother-in-law. 'She didn't have any money. She hadn't got her bag – nothing . . . I'm sorry . . . I don't know where everything goes . . .'

She starts to cry. Timmy watches her fearfully. Above our heads Lynn vacuums away, thumping the machine up against the walls and the furniture.

I have a ridiculous urge to sit down on the floor and laugh. Entirely predictable, once again. It would naturally be at a moment like this that your wife would walk in on you. And I have a suspicion that there's something not altogether unreasonable about her behaviour this time. I think she was just looking for the biscuit tin.

25

The attempts that Summerchild and Serafin have been making at an impromptu lunch-party constitute, I suppose, their first recorded public act as a couple. The news from Oxford, however, I discover when I get the chance to continue my researches, seems to have put rather a damper on the occasion.

'He left a change of address card,' explains Serafin. 'This is how we know. Alexander found it on the hall table.'

'I'm so sorry,' says Tite. 'May I offer my . . .?' What – condolences? Congratulations? He doesn't seem to know. I have the impression that the sudden flood of events has swept even the imperturbable Tite a little out of his social depth.

'It was not entirely unexpected,' says Serafin. 'Though as with most not entirely unexpected events the precise time of its occurrence was.'

'Well,' says Tite – already, by the sound of it, out on the spiral staircase – 'I imagine you'd like to be left to digest this in peace. If there's anything I can do . . .'

'Thank you,' says Serafin.

'Thank you,' adds Summerchild. Yes, they are a couple.

Silence. I imagine he is looking at her. I imagine she is looking at the floor, hand to head. I'm out on the streets again myself, with the tape-recorder to my ear, and it's dark. I've had to wait a long time to find out what happened next. Even after I'd got Lynn back to the hospital they couldn't find anyone to give her any medication . . .

'Just . . . a change of address?' asks Summerchild quietly.

'There was a note on it to say that he was coming back for his books and his bicycle.'

. . . Then after she'd settled and I'd got home I had to sit down in the kitchen and eat the cold joint left over from lunch. My mother-in-law had finished getting Timmy to bed by this time, and putting all the kitchen equipment back in the wrong place. She was sitting opposite me, gazing silently at the cold grey leather on my plate, thinking no doubt about how everything was her fault, while I chewed on no less silently, thinking about the unplayed tapes in the biscuit tin.

'I'd better get back and talk to the boys,' says Serafin finally.

'I'll take you to Paddington,' says Summerchild.

'Thank you. I should appreciate that.'

'I'll turn off the gas.'

The key grates in the lock and their footsteps clatter away down the spiral staircase. Only one guest remains at the lunch-table, so patient and perfectly behaved that they have forgotten about him. Never saying the wrong thing, never showing any signs of unease, still the perfect listener, in spite of there being nothing left for him to listen to. But finally even the tape-recorder runs out of patience, or at any rate out of tape, and switches itself off.

I have emerged by this time on to the open tableland at the top of the hill. I'm very impatient to know what happens next. I walk round trying to find some arbitrary unpeopled spot in the wide warm darkness where I can stop and listen to the next tape undisturbed. But everywhere I go pale shirts gleam out of the summer Sunday darkness with their arms round pale dresses. Everywhere there is sudden invisible laughter, the clink of cans and bottles, the thud of the bass from other tape-recorders. There are also little taut roaring noises indicative of frustration, which come from my own throat. I stop anywhere . . . *here* . . . and turn the machine on. At once there is a shout from out of the darkness close behind me. Nothing to do with me, I'm sure, but all the same I start moving hurriedly from wherever I am to somewhere else, then veer off to somewhere else again.

'Confidential,' murmurs Summerchild into my ear. 'F Tite – S Summerchild. June 21st. I must apologize for any embarrassment you were caused during your visit to the Unit today . . .'

A minute on the subject. Oh no. No, no, no! Say nothing! Just hope that Tite will find it too awkward ever to refer to.

'I think you will have realized how things stand between Dr Serafin and myself . . .'

He's decided on complete frankness. This is going to be worse than the lunch-party itself.

'I see that I should have come to you as soon as I realized what was happening and not let things drift on until you heard rumours or jumped to conclusions. I can only say that at the beginning it was difficult to know what *was* happening, and that once it became clear it seemed so natural as to need no comment or explanation. However, today's events have forced me to see that there are serious anomalies in our situation. I took the opportunity, after escorting Dr Serafin to Paddington this afternoon, of walking back to the department by way of the Parks, and of giving the matter long and careful thought. I came to the conclusion, after considering all the options, that I had only one possible course of action open to me . . .'

He's resigning. Not just transferring to another department – it's too late for that – but departing from the Civil Service altogether. His voice is steady and measured – almost serene. He has found a kind of nobility in defeat. Except that this minute is never going to be delivered – most probably never even typed out . . .

Just a moment, though. I am slowly becoming conscious that what he is saying is not what I was expecting to hear.

'. . . hope we shall find an early opportunity to invite you to join us for a working lunch at the Unit – and this time with a more adequate supply of cutlery!'

What? *What?* I've missed something. I run the tape back.

'. . . only one possible course of action open to me, and that was to explain, fully and frankly, to everyone concerned, exactly what the situation is. I realize that the Unit's working arrangements depart quite markedly from established practice and at one point, as they developed, I did become sufficiently anxious to contemplate requesting a transfer to another department. But I have now become firmly convinced that they provide the best possible conditions for undertaking the type of research in which we are engaged. They may indeed offer the *only* way in which work of this nature can be pursued and I am prepared to defend them very strongly.

'Now that we have set things on a more straightforward footing I hope you will come back and see at greater leisure the work we are doing. Indeed I hope we shall find an early opportunity to invite you to join us for a working lunch . . .'

He's *not* resigning. Far from it. And there's more to come.

'In view of the change in Dr Serafin's domestic situation, which you happened quite fortuitously to hear about during your visit today, you may be concerned about the effect that our working arrangements have had upon our home life. Let me say first of all that there is no reason to think that the departure of Dr Serafin's husband was in any way precipitated by arrangements at the Unit. Their relationship was, as I understand it, already very tenuous. I believe he had little interest in or knowledge of her professional life.

'Today's developments, however, have made me aware of how anomalous my own domestic situation had become. You may like to know that I have now resolved this. After anxious reflection on the question, during and after my walk back from Paddington, I decided I should have to clarify the question with my family. I have now had an opportunity to discuss the matter with my wife and to indicate to her, within the usual limits of discretion suggested by professional confidentiality . . .'

He stops in mid-sentence. He's told Anne. Told her what? Everything, no doubt, in his present exalted mood. Or perhaps nothing. *Indicated* it, by some combination of the sighs and laughs and silences by which he normally indicates, within the limits of professional confidentiality, the events of his working life.

'Is everything all right, love?' he says suddenly, in a very different voice. He's stopped in the middle of his minute to make a phone call. *Love*, though. I wonder if he's ever called her that before. I wonder if he's ever called anyone that before.

'I tried to ring you earlier, only ... Oh, I see. That was Nicholas? He sounded rather ... well, he kept putting the phone down ... The boys are all right otherwise, are they? What about the bicycle ...? No, I mean, did your husband come back for it ...? So he had to mend the puncture before he could ...? But apart from that it went off reasonably ...? Yes ... Yes ... I'm sure it was ... I'm sure you were ...

'Are *you* all right? You sound a bit ... You were asleep ...? Oh, no! I'm so sorry, love, I'm so sorry! It's not that late, is it? Oh, yes, I see, it's ten to two ... I'm sorry – I'd no idea – I was just sitting here working – I'm writing to Francis Tite ... About today, yes – I'm trying to get everything straight ... I suppose it was later than I thought when I got back from Greenwich ... I've told Anne ... Yes ... No, she took it very well. She was very calm, very sensible. We just talked. Or we talked some of the time. A lot of the time we just sat there and ... Eaten? Yes, I've eaten. This was all after dinner ...

'No, Millie was there. I talked about it with Millie. We both talked about it with Millie. She was very calm and collected ... She went upstairs to do her homework. She's got to get up tomorrow for orchestra ... No, they were both very calm. *I* was the one who got a bit ... No, it's all right – I'm fine – don't worry ... It's just that I found it very ... very painful ...

'Anyway, we agreed I should move out ... No, no – it will be better for everyone ... It's the only way, love ... When? How do you mean, when? – I've already done it! I've left ...! Well, I took one of the sleeping-bags ... No, no – I'm in the office ...! Yes! I'm sorry – I should have explained – I thought

211

you realized . . . No, it's all very convenient, as it happens. I've brought the airbed down from the roof . . .

'Oh, I watered the tomatoes . . .

'No, there's enough for breakfast. I'll go out and do a proper shop as soon as things open. I suppose the clam chowder probably ought to be . . . Yes . . . yes . . . I'll make one of my special salads. How early can you get here . . .? You can't stay the night, can you? It's Friday – you could stay the weekend . . . No . . . no . . . Nicholas, yes . . . Of course . . .

'Never mind – *I'll* be here – we can phone each other. We might manage to have dinner here once or twice next week . . . Or breakfast – you could get an early train . . . And if the boys ever stay with Ted . . .'

A moment ago he could scarcely speak for the recollected pain of his departure from Hyde Hill Lane. Now, by the sound of his voice, he has forgotten about it completely. He is drunk on the thin high air at the top of the Cabinet Office. I can see now that it was only a matter of time before he would be spending his nights as well as his days up there. He'll be needing a refrigerator next, to keep the leftovers in . . . a wardrobe . . . they'll be building a loft extension into the roof for when their children come to stay . . .

But already his voice has come soaring back down from the heights. It's suddenly down to ground level again.

'I found the book,' he says awkwardly. 'The book I told you about – the one they were making for me as a birthday present . . . My life . . .'

And now his voice is not just down on the ground – it's disappeared beneath it. No further sound emerges for some moments.

'I went into the kitchen,' he whispers finally. I can hardly hear the words. 'It was in the bin . . . She'd torn it up . . . I could see Millie's writing . . .'

Then nothing more but a few sporadic attempts at reassurance. 'No, I'm all right. It's just . . .' Just what? Just too terrible to talk about, apparently. 'Please don't worry. I'll be . . .' All right, no doubt. Too all right to say the words. Eventually the tape runs out.

I'm down from the heights myself by this time, too. My random movements about the open plain have brought me, I discover without surprise, to the well-known prospect of lights and towers, then taken me down into the hidden world of unsurfaced byways on the front of the hillside. I am on my way to Hyde Hill Lane, of course. What I'm thinking about is the orchestra rehearsal that Millie was going to in the morning. I remember the sunlight in the hall. It was the end of the summer term and the exams were over. It was our first rehearsal during the day instead of in the evenings. Morning sunlight was pouring through the windows in front of us instead of evening sunlight through the windows behind us. I remember the feeling of hopefulness that came with it. And I remember the hope fading as all the scraping of chairs and chatter of voices faded into the A from the oboe and there was still no fuzz of red hair among the cellos beneath me. That was when she gave up playing, and everything else. It wasn't when her father died. It was when he left home.

That was when I walked up the steps I'm now looking at, that was when her mother opened the front door there. After the rehearsal on Friday, June 21st. That was when she spoke to me so oddly and I knew that something was wrong. But Summerchild wasn't dead then; that wasn't the trouble at all. He was in the office, dictating another minute, which I'm listening to now.

'Secret and Confidential', he has begun this time and by the sound of it he has been restored by his night's sleep on the airbed. There is excitement in his voice. Evidently he has amazing new developments in his private life he wants to make known. And he's raised his aim. This minute's not addressed to the Permanent Secretary; it's to the Prime Minister.

I stand where I am in the lane, the tape-recorder pressed to my ear, shocked by the ballooning escalation of Summerchild's unreason. He seems to have lost the last semblance of contact with normal protocol and procedure. I gaze blindly up at the blind windows of the house, waiting to hear to what heights of folly he has ascended now.

'In the absence of the Director, who reports to you personally, I am taking the liberty of minuting you direct myself on
a matter of some urgency.

'I have to inform you that a systematic attempt is being
made to sabotage the Strategy(Quality of Life) Unit.

'I returned to my office this morning, after a brief absence
to obtain various necessary supplies, to discover that my key
would not unlock the door. On applying to Security I was
told that the lock had been changed and that no authority
had been given to issue me with the new key. I went
immediately to seek clarification from Mr Tite, the Permanent
Secretary. Mr Tite declined to see me. His deputy, Mr Le Bon,
referred me to Miss Peel in the Establishment Division, who
told me that she had been asked to arrange a medical
examination for me. She said she knew nothing about the
reasons for this, nor did she know that I had been locked out
of my office. She suggested that I should *go home* and wait
until the medical examination was arranged – a peculiarly
inapposite suggestion, since – as I minuted Mr Tite last
night – I have just *left* home in order to devote myself to my
work. In so far as I now have a home, it is, as Mr Tite well
knows, behind the door which he has locked against me.

'I am informed by Security that the Director herself has not
been issued with the new key. This is an intolerable discour-
tesy. Since, as I have now established, she left her home in
Oxford at 8.45 this morning to come to this office, and since
there is still no sign of her here now (just after 12 noon) I
can only assume that she arrived during my absence, failed
to gain admittance and was forced to return all the way to
Oxford.

'In the circumstances I judged it imperative to secure my
lines of communication by getting back to my desk, and
justifiable therefore to gain access to the office by unorthodox
means. As soon as I had got back into the room I found clear
signs that it had been searched. The airbed had been moved
to provide access to the kitchen. My pyjamas, which I had left

folded and out of sight inside the sleeping-bag, were now lying unfolded on top of it.

'I can only conclude that these measures are part of a concerted attack upon the Unit's existence and I feel it incumbent upon me as a matter of urgency to find out whether they were undertaken with your knowledge and consent, or whether (as I suspect) they represent a flagrant attempt by certain elements in the department here to thwart the Government's will.

'In case distorted reports have been reaching you from other quarters, I should perhaps take this opportunity to give you a full account of everything that has happened in the Unit during the course of the past few weeks. If you have not been kept informed of these developments as they occurred it was not, I must stress, because of any intention to withhold anything from you, but simply because of the pressure of events here.

'As I have explained in my minute to Mr Tite, these have led to an important change in the nature of the working relationship between the Director and myself . . .'

He is interrupted by the phone – has snatched it up before it has completed the first syllable of its ring.

'Where are you?' he cries, and at once his voice is full of joy and anxiety. 'I thought you'd gone back to Oxford . . .! I thought you must have tried to get in and . . .! No, because they've locked us out! They've changed the lock! Francis Tite, yes . . .! Yes, I am – I climbed in! I got out of the window downstairs, in the room where Mrs Padmore used to work! It was rather easy, as a matter of fact. I pulled the upper sash down to make a foothold, then just hauled myself up over the parapet . . . No, perfectly safe! I had to move the geraniums, that's all. In fact I went back down with some of that rope we got for the clothesline – I tied it on to the groceries and hauled them up! That's when they changed the lock, when I was out buying the groceries! They must have been waiting – they must have been watching. Anyway, we're well-provisioned . . .!

215

'No, I shan't . . .! Don't worry – I shan't, I shan't! I did a lot of climbing when I was younger, as you know . . .

'Listen – go and buy a climbing rope . . . A climbing rope, yes! You can pass it up to me . . . What for? For safety . . .! No – for *your* safety! So I can bring you up on the rope . . .! There's a shop in High Holborn – where did you say you were . . .?'

And then there is a long silence. The answer to this simple question, now that he has stopped to listen to it, has brought the whole burbling cascade to a halt. And when at last he speaks again his voice has changed completely. All the wild exuberance has gone. He is very quiet and chastened.

'You mean, at the back of the town hall?' he asks. And I know at once which town hall she's at the back of. It's not Oxford Town Hall. It's not Marylebone, or Manchester, or Mannheim. It's Greenwich Town Hall. She is in the first phone box you come to round the corner from where I'm standing in Hyde Hill Lane.

'You didn't . . .?'

No, she didn't. Didn't go into the house. Didn't ring the bell. Didn't announce her presence.

'And Millie . . .?'

Yes, and Millie. She saw both of them – Anne and Millie. She wouldn't have seen Millie if Millie had been where she should have been, at rehearsal with me. But she wasn't. She was at home, glimpsed through the windows of the house in front of me. And Serafin was standing where I am standing, on this same outcrop of pebbles on the other side of the lane.

'How did they seem . . .?'

There is a silence while she tells him. Though I don't suppose they seemed any particular how. I imagine she scarcely saw them. A glimpse of Millie in the kitchen, perhaps, saying something to her mother. Saying what? Something about her father, about her feelings? Who knows? Probably not. Most likely something about the weekend shopping, or asking if she should take the things out of the washing-

216

machine. Later her mother appeared in the living-room for a moment and seemed to be looking for something in the desk. One or the other came out to the dustbins at some point with a pile of old newspapers . . .

'Listen, there's a train in ten minutes. I'll meet you at Charing Cross . . .'

Another silence. Isn't she going to get the train? What's she saying? She'll miss the train at this rate . . .

'Don't, love,' he says gently at last. 'Please . . . Please don't . . .'

I know what's made her cry. It's not the sight of Anne or Millie. It's the crack in the third step up to the front door, that he saw every night on his way home, that he'd never got round to doing anything about. I'm looking at it now, as we both wait for her to stop crying. If only he'd never said anything about that broken step! If only he'd got it fixed! That broken step is more than any of us can bear.

And there, coming down it in the night, more heard than seen, is a sudden commotion, a wild scrabbling and panting in the shape of a small dog straining against its lead. In the darkness of the open doorway behind it is the paleness of a summer dress. I suppose this is what I've been waiting for.

The dog rushes at me and evolves into *canis erectus* on the end of its lead, drowning the awkwardness of the moment with its yapping. Then it catches the scent of me and subsides as suddenly as it flared up; the smell of me is evidently becoming an established feature of the lane.

'Hello!' says Millie's father suddenly, as she and I turn wordlessly to begin our walk. I start like a murderer at the sound and my finger scrabbles everywhere for the Stop button. Millie has turned to look at me. She is frowning; her lips are parted as if to speak.

'Tape-recorder,' I explain. But it's the biscuit tin that she is looking at, uncomprehendingly, exactly the way Lynn did as I waved it about in front of her at the hospital. 'Tapes,' I elaborate. I give the tin a shake. The tapes shirr plausibly back and forth inside.

She looks away and says nothing. Nor do I. I'm wondering

217

if she recognized her father's voice. It's unlikely – extremely unlikely – impossible. Two syllables, uttered out of nowhere, in the darkness, distorted by reproduction, with the sound turned low, after fifteen years. But it raises all kinds of questions, that brief greeting out of the past. What intimacy can I have with the daughter, when I'm carrying a tin full of the undisclosed and undisclosable remains of the father? Or are father and daughter completely separable entities, which can always live in unconnected parts of my mind?

Another voice has started to talk. Mine, this time.

'I realize all this is rather absurd,' it's saying, with sudden awkward frankness.

'All what?' asks Millie carefully. Yes, all what? I shall be interested to hear.

'All . . . *this* . . .' says my voice. My arms join the campaign. They gesture to indicate the night, the lane, the dog, Millie, myself. And of course as my arms gesture so do the tape-recorder and biscuit tin as well, and the tapes rattle again in the tin, like the money inside a collecting-box, shaken to draw the world's attention to it.

'It's just that going for a walk on my own seems even more absurd,' continues this strange voice of mine. 'My going for a walk on my own over there on the other side of the Park, while you're going for a walk on your own on this side.'

I have the impression that my voice is making some kind of declaration. It all seems rather remote. Because what I'm thinking about is not really Millie – it's Serafin. At what point did she decide to go to Greenwich? Was it some time in the small hours, as she lay sleepless after Summerchild's phone call? Or did she come up out of the Tube at Charing Cross, on her way from Paddington, and instead of walking down Whitehall find herself somehow going into the station? Perhaps she didn't even know quite what she was looking for. It was only when she saw Greenwich on the departures board that the idea came to her . . .

Someone's talking.

'I always used to go for walks with my mother,' Millie is telling me.

'I always used to go with my wife,' my voice might very naturally reply to this. But it doesn't, I note with interest. It maintains a tactful silence.

And what's Serafin going to do? Is she going to get on the train? Is she going to go back to the Unit? I somehow have a feeling, in view of what's going to be happening in two days' time, that there's going to be a painful scene when Summerchild meets her at Charing Cross, which is going to end with her fleeing back to Oxford in shame and remorse.

'But she doesn't get out so much now,' says Millie.

Another thing that my voice might claim in common between her mother and my wife, but doesn't. In fact my voice seems to have taken off in some new direction. It's asking Millie if she remembers the time we did this, the time she said that, the rehearsal when, the first violin who. What I'm thinking while this goes on is that the Unit's chief finding on happiness seems so far to have gone unrecorded. What they have shown, if it needed showing, is that happiness is like economics or heat in seawater. You can make the laws of economics work for short periods of time in small models cut off from the rest of the world, just as you can have a hot bath in the sun-warmed pools of seawater left behind on the beach. But as soon as the neat economic model is reconnected with the unstructured chaos of human affairs, as soon as the tide returns, all gratifying predictivity breaks down, the hot bath disappears at once into the huge reserves of cold in the ocean deeps. Micro-happiness, yes; macro-happiness, I think not.

Soon we are standing in front of the Summerchilds' house again, our circuit of the hillside lanes complete. I have the impression that we have both been silent for some time. Something more will have to be said, some advance made on the progress to date, and I'm interested to know what direction my voice will try. But I'm also much taken up with another question which has belatedly lodged itself in my mind: why Summerchild was saying 'Hello!' He didn't sound as if he was talking to Serafin any more. Perhaps someone had come into the room . . . But the room was locked . . .

219

'I'd very much like to see you again,' my voice is saying, collectedly but surprisingly warmly, surprisingly persuasively. 'Perhaps I could phone you . . . I don't know whether you'd feel like going to a concert . . .' Something is slowly getting under way here, there's no doubt about it. Some awkward, lopsided, half-acknowledged relationship is taking shape in the grey shadow of Lynn's ever-present absence, that will torment and exhaust us both, and bring us little joy. My left hand is now holding both tape-recorder and biscuit tin, I notice, because my right hand, somewhat implausibly, is occupied in holding one of Millie's hands. It's her left hand – her right hand is holding the dog's lead. 'I don't know,' she is saying doubtfully. 'There are various things I have to do . . .' Her hand lies in mine, though, palm downwards, unresponsive but uncomplaining. I run my thumb over the sinews on the back of it.

And yet (I'm thinking) the room was locked and there was no one there for him to say hello to. I have the ridiculous feeling that he was actually talking to Millie. He looked out of the tape-recorder and suddenly saw her coming down the steps . . . His eye is upon us, I think madly – and even as the thought goes through my mind I feel my flesh creep, because I can *see* an eye upon us. In the darkened upstairs window of the house, I am just realizing, is a human presence – a watchfulness – a face. It's her mother, standing back in the shadows, watching us with that same old brooding thoughtfulness. How long has she been there? Was she there before, watching me listen to the tape-recorder?

The face dissolves imperceptibly back into the darkness. She's seen me looking at her. She didn't much like my talking to her daughter when I was single. She won't like my holding her hand now I'm married.

My hand gives Millie's hand a squeeze and lets it go. 'I'll ring, then,' says my voice confidently, as Millie goes up the steps to her front door. 'Give my love to your mother.'

As soon as I'm round the corner and going down the hill, I've put all this nonsense in the lane out of my mind. I've already got the tape-recorder back to my ear. 'Hello,' says

Summerchild once more. It's not a greeting, I realize, hearing it now – it's a question. 'Hello?' he asks again. 'Hello?' But there's no reply. They've been cut off, or else she's hung up in her distress. He puts the receiver down and waits, and when I pass the phone box behind the town hall a few moments later I can't help glancing in to see if she's still there, searching her bag for more change, trying to get through again. But the box is empty, which somehow makes it seem more likely that it was empty then and that she's on her way to the station. He'll meet her at Charing Cross and yes – that's where the confrontation is going to be, conducted in furtive desperation in the midst of the mid-morning shoppers – because I suspect she's heading not for Whitehall but for Oxford.

I'm on my way to the station myself. That eye brooding in the darkness of the window has made me think of another hostile eye, coming ever nearer across the rooftops, peering down through the open skylight above the cloakroom, inspecting the ancient provisions in the cupboard, roaming over the scattered files on the floor . . .

No, I know perfectly well that there is no eye coming over the rooftops. I'm not that unsettled by the affair. In any case I left the skylight securely fastened. The provisions and the papers will all sleep safe until morning, unperceived, non-existent. I can go home, look in on Timmy, listen to the last tape in comfort while I have a bath, and sleep myself, to be ready to write my report in the morning . . .

I just catch the last train of the evening. It's full of returning daytrippers with exhausted children, and ostentatiously drunken youths. I am distracted from all this, however, by some unfamiliar sensation inside myself. I can't quite pin it down. It's some kind of . . . smoothness. Or perhaps weightlessness. Or spaciousness. An outwardness, an upwardness. It seems to have some kind of retrospective connection with the events in Hyde Hill Lane. I can imagine leaping to the conclusion, if I were a different kind of person, that it was a faint twinge of happiness.

The lighted towers outside the windows revolve gravely anti-clockwise in the night, smiling very slightly to themselves.

26

The scattered files leap back into existence as I turn on the light. The close stillness of the air is re-created exactly as it was, undisturbed by any draught from an opened skylight, its intimately known smell of dust and old paper untainted by any lingering trace of human exhalations. My succession to the kingdom is still unchallenged.

I put the biscuit tin and the tape-recorder down on the desk between their photographs. I switch on, then slide up the window sash to let some air into the room. On the dusty square far below two belated tourists are moving uncertainly about, stopping and changing direction at random, living metaphors of the human condition. Behind my back Summerchild is walking about the room in much the same way, from time to time groaning and uttering little despairing sighs. He's not sure whether Serafin is going to ring back or catch the train; he's trying to decide how long to wait for the call before he rushes to Charing Cross. Suddenly the footsteps stop. He's decided she's not going to phone; I knew from the first that she wouldn't. I wait for the usual juddering as the door is dragged open, for the usual dying clatter down the spiral staircase . . . There is no juddering, though, no dying clatter, only a few faint sounds I can't quite place – the abrupt movement of fabric against a hard surface, a rattle, a scrape. Then the brooding silence of an empty room.

Naturally, as soon as I think about it – the door's locked and he can't open it. He's left the way he came in – through the window. I haul myself out after him to see where he's gone, with the same rub of my clothes against the window-sill as I hoist myself up, the same rattle of the raised sash as my back catches it, the same scrape of my shoe against the frame as I squeeze one leg through the gap and ease myself cautiously out on to the slates. I look over the parapet, straight down into the darkness of the garden behind Number Ten, five floors below. Even in the blackness I can see one thing down there with great clarity – myself, an unconscious huddle of broken bones, waiting to be found by the security people in the morning. I move back behind the parapet and control my panic. Summerchild was a climber when he was younger; I wasn't. I put my head over the edge again, not looking down into the darkness at the bottom this time, but shifting my gaze slowly down over the bricks immediately beneath me, course by course, until they come to the lintel above the window on the fourth floor. This was the Clerical Officer's room. What Summerchild was doing, presumably, was shifting his body backwards over the edge, and then hanging from the parapet while he felt with his feet for the top of the sash he had left open below . . .

I get back behind the parapet again. I feel a kind of sick electricity run through me, as if a current were being induced in my flesh by the magnetic attraction of the emptiness below. Even allowing for his youthful experience, it seems to me that Summerchild has now lost all reasonable judgement of danger, all normal assessment of the possibilities of the world around him. To hang down that wall, with forty feet of nothing underneath him . . . in the dark . . . No, not in the dark! I'm in the dark – he's doing it in broad daylight – visible to every policeman and security officer around Horse Guards Parade, his fall watched by every tourist . . . But I don't want even to think about it. I firmly imagine Summer-child safely arrived inside the Clerical Officer's room, on his way downstairs to Charing Cross. After all, he has two more days to live – and he was found nearly quarter of a mile away, not down there in the Prime Minister's garden.

I haul myself unsteadily back in through the window and go to the cloakroom to wash the memory of the parapet off my hands. Then, as I shake them dry, I think I hear a faint noise in the room behind me. I listen, my hands petrified in mid-air . . .

Yes – a scrape of shoe on window frame, a rattle of the sash as something catches it . . . Breathing . . . Someone climbing in through the window – someone in the room . . . I spin round, more frightened of not seeing than of seeing.

But there's nothing to see. Only the tape-recorder turning and the breathing of someone who was in the room fifteen years ago. Of course. I'm losing my own sense of judgement.

My scalp still tingles, though. This unseen presence in the room is as real as living flesh and blood and even more alarming. Who is it, moving a chair three feet away from where I'm standing? Sitting down . . . Pushing back papers on the desk . . . breathing, audibly *breathing*! Then the vocal chords close on the escaping breath to make a new sound – the sort of long unconscious growl of complaint that a man might utter when he turns over in his sleep, or release in the privacy of his own room to vent his feelings.

Yes, my invisible visitor is in his own room. In his own home, in fact; it's Summerchild sitting on the opposite side of the desk from me. That's why he's breathing so hard – because he's just hauled himself up over the edge of the parapet. He's come back.

He hasn't been to Charing Cross. He hasn't had time even to get halfway down the stairs. I don't understand this change of plan . . .

He groans again. That same sustained low roar of anguish and frustration.

Yes . . . I think perhaps I do understand. He has been hanging from the parapet, reaching with his feet for the unseen foothold on the lowered window sash beneath him – and the foothold has gone. Someone has closed the window. They've locked him out of his office and now they've come back and shut up the Clerical Officer's room as well. His little bolt-hole has been closed – but with him inside it.

There are no more groans. His first spasm has subsided and he is sitting here thinking hard, as he has been trained to do, about the implications of the situation. They are quite interesting and he is going to need all his professional powers to deal with them. Or so it seems to me, because I'm thinking about them myself, no doubt in much the same kind of way, listing the same options, arriving at the same recommendations.

The options are two, and they are a long-married couple: I can do something, or I can do nothing. I can ring Tite and get myself let out, or I can wait.

If I get myself let out, I might still just reach Charing Cross in time to meet Serafin's train. But once I am out I shall not be allowed in again. I shall have met Serafin, but we shall be homeless.

If I wait, Serafin will arrive at Charing Cross and find no one to meet her, whereupon she will have a rather larger number of options open to her. Of waiting or not waiting, of coming to the Unit and finding the door locked, of returning to Oxford, of entering a nunnery or going back to Saratov. All of these will be more or less disastrous to my hopes. But she also has one option which might turn out to offer some hope of salvaging something from the wreck: she might phone.

Now Summerchild and I are both Serafin, reaching the barrier and finding no one, then running the list of options through our single conjoint head. What are we going to do?

At this point our two Serafins, Summerchild's and mine, diverge. Mine hurries across the concourse, head down in shameful flight, to bury herself in the Bakerloo. Summerchild's phones. Plainly she phones. Surely she phones!

I'm Summerchild, not Jessel, for present purposes, and my Serafin's going to phone. So I wait.

I wait in silence. What I'm thinking about, now that I know she's going to phone, is what we're going to do next. All my plans have an air of frank unreason. I'm going to get her to come here and hide in the building while I phone Tite, so that when he opens the door she can rush in behind him . . . We're going to overpower him and snatch his key . . . All right, then – morally overpower him and persuade him to hand over his key . . . Barricade ourselves inside . . . Defend our home together . . . Go out only singly for provisions . . .

I've clearly lost all contact with reality. No, I haven't. I'm going to be very down-to-earth and practical. 'Listen, love,' I'm going to say reasonably when she phones, 'we can't decide the rest of our lives like this, in a sudden panic, before your change runs out, our voices half-drowned by the noise of the station. Go back to Oxford, have a think about things, and then ring me quietly from that phone on the sideboard in your own dining-room. I'll be by the phone here all day – all weekend. I won't do anything until I hear from you. We'll sort things out somehow.

'And listen,' I'm going to say, 'the sun's shining. I've put the geraniums back outside the window. I'm making one of my famous salads for lunch. Nothing's changed.

'Because listen, love,' I'm going to go on, before we're finally cut off, raising my voice over the station loudspeakers and their time-honoured litany of inner and outer suburbs. And then, against the clock, against the confusion of the world, I'm going to say all the things I've never said to her. All the true and tender things, all the soft unreasonable things.

So we wait, Summerchild and I, for the phone to ring. Trains come into Charing Cross and people get out of them. How many trains and where they come from I find it difficult to estimate, because by now we're waiting at different speeds – me with my finger on the fast-forward button, Summerchild without the benefit of any of the controls which the present offers us over the past.

'Listen,' we're going to say. 'Listen . . .'

A slight blip breaks the even hum of the tape. Some small event has occurred. I run the tape back and creep forwards again at Summerchild's speed. The blip becomes a soft click. I run back and play it again. *Bluck* . . . Yes - it's the receiver being lifted. He's given up waiting. He's calling out.

226

I knew she wouldn't phone.

Two more clicks, like the first but not so solid. He's moving the receiver rest up and down, trying to get a line. Who's he calling? Her sons? 'Is your mother back . . .?' – How can she be back yet? Tite, then? 'There seems to be some ridiculous misunderstanding about the lock on my door . . .' Anne? 'Please don't ring off. I've been thinking about things. Listen . . .'

British Rail, more likely. 'Are the trains from Greenwich running normally . . .?'

He presses the receiver rest again, and again. He rattles it up and down, in growing agitation. Then slams the receiver down.

I see. They've disconnected his phone.

And at once the tape runs out.

So what am I doing? Raging helplessly up and down the room? Beating my hands against my head in despair? Possibly. But whatever I'm doing I'm now suddenly stopping doing it and laughing aloud to myself instead. Because I'm thinking: So that's why she didn't ring!

I'm wrong about this, surely, but at least it gives me a few more minutes' happiness, which I can't imagine anyone would begrudge me in the last days of my life. It was, after all, the substance we were trying to isolate in our little laboratory up here under the eaves.

So now I'm Serafin again, Summerchild's Serafin. I've rung from Charing Cross and been told by the switchboard that the Unit's extension has been disconnected. On hearing this I've hurried straight round to the Cabinet Office, along the corridors, up the winding stair . . . Now I'm pushing at the door and finding it locked, just as Summerchild said. 'Stephen!' I'm shouting, hammering on the heavy panels. 'Can you hear me . . .?'

Only I'm not.

How could I be? I'm on the main line out of Paddington, staring sightlessly at the flying wastelands of the western suburbs.

No, I've been turned back by Security! Yes! If they've changed the lock and cut off the phone they'll obviously have cancelled the Director's security pass as well!

So I've . . . what . . .? I've gone round the back of the building. Yes. I'm standing in Horse Guards Parade, gazing up at the little window five floors above, waiting patiently for the moment when Summerchild catches up with my thinking and looks out.

That's why he's at the window now, and me, Jessel, with him, gazing down into the Parade, trying to see someone pacing slowly back and forth among the purposeful midday walkers, or an upturned face and an arm suddenly flung up to wave. No one . . . What am I going to do if she *is* there? Wave back. What else *can* I do from up here? Shout inaudibly . . . Write 'I love you' on a sheet of Government writing paper, fold it into a dart and launch it . . . only to see it turn back in the breeze and fall in the garden of Number Ten, at the feet of the Prime Minister . . .

She's not down there, though. I can tell him that, even from fifteen years off. – No, well, she waited all this time, then she went off to look for a phone – she's going to ring Alexander and tell him where to find the things for lunch. She'll come back sooner or later. She'll have to. There's no other option still open. Events have simplified our situation even as they have made it more difficult.

So we wait at the window. Suddenly I stiffen. There's a figure moving slowly through the dappled shade beneath the lime trees outside the back wall of Number Ten . . . A woman – broad-hipped, Slavic . . . It's her! A huge, implausible noise comes bursting out of somewhere very close indeed to the inside of my head. 'Elizabeth!' I roar, in a voice I have never before heard coming out of me. Two policemen standing just beyond the Cadiz Memorial turn to look up in our direction, and so does a man crossing the Parade beyond them, whom I think I recognize from a joint committee I once sat on at the Home Office. They look startled; no one in the whole history of the Civil Service has ever shouted out of the window of a Government building before! Even the woman has turned to look.

She's not Serafin, of course. She's nothing like her.

Nor, for that matter, did I shout; I'm not *that* far removed from myself. On the contrary, I've become very silent as I gaze down into the lost world below. I'm only just beginning to realize quite how isolated I am. No one in the department knows I'm here – they think I'm anywhere but. No one's going to unlock this door again until Establishment want the premises for some other use. No one's going to hear me banging on the door in this remote corner of the building. The only way I'm going to get myself released *is* by shouting out of the window.

Also it's Friday. Fairly well on into Friday afternoon, I think, by this time. If I don't shout in the next few hours there's going to be no one but weekend tourists left to shout to until Monday.

I lean out over the sill, drafting a possible text for the shout. 'Help,' I murmur experimentally.

No! Redraft that from top to bottom!

'Excuse me,' I try. Yes, that's a possible formulation. I raise my voice slightly and say it again. The two policemen I'm addressing, down there five floors below by the Memorial, turn and walk slowly away in the sunshine.

I find it difficult to imagine premeditatedly speaking very much louder than that, which makes me think that possibly the time is not yet ripe for a minute sent through these particular channels. In any case my mood is changing once again. I'm beginning to feel that I might do a lot worse than stay up here for the weekend. I go and check my supplies in the cloakroom. Plenty. Yes, I'll stand my ground. I'll make no decisions until they're forced on me; the classic strategy of my trade.

I have to think in terms of rather longer perspectives, after all. The fact that Serafin has still not appeared beneath the window means that she didn't try to ring me from Charing Cross. What she has done, I think, is exactly what I was going to urge her to do if she *had* rung – she has gone back to Oxford, so that she can phone me calmly and unhurriedly from her own dining-room. When she does and discovers that the office phone is disconnected, she will come back to London and start hammering at the door, or waiting beneath the window. But that will take time. I now expect her not before the end of the afternoon at the earliest and, more probably, by the time she has sorted out the domestic problems that crowd in upon one as soon as one sets foot inside one's own front door, not before this evening.

Just possibly not until tomorrow, Saturday.

All Summerchild's courage and hopefulness have returned, now he's got this sorted out inside his head. The sight of his provisions in the cloakroom has reminded him that it's long past lunchtime and he's fixing himself a substantial meal. There's no longer any need to hover between door and phone and window; I shouldn't be surprised if he took the lunch up on the roof and ate it in the sunshine.

Back here, meanwhile, in the unreal wastes of Sunday night where I live, I can only look to the biscuit tin for refreshments. The next tape – that's my nourishment.

I carefully set aside the tapes I have already played. Only one remains.

27

The last tape.

Or so I assume. There's no date on the label. Perhaps it's unused; the tape is all in the lefthand chamber, either run all the way through and back, or rewound – or never started.

I turn it over in my hands. Now that the end of the road is finally in sight, as it has seemed to be so many times before, I feel the same reluctance to take the last few steps. I don't want to know what happens. I want to creep away and leave Summerchild where I've thought him through to, in the cloakroom happily making his belated lunch, knowing his love will return. A kind of sweet feverish lightness comes into my hands, as if they are just about to throw the tape out through the open window and put an end to it all. When the staff look out of the windows of Number Ten in the morning there'll be litter in the garden to be cleared and that's all that will be left of Summerchild – a shattered cassette and a tangle of spilling tape.

Perhaps it was the same with the shattered body and the tangle of spilling guts. Yes, because that's the way these things happen. Lightly. I can feel the frightening lightness in my hands spreading to my chest and stomach and legs . . .

However, I put the tape into the machine.

I press the button and what comes out is silence – recorded silence, though, the sound of silence, a faint expectant murmur, as if the machine is waiting with some curiosity to hear what Summerchild will say.

What he says is nothing. He has switched the machine on because something inside him seemed about to get itself said. Something was forming – a minute, a memorandum. A poem, a confession. The thoughts and feelings were massing for a breakout. But now he sits watching the tape turn, hypnotized by the little red light, and no words come. His mood has changed again since his cheerful preparations for lunch. Or maybe not even lunch was such a happy event. Maybe I'd lost him already.

Anyway, time has passed since then. But how much there is no way of telling. The sun has gone behind clouds. Or behind the horizon. It's dark – it's the middle of Friday night. Or it's Saturday afternoon – it's Sunday morning. The only certain thing is that Serafin hasn't come. And won't. Even Summerchild knows that now.

No – will come! May come. May yet come.

The tape turns and still Summerchild can't find what it is he wants to say. I fast-forward, then stop guiltily, as if I had caught myself feeling impatient at a deathbed. I rewind and tiptoe through the silence again at the speed he lived it. It is extraordinarily eventless. He's not walking up and down the room, or muttering, or sighing. He's sitting thinking what he wants to say – and doing literally nothing but think, motionless, scarcely breathing. I put my ear right up against the loudspeaker. I believe I can distinguish occasional very faint variations of the background murmur, as if he were leaning a little further forwards in his chair, or moving his hand slowly over the surface of the desk, or turning his head to look at the open air outside the window. Then my straining ear tires and even these tiny anomalies slip away from its grasp. The thought comes to me, made not less but more discomfiting by its patent illogicality, that somehow Summerchild is already dead and that those small sounds I thought I could hear are the last involuntary stirrings of a corpse.

A faint click explodes next to my ear, followed by the deadness of unrecorded silence. I jump back from the loudspeaker, the sudden nothingness reverberating inside my

232

head like the slam of a door. The abrupt death of the sound is testimony to Summerchild's still being alive. Then at once the expectancy resumes; he's switched on again. But scarcely have I got my ear back to the loudspeaker than the murmured silence has stopped. Then resumed. Stopped again. Resumed again . . .

There is something painfully ridiculous about these mute attempts at speech – and something even more ridiculous about the optimism with which each next attempt is made the very instant that the last has been abandoned. But when I reflect upon it I realize that this immediacy is almost certain to be illusory. There is no way of knowing how long the machine was off each time. In these unrecorded intervals whole hours may have elapsed – whole days – lifetimes of reflection and preparation to speak.

So I keep vigil through the night. The long quietness of the dying man's breath scarcely disturbs the air. In its indentation in the pillow my father's face lies as precisely accommodated as a jewel in its box. It's so familiar to me! So painfully familiar. A nurse is holding a mirror to his lips and when I look in the mirror I see that the face is mine . . .

I wake in a panic of confusion and guilt. It's the silence that has woken me. The total silence. The quiet breathing has ceased. I've missed his death, I've slept through his last moments . . .

I fumble stupidly at the machine. Yes, the tape has come to an end and switched itself off. The long-awaited words have been spoken, everything has been made clear at last, and I have not heard. I run the tape back, feeling absurdly indelicate about it, as I were shaking the corpse back to life and making him breathe his last all over again. But breathe is all he does. There is no last blessing for his patient investigator, no final 'Rosebud'. Wherever I stop the tape and try it, nothing but the sound of silence. Silence and silence and then the end of silence.

I realize that there was nothing much I could have learnt from this last tape, even if Summerchild had talked all the way through it, even if he had left a personal message for whoever it turned out to be who was obliged to listen to it. All the same, I feel a leaden disappointment come down on my heart. I want to know what *happened*! Didn't she come, then? Obviously she didn't. I knew she wouldn't. And even if she had it wouldn't have made any difference. I suppose secretly, though, I hadn't quite given up hope. I still thought that somehow – I can't imagine how – everything was going to work itself out, that what happened wasn't going to happen after all.

Perhaps she did come. Perhaps she stood down there in the square, waiting for him to look out of the window – was standing there even while he was sitting in silence at his machine, even while I was sitting here listening to him . . .

Well, there's no way I'll ever find out now.

On second thoughts, though, I suppose there is. I could try asking *her*. That's where the last trace of information is lodged – inside Serafin. She's still in Oxford – I have the address written down in my file. I have the phone number – I could try phoning her . . .

I go clattering down the spiral staircase into the great dark emptiness of the building below. I remember the office I phoned from before and push open the door, but can't find the light-switch and can't wait to look for it. It doesn't matter – I remember where the phone is from last time, and there's just enough light spilling in from the corridor to dial by . . .

As soon as the number starts to ring I long quite violently for her not to answer it. It rings five times . . . I have no idea what I'm going to say . . . Seven . . . She's not there. I begin to calm down. Nine . . . Ten . . . Even feel a little disappointed. I'll let it ring twelve times. The phone's probably still in the dining-room, exactly where it was the first time she got a call from Whitehall. Thirteen . . . She's probably in the middle of a tutorial, just as she was then. I can't help imagining that it's even still as dark in her house as it is in this office. Fifteen . . . She's struggling blindly across the hall, falling over the bicycles . . . manhandling pieces of falling cardboard . . .

No answer. I go to put the receiver down. 'Hello?' it suddenly gasps at me.

I scramble the receiver back to my ear, but now I'm the one without words, because that gasping note in her voice, that suggestion of confusion and alarm, has brought an appalling realization to me: I have phoned her in the middle of the night. She's been struggling not across the corridor from her study but downstairs from her bedroom. I've done just what Summerchild did. I wonder if the memory of that mad and terrible earlier call is now sitting in her mind as well, at the other end of the wire.

'Hello?' she says again and I can't think how to explain simultaneously both why I am calling and how I have come to lose touch with the time of day. 'Hello?' she says, and it seems to me that I have been listening to that voice all my life. I feel I must make it immediately clear to her that I know a great deal about her and that I understand and sympathize. But where to start?

'Hello?' she says patiently. She knows there's someone here, waiting to speak. The anxiety in her voice is softening now. It's beginning to have a suggestion of the eagerness and encouragement I have heard before, as if she were leaning towards me over the desk, nodding and smiling, urging me on to speak out and develop my ideas. 'Hello?' she coaxes, and I feel that before I ask my questions I should like to tell her everything I know already. About how I have reconstructed their life in the office – how I have discovered their lost valley on the roof. About how I saw Summerchild coming up the lane. About Millie and Anne. About Timmy and Lynn.

'Is that you?' she says, before I can find the words to start. This is why she hasn't rung off, this is why she is anxious about getting a call in the middle of the night, but not alarmed – because she was half-expecting it. I hold my breath. Who does she think I am? Someone from the television company, perhaps . . . No – a mad and terrible idea has run down my spine. She thinks I'm Summerchild.

'It *is* you, isn't it . . .' she says, very gently.

There's nothing I can say.

'Just tell me where you are . . . Just tell me you're all right . . .'

I've recovered from my moment of vertigo by this time, of course. I know perfectly well who she thinks I am – one of her sons. Nicky, presumably, still lost and delinquent after all these years.

'Alex?' she says. 'Alex . . .?'

Alexander was her good son, the one who looked after her and never caused her any trouble.

I'd like to put my arms round her. What I'm imagining is my own son calling, lost and gone, unable to say anything to me.

I've missed my chance with her, though. There's nothing I can tell her now, nothing I can ask, if indeed there ever was. 'I'm sorry,' I find myself saying, absurdly, now it's too late to speak. She doesn't reply. 'Don't worry,' I tell her, helplessly. 'Everything will be all right.'

There is a silence. 'Who is this?' she says, in a different voice.

'No one,' I say, and no one is who I am. 'Nothing. Wrong number.'

I put the phone down. What I'm wondering now is whether by any chance Alexander's wanderings have taken him back to his mother's homeland. Has someone come across him there and been given some kind of hints about the past? Is this how the story has surfaced again? Is this why I'm here in the empty darkness, almost as mad as Summerchild himself?

By the time I've thought this, though, I'm no longer sitting there in the dark – I'm running back up the spiral staircase with a new thought in my head, come to me out of nowhere. What I've realized is that I've still got a possibility in hand upstairs after all. That wasn't the end of the last tape – it was only the first side! There may be something on the other side. There is, there is. I'm as certain of that as I ever have been of anything.

I miss my footing on the stairs in my haste and fall into the room like a missile. I snatch the tape out of the machine and turn it over, all the delicate reluctance I felt at broaching the end of the story evaporated. I shouldn't like to be seen by anyone at the moment, I realize; I've lost all sense of proportion and dignity, like a man in the grip of some uncontrollable craving.

I was right, though. There *is* something on the last side of the tape. And Summerchild has recovered his powers of speech.

28

He is dictating another minute or memorandum of some kind. But this time there is no addressee given, no date or security grading, and his language is informal, as if he were writing to a friend. Perhaps he is. His voice has recovered all its old diffidence. His words are dragging their feet again, reluctant to go forth into the world. He sounds thoughtful, almost dreamy.

'I suppose,' he says, 'we have to consider the Unit as effectively having been wound up.'

He thinks about the matter. I wish I knew exactly when he was saying this. Whether it was the Saturday or the Sunday by this time. Whether it was day or night. I wish I knew even *where* he was saying it. I suppose sitting at his desk, looking dreamily up towards the window . . . But somehow I don't think it is. There's something different about the acoustic. It's bald, without resonance.

'I'm not sure exactly where we went wrong. Each step seemed reasonable enough at the time . . .'

Each word of all this seems reasonable enough now, for that matter. It's this very reasonableness that makes the unreason of saying anything so vertiginous. Why's he resorting to speech again? Is it a kind of last testament? And *where's* he saying it? 'He's not in the same place as me, I know that,' I say aloud, and the sound of the words inside the room is full and rounded.

'I don't know how much longer I shall be able to remain

on the premises here,' says this curiously attenuated voice of his. 'But I think I'd like to use the time to put on record . . . what our findings were before we were disbanded. I'd like to work out, if only for my own interest, exactly what we achieved. These are going to be rough notes, rather than firm conclusions . . . Tentative hypotheses . . . Provisional findings. The Director has been submitting interim reports. Perhaps we might think of this document as being in the nature of . . .'

He hesitates. He has been interrupted by a strange noise, like a blast of steam from a locomotive. Then the valve is closed again.

'. . . a final interim report,' he concludes and at once the noise starts again. The locomotive is pulling out of the station, its mighty blasts of steam getting gradually faster and faster. He's not . . . on a railway station? Fled to Russia . . .? Yes, I remember the last time I heard a steam train on this tape. That was Serafin, crying her way out across the steppe.

No, this is a different sort of locomotive. It's laughter. 'Final interim report' – he's made a joke and now he's snorting away to himself. Have I heard him laugh before? I don't think I have. His whole character is changing.

But the locomotive has been overtaken by another form of transport. The archaic chuffings of the escaping steam have been replaced by something much more modern – a smooth mechanical howl with a characteristic whining edge to it. A plane is passing overhead, rather low, on its way to touch-down. And now of course I know where he is.

I switch the tape-recorder off and join him. I want to be in precisely the same place as he is, to see precisely what he's seeing. I clamber on to the draining-board, thump open the skylight, and stand the machine on the edge of the hatchway, just as he must have done. I get my foot on to the stopcock, then heave myself out over the unlit emptiness beneath and up into the cool dark abundance above.

I stand still for some moments in the blackness, blinded by the memory of light. Then the sky separates itself from the

horizon of roof-crests and chimney-stacks. There is a suggestion of stars up there, muddled by the summer haze and
dimmed by the shine of the city. Now the whole valley is
beginning to emerge from the night, as sombre, in the flat
grey urban half-light, as a landscape of spoil-heaps. I take the
tape-recorder up to the further end of the gully where I
guess he must be, sitting in one of the chairs they put out to
catch the afternoon sun, and switch on again. But the dicta-
tion has not resumed. There is nothing to hear but the
aircraft dwindling into the west. I strain my ears into the
shush of the tape. I begin to discern a murmur which I
suppose must be of distant traffic, and some brief, harsh cry
that might be a bird of some sort, or a shout of human
derision in the streets below. Then another aircraft, but this
time high up and far away, coming and going in the shifting
currents of the sky. I'm not sure, though, which of these
sounds are coming from the tape-recorder and which are in
the air around me. Because, yes, they are all the sounds of
the night. He's not sitting here in the afternoon sunlight. He's
in the dark, like me, and it's far on into the small hours. Of
Sunday night? It could be. The sounds have a kind of Sunday
night desuetude. I believe my world and his have become
precisely consonant.

But what's he doing now? There is a sudden creak, a
wincing squeak, as of chalk on blackboard. A dislodged slate
moving out of place, perhaps. I think he's walking up the
slope of the roof . . . I can hear the tiny crunching sounds as
the slates give a little to take his weight. He's been distracted
by the plane – he's gone up on to the pitch to watch it go
winking away down into the west.

I follow him up, awkwardly, on all fours, snatching gratefully at the familiar cliff of chimney-stack halfway. The bricks
are still warm, still full of stored sunshine. Something moves
against my fingertips; the crumbling dry remains of the old
clothesline. I can hear him pattering about above me, moving
as lightly and surely over the dark hillside as a mountain
goat. I move cautiously on upwards after him. I didn't like

doing this in daylight; in the darkness, with Summerchild dancing around ahead of me, it's even worse. What I resent about him more than anything else, I think, is this easy lightfootedness on the heights, this indifference to the great magnetic emptiness beneath him.

It's all right for him. He used to be a climber in his youth. This is his world. I imagine him at university, for that matter, climbing in and out of college. It was that kind of university – he was that kind of undergraduate. Over the roof of the dining-hall. Up the spire of the chapel. I see him, nonchalant in gym-shoes, his trousers tucked into his socks, jumping the chasms of night between one medieval cornice and the next, and saying nothing about it in the morning. Doing famous deeds by stealth, under the cover of darkness.

Yes, he was a *night-climber*. Of course.

I stop – he's talking again. The voice is coming out of the machine, in the gully below me, but it's remote and faint, because he's sitting astride the crest just above me.

At first I can't catch the words. He must be talking to himself up there rather than dictating. I think he's forgotten about the machine altogether. Then, shouted aloud, clear and exultant: 'But we did! We found it!'

I can guess what he's talking about – and I can guess what he's doing. He's not *sitting* on the pitch of the roof – he's *standing* on it. He's balanced on the narrow lead flashing that crowns the south and north slopes, with the whole world of Government beneath his feet, and nothing to hold on to but the darkness.

I crouch close against the slates, sick and frightened.

Now he's talking to himself again. Or talking to the world at large. Odd phrases come out of the night at random as he turns to address different points of the compass.

'. . . discovered a number of its properties . . . Transparent, weightless . . . radiates light and energy . . . mildly hallucinogenic . . .'

Now what? Oh, yes – he's laughing again.

'. . . but inherently unstable . . . rapidly decays into a dense black inert material which is very hard to dispose of . . . only in laboratory conditions . . . further research . . . whether it can be manufactured in bulk . . .'

I edge my way shakily upwards and seize hold of the flashing on the pitch with both hands.

'Unfortunately,' says Summerchild, 'we have not been able to preserve a sample for further study . . .'

His voice dies away. As I haul myself up the last couple of feet and look cautiously over the top I see what he's become absorbed in.

The city's turned inside out since I was last here. Now almost all the light is from below instead of above, striking upwards on to façades and monuments, rising like a sulphurous exhalation from the canyons of unseen streets. Between the shining valleys, the roofs are left as a jumbled highland of shadows. This is what he's gazing at. He's holding his hands around his eyes to block out the fume of light rising from Whitehall on the other side of the ridge, and he's following the complex grey cordillera first to the Scottish Office, then past the illuminated lantern on top of the Horse Guards to the twin towers and masts of the Admiralty.

That's the way he's going to go. Those are the hills he's going to take his walking holiday in this summer.

Not, I think, that he knows it yet. What he's looking for is simply a way down. There must be one somewhere, among all those complex plunging verticals. He's just realizing, as he searches silently for the start of the route, that he could be on the first train to Oxford. Or just possibly the first train to Greenwich.

And he's off! I can hear him running lightly down the slope towards the edge. Then silence. He's over the parapet and gone . . .

No, not yet. He's gone back down the slope he came up – this is why the sound of it registered – and turned the tape-recorder off. He's climbing back into the room with it – taking the tape out and hiding it in the biscuit tin where I found it. He wants some last trace of their life up here to survive.

He'll be back, though, unobserved and unrecorded this time. And this is the way he'll go – over the pitch beside me, down the slope in front of me, and into the chasm that separates the upper storeys of the Cabinet Office from the Scottish Office. It's filled now by the shine from some kind of security lighting below, but as he sees it, I should imagine, in those still careless times, it's as dark as the pit.

Down he'll go, down . . . But he won't get right down to the ground. He'll get as far as the shoulder that connects the two buildings, which I think I recall is at first-floor level, and somewhere below that, I presume, he'll discover his way is barred. So he'll cross the shoulder, and climb the two floors up the vertical cliff-face beyond, to see if there's a way down further along, from the roof of the Scottish Office.

Here he comes now, as I watch, up from the depths on the far side of the chasm, all his youthful powers restored, all the old cunning back in his nerves and muscles. He balances from one insubstantial toehold to the next, braced by finger-holds too shallow to see, moving with the same insane logic that has brought him, foothold by foothold, toehold by toehold, all the way up here out of his level life below. As soon as he and Serafin found themselves face to face in that little attic room the climb began. And then I start to think about all the skill that he deployed in getting her into that room in the first place, all the threats of Kilburn and Croydon, all the disingenuous manoeuvrings in Northumberland Avenue. It seems to me now, as he hauls himself over the edge of the cornice on the Scottish Office, that it wasn't entirely for the benefit of the department, after all. The climb had already begun.

He moves away along the back of the building, then leans out over the edge to search the sheer wall beneath. I can't watch. I keep my head lowered for some moments, concentrating on the backs of my hands, blanched against the black of the lead along the pitch . . . When I look up he's pulled himself back – he's disappearing round the Whitehall side of the roof to try there. A long time goes by, in which I begin to think about my own nervously cramped position, half-kneeling on the slope, clinging on with both hands. I can't help reflecting that it's Summerchild who's got me up here. I should never have thought of Millie again if it hadn't been for him. Sooner or later I'm going to be exploring the rooftops in the dark myself, looking for a way down where none exists . . .

But he's way ahead of me. The next time I catch a glimpse of him he's off the Scottish Office and on to the Horse Guards. On and on he goes, like the Flying Dutchman, leaving me further and further behind with my cramp and my vertigo. By the time he's climbed up again, on to the roof of the Admiralty, most of the short summer night has already gone. There's no way back now. When finally he reaches the cornice above the little yard on the other side, though, it's light, and he can see a way down as clear as a staircase. He rests for a few moments; he's not still an undergraduate, after all, and he's painfully tired. The first rays of the rising sun catch him and light him as brightly as Icarus. Any moment now he's going to be spotted. He lowers himself over the edge and feels with his feet for the sash of the window below. His arms are as weak as sun-warmed wax . . .

I clamber backwards down the roof, still on all fours, like some animal out of its natural element, almost too stiff to move. The stars have faded and the sky in the north-east is as pale as my shaking hands. I don't know how long I've been up there. The tape has run silently to its end and switched itself off a long time ago.

Yes, that's the way he went. There's nothing more to know.

I lower myself through the hatch, suddenly too tired to think. I wash the dust of the roof off my hands as best I can, then muddle the scattered files about the office floor until they make a sort of mattress, with a heap of files beneath my head and a hollow for my hips. I stretch myself out on this bleak bed and pull an empty folder over my face to keep out the dawn light. Halfway down into the depths of sleep the water gets cold and I move back up into wakefulness. I pull sheaves of papers over me to make a blanket and break up boxes as a cover to hold the papers down. In the midst of this confusion of dreams and waking another hypothesis comes to me. Perhaps he wasn't trying to get down to ground-level at all. His intention was to stay up exactly where he was, and what he was doing in that great expedition over the roof of Government was simply this: he was walking his world . . .

Down he went, one way or another, none the less. And this is why, when Serafin at last came back from Oxford that morning, as he had known she would – my last coherent thought, this, as clear as the square of daylight at the window above me – this is why she failed to find him.

29

On the desk in front of me lie two human hands. They are alive, but perfectly still. One of them is sitting, poised like a crab about to scuttle, the fingers steadying a fresh sheet of Government-issue minute form. The other is holding a grey Government-issue ballpoint, poised to write.

Slid tidily back to make room for the minute form are three folders. *Subject*, demands the label on the top one, and then answers, in the small neat letters characteristic of this grey pen and these two pink hands: Summerchild. Beyond the desk, the plain maroon carpet. At the edge of the carpet, the filing cabinet, the hatstand, the two upright chairs, etcetera. The jacket of a pale grey summer suit, net curtains. The sound of phones and muffled voices. 'Bartlett', 'Kyle', 'Gedge', etcetera. My own voice: 'Jessel . . . Yes . . . No . . .' Etcetera, etcetera.

I am back in my own office, about to write my report, and all my world is back in place around me. My suit is even crisper than it usually is on a Monday morning, my shirt even whiter, my tie even more spotless; I've just bought them all at a gent's outfitters in the Strand, on my way back from an early breakfast in the Regent Palace Hotel. My scuffed weekend shoes, that I was too mean to replace, are hidden under my desk.

Summerchild, too, was wearing a suit that last Monday morning of his life. I discovered this from my bedclothes when I woke up – they included, among the mass of other crumpled papers, the post I took up with me to the garret room on Friday, and in one of the envelopes was the full inquest report I'd sent for earlier in the week. The suit (mid-grey, chalk stripe, single-breasted) I understand; it was what he was wearing when he left home on the Thursday night – it was probably the only clothes he had with him. But he was also wearing a tie. There's something distinctly odd about the idea of his sitting up in that hot little room all through the last weekend of his life in a tie. A slight mystery remains about this, to my mind. Maybe he simply felt it was demanded by the suit. Maybe he was so preoccupied that he never got round to taking it off. Or maybe he *wasn't* wearing it during the weekend – wasn't even wearing it when he climbed up on to the roof. It comes to me that this is just possibly why he went back. Not simply to put the tape into the tin, but to fetch his tie. Because he was heading not for Oxford or Greenwich, but for some other place entirely, some place where ties are worn. Tite's office, to have the whole thing out. Number Ten, even. The House of Commons – the Palace. By the end of that night all sense of what could be done in this world and what couldn't must have become very remote. Perhaps he was dressing to meet his maker. I have a picture of him now *taking flight* from the roof of the Admiralty . . .

Or maybe I've somehow got everything entirely wrong – misunderstood everything I've heard. Maybe he'd never left home. Maybe he set out that morning as usual from his house in Hyde Hill Lane, just as Anne allowed people to think at the inquest. Or maybe . . . Yes, because where did the tape-recorder go? Was it taken away by Tite, when he went through everything else? Or is it possible that Summerchild took it back up on to the roof with him? Perhaps somewhere, in Tite's desk, or in a detritus of broken pieces at the bottom of some unexplored airwell halfway between the Cabinet Office and the Admiralty, there is a further tape that explains everything, absolutely and unambiguously, once and for all . . .

No, I know where it is. It's back in Oxford.

Because, yes, she did go back to him that morning. She did all the things he had calculated she would. She hammered on the locked door – she called to him – she went round to the back of the building and stood gazing up at the open window. Stood for an hour or more – tried the door again – stood for another hour . . . Until at last she saw a movement inside the room. Back she ran, full of the emotion that was the subject of their inquiry. At the top of the spiral stairs the unlocked door juddered open in its frame just as it always had. And there he was, hunting through the files they had created, then turning to look up at her as she burst into the room, becoming as he did so old and silver-haired and entirely other.

'Please sit down,' said Tite gently, pushing the files aside and setting a chair for her. 'I'm afraid something rather terrible has happened . . .'

This is why she went back to Oxford with her son's tape-recorder and vanished from the record of the event. Because Tite persuaded her that, for all their sakes, anything was better than the truth.

My hand moves. 'Confidential', it begins, 'Summerchild'. It shifts to the next line. 'Mr Hurren', it enters on the left. 'B Jessel', it adds on the right. My brain is composing its own minute at the same time. 'More confidential still', it begins. 'Millie', it thinks on the left. 'But then Timmy', it adds on the right.

Off goes my hand again, with steady and confident speed. A brief résumé of the affair is what Ken asked for. A brief résumé he will get. 'I have made a very full investigation into the circumstances of Mr Summerchild's death,' writes my hand, which knows so much better than I do how to be clear about these things, 'and have found nothing to suggest any possible breach of security. Although the Coroner's jury returned an open verdict, all the evidence points to a simple accident in the course of a rather foolish feat of bravado. Mr Summerchild was not engaged on work of a sensitive nature and there is no suggestion of any involvement with the intelligence agencies, or with any foreign power.'

This meets the case, I think. There was also the question of a colleague who 'subsequently defected'. Yes, well, that might be Alexander . . . Or maybe, in the aftermath of Summerchild's death, Serafin did make some kind of trip herself back to the land of her fathers. I have a sudden clear picture of her, head-scarfed and penitent, prostrate before the ancient black and gold Mother of God in some remote Russian monastery . . .

'No colleague of Mr Summerchild's has so far as I can establish ever defected,' I write.

What else? Nothing else. *The need to know* – this is the formulation that controls the distribution of sensitive information in the Government service these days, and no one needs to know any of this. 'Unless you have some especial interest in the details of the case,' I conclude, 'I suggest that as a matter of normal good housekeeping the original files should now be destroyed.'

And off the minute goes. I think, like Tite before me, that this is about the best I can do for them both – indeed, for all of us.

I watch as two pink hands shift the Summerchild file to one side and pull forward the one marked 'Joint CO/Treasury Overview Meeting, Sunningdale'. A small familiar sound is audible in the room, issuing from a point about eighteen inches above the hands. A sigh, experience tells me.

Monday, yes. Another week, another file.